THE
CREATIVE
VISION

The Symbolic Recreation of the World
According to the Tibetan Buddhist Tradition
of Tantric Visualization

Otherwise Known as

The Developing Phase

HERBERT GUENTHER

LOTSAWA

Production Coordination: Matrix Productions
Cover Art: Cynthia Moku and Video Arts
Copy Editing: Russell Fuller
Book Design: Merrill Peterson
Production Artist: Kim Freeman
Typesetting: The Composing Room of Michigan, Inc.

Library of Congress Cataloging-in-Publication Data

'Gyur-med-tshe-dban-mchog-grub, Dge-rtse Paṇḍita,
    b.1764?
    The creative vision.

    Translation of: Bskyed-pa' i rim-pa cho-ga dan sbyar-
ba'i gsal-byed zun-jug snye-ma.
    Bibliography: p. 160
    Includes index.
    1. Yoga (Tantric Buddhism) 2. Tantric Buddhism—
China—Tibet—Doctrines.   I. Guenther, Herbert V.
II. Title.
BQ7805.G982513 1987   294.3'44   87-2799
ISBN: 0-932156-03-7

Printed in the United States of America

9 8 7 6 5 4 3 2 1

To Nena

ACKNOWLEDGEMENTS

While preparing the translation and writing this book I have been extremely fortunate to benefit from correspondence and fruitful discussions with friends and colleagues, artists as well as writers, philosophers, and scientists. I am particularly indebted to professor K.J.G. Haderlain, David Higgins, Mariana Neves-Anders, and, last but not least, my wife Dr. Ilse Guenther. I have also received important information from professors Eva and Lobsang Dargyay. Lastly, I wish to thank my publisher Merrill Peterson for his valuable editorial suggestions.

CONTENTS

INTRODUCTION   vi

PART ONE   WESTERN PERSPECTIVE   1

   Prelude   3
   Being's Holomovement and the Two Realities   4
   The Symbolic Re-creation Process   10
   In-depth Appraisals and Phase Transitions   21
   Imagination and the Symbolic Re-creation of the
      World   30
   The Imaginative Recapitulation of Morpho- and
      Ontogenetic Processes   47
   Conclusion   57

PART TWO   EASTERN PRESENTATION   59

   Prologue   63
   Introduction   63
   Preparation   65
   The Main Part   74

CONCLUDING REMARKS   105

NOTES   111

REFERENCES   160

   Works in Western Languages   160
   Tibetan Works   162

INDEXES   168

INTRODUCTION

The Creative Vision addresses itself to an individual's creative vision of himself and his environing world. Its subtitle, "The Symbolic Re-Creation of the World," paraphrases the Tibetan term *bskyed-rim* (*bskyed-pa'i rim-pa*), rendering the Sanskrit terms *utpattikrama* and *utpannakrama*, both of which may be translated, more or less literally and hence rather inadequately, as developing phase or phases. The first Sanskrit term emphasizes the process and the second emphasizes its result or product.

Re-creating one's world and by implication oneself through vividly experienced symbols is discussed in a relatively small work, the *bsKyed-pa'i rim-pa cho-ga dang sbyar-ba'i gsal-byed zung-'jug snye-ma* ("The ear of corn symbolizing the unity of the human and the divine—the shining sun of the developing phase with its attendant ritual"),[1] by 'Gyur-med tshe-dbang mchog-grub, also known as the Kaḥ-thog dge-rtse paṇḍita. He was probably born in 1764, but the year of his death is unknown.

This small but important text is, to a certain extent, an excerpt from the author's larger *gSang-sngags nang-gi lam-rim rgya-cher 'grel-pa Sangs-rgyas gnyis-pa'i dgongs-rgyan* ("The ornament that is the Second Buddha's [Padmasambhava's] sense-bestowing world design—an exhaustive commentary on the psychic progress in the individual's existential approach to life's meaning"), which was written in 1805. Unfortunately, the excerpt from this work has been transmitted to posterity in rather poor shape. Rampant with omissions and abounding in misspellings, at places it is even illegible and, worst of all, quite garbled. We can only surmise the reasons for this deplorable condition. The work may have been hurriedly written, and the person who took down the notes to be elaborated in the body of the text was not always attentive. The printing blocks were probably carved by an illiterate craftsman and never passed through a corrector's hands. However, these defects could be mended by consulting the author's larger work and by referring to other works similar in content.

A translation of a text like this one presents enormous difficulties. First no two languages are sufficiently alike to permit a mechanical transfer of the style and meaning of an original text from one language to another. Further, translating is above all an ongoing hermeneutical process that demands the utmost of the translator. A translation deserving of the name must be faithful to the substance—the meaning of the text. If the text contains a word that has no English equivalent, it must be paraphrased rather than be replaced by a word from another language— in the case of Tibetan from Sanskrit—whose semantic value may be quite different from the connotations the original word aroused in the mind of the person who used it. Apart from being thoroughly trained in the language of the text to be translated and highly sensitive to the subtleties of one's own language, the translator must know both the subject matter of the text and the context in which it was conceived and composed.[2]

'Gyur-med tshe-dbang mchog-grub's work belongs to a group of texts that favor an existential-experiential rather than epistemological approach to one's enworldedness (rgyud, Skt. tantra), involving self-exploration coupled with self-interpretation and world interpretation. As a "way," such an approach involves a progressively deepening understanding of how the nexus of meanings, which is what we call world, evolves. However, as the Buddhists noted long ago it is more correct to speak of various approaches that reflect differences in and levels of an individual's intellectual acumen, which is always interpretive in nature. "There is no such thing as a way or ways in consciousness; individual ways turn up merely by virtue of consciousness making itself understood," says Klong-chen rab-'byams-pa.[3]

Following the Indian predilection for systematization and classification, the Tibetans accepted nine ways or spiritual pursuits (theg-pa, Skt. yāna).[4] Three of these are more or less well known in the West because they fitted easily into the framework of traditional Western philosophical systems that acted as powerful fore-structures or fore-conceptions in presenting and interpreting Indian philosophy in general and Buddhist philosophy in particular.[5] These three pursuits are (1) the Śrāvakayāna— the way of those who listen and who, as social beings, make others listen too; (2) the Pratyekabuddhayāna—the way of those who autistically withdraw as each-a-Buddha-for-himself; and (3) the Bodhisattvayāna— the way of those who have a strong social awareness and who have become reflectively aware of the meaning of the mundaneness of ordinary mentation. In general, the first two pursuits constitute the Hīnayāna, a rather conservative movement that, philosophically, represents a naive realism. The third pursuit constitutes the Mahāyāna, a more comprehensive movement embracing all the varieties summed up by the term *idealism*. However, from the holistic viewpoint that gained precedence in the development of Buddhist thought, these three pursuits rank rather low because they tend, precisely because of their excessively rational and reductionistic character (realism being as reductionistic as idealism), to diminish and ultimately even eliminate one's humanity. Certainly a world minus ourselves is a contradiction in itself, and a human being as a barren abstraction sheds little illumination on his or her concrete en-worldedness and, to say the least, remains emotionally and spiritually unsatisfactory.

Once we understand the inadequacy of logical induction or deduction as a way to impart meaning to our lives, we can "move on" to probe the forces working in and through us and to create a world in which we can live because it encompasses much more than mere thinking. This moving on is the concern of the next six approaches, referred to by the term *Vajrayāna*—the pursuit of the indestructible, ever dynamic core of Being. Each of these approaches constitutes a specific way of weaving the tapestry of one's existence. The point to note here (a point that we cannot overemphasize) is that without prior realization of the shortcomings of the preceding pursuits, the arduous task of weaving one's existence into a richer and more satisfactory tapestry remains ineffectual and may even become counterproductive. This realization was admirably expressed by Johann Wolfgang von Goethe in *Faust* (1984, p. 13).

I've studied now, to my regret,
Philosophy, Law, Medicine,
and—what is worst—Theology
from end to end with diligence.
Yet here I am, a wretched fool
and still no wiser than before.
I've become Master, and Doctor as well,
and for nearly ten years I have led
my young students a merry chase,
up, down, and every which way—

(Habe nun, ach! Philosophy,
Juristerei und Medizin,
Und—leider auch—Theologie
Durchaus studiert, mit heissem Bemühn.
Da steh' ich nun, ich armer Tor!
Und bin so klug als wie zuvor;
Heisse Magister, heisse Doktor gar,
Und ziehe schon an die zehn Jahr

Herauf, herab und quer und krumm
Meine Schüler an der Nase herum—)

Such awareness stands in marked contrast to the widespread anti-intellectualism in the Western world that, frankly, is merely the attitude of those who, in contemptuously dismissing what they have not studied and perhaps cannot comprehend, proudly make themselves ridiculous without knowing to what extent.

The six approaches we have mentioned divide into two sets of three. As stated in the *Rig-pa rang-shar* (p. 815):

The rDo-rje theg-pa (Vajrayāna) is said to be of two varieties
An outer one, which is the capableness tantras (*thub-pa rgyud*),[6]
    and
An inner one, which is the activation tantras (*thabs-kyi rgyud*).

The first set comprises the so-called Kriyātantra, Ubhayatantra, and Yogatantra, usually referred to by their abbreviations of Kriyā, Uba (sic), and Yoga.

The Kriyā emphasizes the importance of ritual activities ranging from ablutions to eating and drinking, clothing and other ceremonial expressions, performed either by a person alone or by a social group to which the performer belongs. Apart from drawing attention to the individual's embeddedness in and obligation to a social setting, these ritual activities are performed simply because it is proper to do so.

The Uba (which means "both") is, as it were, suspended between two objective levels: a mechanistic one below, the ritual and whatever pertains to it, and a qualitative one above, the meaningfulness of the inner forces with which one attempts to establish a relationship. It thus mediates between external, observable, and easily inimitable acts and one's attempts to tune in to psychic forces presenting themselves in symbolic representations of visual and acoustic patterns, subsequently graphically concretized.

The Yoga emphasizes tuning in to the psychic forces, whereby the individual places himself or herself in a network of varying subjective relationships with these forces, which assume anthropomorphic features. This triad of approaches is superior to the preceding one primarily because a world that includes us has been set up where we feel ourselves capable of "doing something." Nevertheless, this triad also has its pitfalls. Though it certainly constitutes an opening up that manifests in the establishment of a kind of partnership both with others and with a nonpersonal world, it also is marked by closure due to structuring this experience in rational terms, elevating it to the dubious heights of absolute truth. The ensuing rigidity has been patently exhibited by the cultists of every religious denomination, presenting a pitiable mixture of laughable imitation and impervious close-mindedness.

These pitfalls and shortcomings were clearly realized by the Buddhists who classified this triad as outer and defined it in terms of its preoccupation with externals on the physical level and with representational thinking on the mental level. What had seemed a promising start after the individual had been reinstated in the scheme of things ended in utter stagnation. In other words, this triad of pursuits did not go deep enough and so fell far short of providing an understanding of life's dynamics. Penetrating to what, from deep within, holds the universe (including ourselves) together is the concern of the last three pursuits: the Mahāyoga, Anuyoga, and Atiyoga, abbreviated as Mahā, Anu, and Ati. Actually, this triad follows directly from the preceding one. Specifically, the Mahā is related to the Yoga such that what in the Yoga is dealt with representationally is in the Mahā dealt with experientially.[7] We initiate the deeply felt understanding of the identity of the forces working in us and the universe, whereby every form of dualism is undercut and whereby we come to "know" ourselves to be both the whole and yet only a part of it, by activating our inner potential, which is inseparable from that of the whole. Though we speak of inner, as does the passage quoted from the *Rig-pa rang-shar*, we must understand that what is so designated is an interiority that has neither a within nor a without.[8] Allowing that language sets reifying traps for us and that we habitually fail to recognize the tricks it plays on us, we may state that this activation is systemic in the sense that it involves the system as a whole and that an essential feature is its autocatalysis. That is, it reinforces the processes that lead to an ever deepening appreciation of life, which if singled out for descriptive purposes is the concern of the Anu and which is already holistically operative. The activation of the whole system's potential and its holistic appreciation are complementary; the one is not possible without the other. The dynamics of this complementarity, which we can only assess and access by first focusing on the one or the other of its features because the limitation of language makes it impossible to capture the whole, is the subject matter of the Ati or rDzogs-chen approach.

We can now state explicitly that the inner variety of the Vajrayāna is indicative of pure process thinking. Again, a word of caution is necessary: language can only present the triad of this inner variety in linear form, but linearity, like circularity, is an abstraction and as such misses the point. We must realize that only the whole, the Ati or rDzogs-chen, can concretely express its dynamic unfolding through what is termed activation or, in a human being's microscopic reality, appropriate activity, while appreciative discernment links the experiencer with the whole, the macroscopic reality. In Buddhist terms, appropriate activity, the activation of the inner potential (*thabs*), is the developing phase (*bskyed*) that leads to a new dynamic regime; appreciative discernment (*shes-rab*) is a holistically inspiring and deeply felt presence and operation (*rdzogs*). Their indivisibility or complementarity is Being's superholistic dynamics (*rdzogs-chen, rdzogs-pa chen-po*).

In the *rDo-rje sems-dpa' snying-gi me-long* (p. 330) we are told:

> *bskyed-pa* or Mahāyoga
> Is like the foundation of all that is;
> *rdzogs-pa* or Anuyoga
> Is like the way that all that is follows; and
> *rdzogs-pa chen-po* or Atiyoga
> Is like the goal that all that is reaches.

The goal of which the rDzogs-chen thinkers speak is the whole, Being's pure potential, a singularity forever unfolding in renewed meaningfulness. In light of the above discussion, we may now position the text translated and commented upon in the following two parts of the book within the framework of Buddhist thought and indicate the significance it may still have for modern man.

First, the text falls under the Mahāyoga pursuit, which, as noted, is process oriented. This implies that structuration, through which any process manifests, is kept fluid and is not allowed to become static or rigid. In the context of a living human being, this means that particular individual's creative self-transcendence. The endogenous dynamics of such self-transcendence cannot be reductively explained but can and must be experienced directly. Such an experience, indistinguishable from a deeply felt understanding, is holistically active on every level of reality, and the symbols through which it manifests are a challenge to probe still deeper, not a lifeless end in themselves. In the immediacy of this experience self-transcendence becomes self-cognition, which is ultimately possible only by doing, hence the insistence on the activation of one's inner potential.

Second, the symbolic re-creation of ourselves and our world starts from our embodiedness and enworldedness, which, on the basis of the Vajrayāna's acceptance of a human being as an integral aspect of the overall scheme of reality, highlights the ineluctable presence of the person's body as animated by spirit or consciousness, its organizing principle. This recognition undermines and makes somewhat ineffectual the notion of the body as an object, physical or otherwise. My body is never an object but always a mode of experiencing myself and ordering my world. It is thus a formulated and formative energy; to use mythological-religious language, it is of a deiform nature (*lha*) with a distinct gestalt quality (*sku*).[9] In the immediacy of such self-experience the drab world of egocentricity has dissipated and a vast realm of meaning and beauty has opened up. This experience of one's body as a gestalt and reliving it in new live circumstances concretely illustrates how life casts certain formal aspects into a new semantic context and brings them into a live exchange with the environing world.[10]

The experience of one's embodied existence presenting a gestalt quality, characterized by autopoiesis[11] and self-transcendence, carries with it strong visual elements—"seeing with fresh eyes," "seeing oneself in a different light." However, with respect to speech (*gsung*), which presents another dimension of one's hierarchial organization, the situation is quite different. Somehow we have put the life of speech into a highly inadequate formal framework, the vowels and consonants, as this framework is called in Indian and Tibetan texts. In addition to being primarily of an audible nature, vowels and consonants also exhibit visual patterns, singly or in combination. A tone-image may exhibit any or all of the nuances of light and dark colors. It is an utterance as originary disclosure, Being's or the whole system's announcement of itself to itself, that the life of speech, and with it its creativity, shines forth. In the words of Arturo B. Fallico:

> Original utterance is thus a full program of purposing. It is the undivided matrix of activity. It contains the initial pattern of feeling, action, and enhanced being such that in any single utterance a complete purposive world can be uncovered.[12]

Our author, 'Gyur-med tshe-dbang mchog-grub, says next to nothing about the audible quality of utterance. In a very sketchy manner he refers to utterance on its way to becoming a spoken word in its visual aspects such that the elements that go into the formation of the spoken word may be imaginatively arranged like stars encircling the moon, or as revolving around a person's head like a firebrand, or as going forth and back like a king's emissary, or as buzzing like bees whose hive has been destroyed. The last of these illustrations is his only reference to the audible character of the constitutive elements in utterance. Most of this section in his work is taken up by quotations describing and eulogizing the rosary used to keep track of how many times one has muttered the rigidly prescribed formulas associated with the imaged gestalt quality of

the deiform energy. Here he seemingly forsakes the position of the Mahāyoga and reverts to the lower Yoga position with its emphasis on
externals. Since this section has little to do with creativity, it has not
been translated.

The same holds for the third section, the transmutation of mentation
into the sheer lucency of pure experience as one's resonance with the
whole (thugs). Here our author says even less than in the preceding
section perhaps because this linking backward to the primal origin as a
new beginning is the topic of the Atiyoga (rdzogs-chen) rather than that
of the Mahāyoga (bskyed-pa), with which our author is primarily concerned.

The Creative Vision is structured in two complementary parts. Part
One starts from the Western perspective and shows that the so-called
Eastern insights are not so alien as they are often believed to be and that
the holistic view of human beings and the world is intimated and often
clearly expressed by great artists, painters, musicians, and poets in particular. We should not, however, overlook the contributions of modern
science that have thoroughly discredited the old reductionism, even if it
is still held widely in the humanities where it is most out of place. In
particular, this part explicates the highly technical terms employed by
the Tibetans in their account of experiential processes, in the light of the
findings of modern science whose concepts of symmetry, holomovement,
complementarity, self-organization, and many others have proved themselves to be extremely helpful in understanding Buddhist process thinking. The internal structure of this part follows the structure of the Tibetan text and so is intended as a modern running commentary on a
Tibetan text.

Part Two presents the translation of the Tibetan text along with
copious notes clarifying, primarily on the basis of Tibetan sources but
also by drawing on Western material, the indigenous ideas and their
often tacit implications. This translation illustrates how the Buddhists
attempted to enrich their world through an imaginatively sustained re-
creation and reinterpretation; the same problem that faces us today more
than ever and is touched upon in Part One.

The complementarity of Parts One and Two poses a particular challenge to the reader. By reading an early nineteenth-century text whose
ideas originated more than fifteen hundred years ago, we may learn not
only what people once knew and believed to be an answer to man's ever
present problématique, "the problematic nature of an evolving situation
which becomes manifest in ever-changing elusive aspects which may

become transitorily recognized as 'problems'" (Jantsch and Waddington, 1976, p. 37); we may also realize what we now believe to be an answer may need some rethinking. Maybe we must take seriously the paradox that the old is not so old and the new not so new.[13] On this mystical note we shall conclude our introduction to the creative vision of ourselves and our world.

PART ONE

WESTERN PERSPECTIVE

The world must be romanticized.
Thus one rediscovers the original meaning.

(Die Welt muss romantisiert werden.
So findet man den ursprünglichen Sinn wieder.)
—Novalis

PRELUDE

The quest for meaning has often been equated with rational thought because *within* a particular framework or paradigm, its major operation of logical induction and deduction has worked extremely well. However, the rational approach tends to see the "world" as an external, allegedly "objective" totality of entities from which, ironically, the experiencer is excluded and, as an insufferable nuisance, is relegated to some inaccessible region. Carried to its extreme, the rational approach has devastating effects. It impoverishes one's world by attempting to reduce its rich tapestry to its barest threads and thereby overlooks and leaves out most of what makes life worth living.

Nevertheless, however abstract the model of the world created by the rational approach may be—be it the philosopher's world of realistic or idealistic, monistic or dualistic tenets, the physicist's world of interacting forces responsible for the structuration called the universe, or the artist's world of aesthetic forms and color schemes—there is in each such model a "hidden" order or beauty, a gestalt quality that seems to have its own life. Not only does it draw the disparate elements in a model together into a harmonious and consistent whole, it also arouses in the experiencer a feeling of being an integral part of an evolving universe in whose dynamics he or she actively and creatively participates. With this emergence of appreciation, the "world" has become again what it has always been—an appreciated and experienced world.

In thus distinguishing between a rational approach to the world, which we believe to have general validity simply because we have imposed upon it an intellectual interpretation that reflects the features of our own rationality, and an appreciative approach, by which we relate to reality in terms of all kinds of value experiences and which we deem to have a higher validity, because through such experiences we can recapture the feeling of being alive and to stream rapturously into the world within and around us, we must remain aware that either approach pursued as an end in itself tends to become increasingly sterile and rigidified as a specific structure. Furthermore, this distinction between a commonly accepted reality and a higher-order reality[14] easily lends itself to the construction of a dualistic, static world view, as may be gleaned from the prevailing reductionism in early Hīnayāna Buddhism and its rather naive teleology, aiming at a recognized and preestablished goal. By contrast, thinkers in the subsequent periods in the history of Buddhist thought, as it unfolded in the various trends of Mahāyāna and, specifically, in Vajrayāna Buddhism, tended increasingly to eschew the older structure-oriented way of thinking and to emphasize the dynamics of processes that are primarily geared to a system's self-organization and self-renewal. Here we should note that the term *system*, like its scientific and philosophical variants, *totality* and *Being*, is used in an all-inclusive sense, at once referring to both the macroscopic and the microscopic, the whole and its parts, not the least significant of which is the experiencing individual who interprets himself in relation to the whole. On the basis of this process-oriented thinking, the above-mentioned distinction between a lower-order, commonly accepted reality and a higher-order reality points to degrees or autopoietic[15] levels of insight within the total system's self-organization dynamics, which is the system's thrust toward optimization.[16]

BEING'S HOLOMOVEMENT AND THE TWO REALITIES

In a process-oriented view the commonly accepted reality is experienced as a lighting-up,[17] which in this process breaks up into smaller light packages such that, as an inordinate addiction to and preoccupation with its own creations, it is responsible for the joys and sorrows that the six kinds of living beings experience as "happening" to them. As one's intellect it structures the world in terms of causality and is responsible for the various philosophical systems that provide the rationale for its short-range perspective. As value/meaning dynamics it expresses one's deeply felt understanding, akin to an undivided, holistic appreciation of reality and is responsible for a qualitative perception of the world as being an ornament to itself by its autopoiesis. And as Kun-tu bzang-po, the universe as a harmonious whole, it is the total system's, Being's holomovement (a term coined by British physicist David Bohm)[18] in its spontaneous and dynamic thereness.

However, in its lighting-up Being may go astray into a state of opacity that marks each of the six niches in which the six kinds of living beings hole themselves up; or it may come as the autopresencing of ten autopoietic levels in a person's psychic development—worlds of transparency and purity and symbolic significance; or it may be felt to be there as the purest of the pure—the total system's originary awareness that in its dynamic is its holomovement. In whichever way one may specify these nuances and modes of the lighting-up process, it abides in its own effulgence, like the sun or the flame of a lamp.[19]

We must note two points in this connection. One is that the "going astray into a state of opacity," associated with what is commonly called samsara—a running around in circles and a groping in the dark—is only one of the modes or field patterns in which the lighting-up process may manifest. Hence, while this process is what is otherwise termed the commonly accepted reality, not all of it is a going astray; there is the lighting-up as worlds of symbolic significance, which are also manifestations of the commonly accepted reality but are not the opacity that marks Being's having gone astray.

The other point is that this lighting-up is a holomovement. As the indigenous Tibetan term *gzhi-snang* implies, the whole, not merely an aspect of it, lights up and, as the specification of this lighting-up as a projective glow or effulgence intimates, may be conceived of as the projection of a higher-order or higher-dimensional reality. This higher-order reality is always present, without being anything or being such that it could be reduced to some thing or other. This presence is its spontaneity and uncreatedness, which from the viewpoint of thematizing thought, engrossed in quantification and concretization, is "nothing." However, it is not some nothingness or emptiness or void, the misleading rendering of the Tibetan term *stong-(pa)-nyid*, which is based on the mistaken translation of its Sanskrit equivalent *śūnyatā*. Rather, this higher-order reality is an all-inclusive ground that is itself not grounded anywhere. To use an analogy, it is like the vacuum in modern physics, an immense "sea" of energy, omnipresent and ever active. Whatever surfaces from this sea or, as the Buddhists would say, lights up, is a "quantized" wavelike excitation, spreading out over a broad region and manifesting as one or another niche that is a subtotality of the overall totality. We can study and explore any such sub-totality provided that we remember that it is a derivative, an effulgence whose true meaning we can access only when we take into account the higher-order reality of which it is a fluctuation in the sense of surfacing from and receding into it.

In speaking of this totality as all-inclusive, we must not slip back into regarding it as some container, which has a definite and limited dimension, a static notion not in keeping with the dynamic immensity of this totality. However, continuing the metaphorical container diction—

bearing in mind that all language is metaphorical—to its logical end, it follows that mentation, intelligence, consciousness, or whatever other term we may use to refer to the specific operations of the system's functional organization is included. On this basis intelligence points to the system's self-organization deriving from its excitation. It also follows that such intelligence/excitation is not some kind of mechanical problem solving that presupposes the existence of an unambiguous answer and thereby contradicts the very dynamics of life's creativity as the ongoing unfoldment of its totality. Being's undivided wholeness, as we have seen, is analogous to an immense sea of energy, which, although nothing as such, is ever active in the quantization of itself through its radiance or effulgence or lighting-up. This very activity is the totality's excitatory intelligence in the process of organizing itself as a consistent whole. In emphasizing processes involving spontaneous structuration, which in living systems such as human beings manifest in a multilevel autopoiesis and its systemic connectedness by homologous dynamics, the Buddhist thinkers seem to have intuitively discovered the principle of evolution as an open-ended learning process. As such the principle of evolution does not attempt to "explain" the universe, that is, to reduce all phenomena to one level of interpretation, but rather offers clues to gaining an understanding of our role in the drama of evolution—finding the meaning of our life.

Klong-chen rab-'byams-pa has most succinctly summed up the indivisibility or complementarity of the two reality modes, experienced as the paradox of there being a presence and yet nothing, as the individual's starting-point for self-renewal and self-transcendence, in the following words[20]:

> Here, in the first place, it is important to be aware of Being's abidingness.
> Although there are many interpretations of it according to the various disciplines,
> The indivisibility of two realities as the thrust toward its autopoietic and autocatalytic certainty
> Is the arcane treasury of Buddha-experiences.
> As such it is a sheer lucency which also is Being's originary awareness[21]
> Our authentic individuality[22] that from its very beginning had nothing to do with an essence and with thematic proliferations;
> Like the sun in the sky it is a spontaneous presence and uncreated.

Since in its thereness it has atemporally abided in utter purity,
unmarred by anything that might be construed as its essence,
Its indivisibility of being a presence and yet nothing, can
neither be affirmed nor negated, nor does anything go into it
or come out of it.
All thematizations have come to rest in it because, in view of
the fact that it lies beyond the sphere where the distinctions
made within the concrete framework of the commonly
accepted reality have their relative validity,
It also lies beyond the two realities postulated by the intellect.
The indivisibility of two realities is not such that it can be
affirmed or negated as some thing.
Since the paradox of there being a presence and yet nothing,
arising out of Being's expanse, is not constituted as a duality,
This reality, too, is referred to by the term indivisibility.

When one properly investigates what is commonly referred to as
the two realities, one will find that
All the elements that make up samsara, which is Being's
lighting-up process going astray,
Are because of their having no reality of their own and because
of their deceptiveness precisely what is considered to be the
commonly accepted reality.
By contrast, the elements that make up nirvana, a sheer
lucency, profound and calm,
Are claimed to be the higher order reality which as such
remains invariant.

The varied phenomena of the commonly accepted reality
Are like a magic show, a reflection of the moon in water, an
image in a mirror and
Are not something existing of their own.
When one critically examines that which so lights up,
It turns out to be like the sky, an open nothingness and as such
having no defining characteristics
Because it has neither grounding nor rooting nor anything
substantial about it.
When one does not examine it, it provides various delights, like
a magic show,
Stemming from a universal interconnectedness that in itself is a
going-astray due to one's ingrained tendencies.
All this is like the hallucinations of a person who has eaten a
datura fruit.

Since this very fact that all this is nothing in itself and has no
    individuality about it,
Is what constitutes Being's abidingness in it,
It is called the higher order reality, while that which lights up
    as this or that is the commonly accepted reality.
Because the latter reality, ever since it has made its presence
    felt by its lighting-up, has not been something that could be
    affirmed in terms of birth and so on,
This paradox of there being a presence and yet nothing is the
    indivisibility of the two realities.

Since there is nothing that would allow us to make a clear-cut
    distinction between and separation of
The higher order reality which is Being's expanse and the fact
    that there is no essence whatsoever to be found,
Because samsara is not given as something in itself, although
    there occurs a lighting-up,
The indivisibility of samsara and nirvana in this sense is what is
    meant by their identity[23].

A mind entertaining perverted notions about reality as being
    otherwise,
Is completely bewildered about the meaning of Being's
    abidingness.

To the extent that there is such a lighting-up in terms of
    Being's dynamics going astray, the relationship between cause
    and effect has its validity.
Therefore in this context it is important to know what is good
    and evil and what to accept and what to reject.
The higher order reality which remains invariant is such that
It is a sheer lucency, the system's thrust towards optimization, a
    spontaneous presence, and this is also what is meant by
The indivisibility of the system's qualities of being open-
    dimensional, radiant, and excitatory-intelligent.[24]
This, indeed, is the spontaneously present configuration
    (dkyil-'khor)[25] that constitutes one's situatedness;
It has been atemporally there, utterly complete, and as such the
    energy that makes the individual strive for limpid clearness
    and consummate perspicacity;
Pure in every respect, free from thematic limitations, and free
    from all bias;

Profound and calm, experienced as a gestalt quality and an originary awareness, neither of which can be added to nor subtracted from the other.

The reference to a configuration, which is a key term in the literature that deals with the symbolic re-creation of ourselves and our environing world, points to the individual's a priori situatedness in a world and to the task lying ahead. In the words of Erich Jantsch (1980, p. 251), in this task "it is of primary importance that the openness of the inner world, for which no limitations are yet in sight, is matched by a similar openness of the outer world, and that it tries actively to establish the latter." This, however, is possible only when the individual is aware of his situatedness. Klong-chen rab-'byams-pa outlines this program:[26]

When one thus knows Being's abidingness one has to develop its potential creatively.
Here, as a beginning and a preliminary step
One has to take refuge and raise one's mentation to its higher level of limpid clearness and consummate perspicacity.
Then, one has to cultivate by creative imagination, the developing phase as detailed in the outer, feedback relationships dominated, and inner, intrapsychic dynamics dominated, aspects of the existential approach to the mystery of Being.

According to Klong-chen rab-'byams-pa, the program itself is an ongoing process[27]

Thus the outer world is transmuted into realms of the imagination and the sentient beings in it into gods and goddesses;
One's live body is transmuted into a beautiful palace, and one's speech into the creative evocativeness of a first utterance, and
One's mentation into the radiance of a deiform energy, whereby the addiction to and preoccupation with the vulgar ceases.
This is the burning away of the dirt of the obscurations that accompany the creativity of Being's dynamic expanse.

However, the charm, desirableness, beauty, and attractiveness of the images conjured up in this symbolic re-creation of ourselves and our world are so strong that the individual may come under their spell to such a degree that this symbolic re-creation becomes an end in itself and no longer serves the individual's evolutionary purpose. So the next step is to embark on the fulfilling phase, which is strictly a holistic, autopoietic, and autocatalytic process, not a static end-state. This is borne out by Klong-chen rab-'byams-pa[28]

> After this symbolic re-creation of one's self and the world one
> will have to develop the fulfilling phase in such a manner
> that
> Experience is understood to be nothing objectifiable, even if it
> comes in the images of the symbolic re-creation process, and
> that
> Experience is a sheer lucency taking shape in gestalt qualities.[29]
> This is Being's intentionality as detailed in the texts dealing
> with one's existential approach to certainty.

As he explicates in his own commentary to this aphoristic statement, by understanding experience as being nothing objectifiable, having neither an external nor internal reference, the preoccupation with the magiclike images is undermined, and by understanding it as being a sheer lucency, the notion of and preoccupation with it as being some "nothing" is undermined.[30] That is, the fulfilling phase is nowhere else than in the developing phase and the developing phase is itself a process and not a thing. While in the developing phase, the individual is actively engaged in transmuting his dense and murky mentation into a dynamic, luminous, deiform energy, visualized in images of a personal "I" and a personal "Thou." In the fulfilling phase the appreciatively felt experience of this very activity is of primary importance such that here the system's gestalt quality and dynamics, its lighting-up and its being nothing at the same time, are made the "way," which thus turns out to be the individual's coevolution with himself.

THE SYMBOLIC RE-CREATION PROCESS

The symbolic re-creation of the world is referred to by the technical term *bskyed-rim*, which has been rendered as "developing phase"—a makeshift term since there is no English equivalent to express the richness of the programs inherent in it. The term describes an iterative feedback process between the outer and inner world. It implies the co-ordination of the conditions for simultaneous differentiations that retain a dynamic interconnectedness. In this process "reality," as commonly and naively understood, is changed by our mental image of the situation, which in turn,

strongly influences this image and limits its creative scope. We know
that the frequencies of the environing world that reach us are not accepted passively and merely registered but are met actively by the organism in
its holistic self-organization and relationships to the environment whose
structures reflect the structures of our inner world. Buddhist texts speak
of this inner world as *bcud* which literally means "elixir" but is her-
meneutically explicated by Klong-chen rab-'byams-pa as: the possibility
of interpretively experiencing one's actions and emotional responses to
the world in which one lives in terms of varied feelings of happiness and
sorrow,[31] and of the outer world as *snod*, literally translated as "vessel" or
"container" but understood by Klong-chen rab-'byams-pa as: "a lighting-
up of the five fundamental forces in images of their dynamics."[32]

At the interface between these existential coordinates in the individual's self-interpretation and individuation as authentic subject, a new
perspective may evolve or, more importantly, be initiated. Perspectives
have a bipolar structure in always being a perspective *from* a perceiver
and *of* a figure with background. Only to the extent that in this context
the experiencer is at the center of experience does he figure prominently
when it comes to defining what is meant by the term *bskyed-rim*, which
in addition to being a developing phase now reveals itself as a deeply felt
transformative experience. According to sGam-po-pa (1079–1153),
probably one of the earliest Tibetan authors to give an overview of this
technique of creative experimentation, its gist is

> to restore radiance to mentation through the felt image of it as a
> deiform energy, by having repulsed mentation's trend to end up in
> the common subject-object dichotomy.[33]

The specification of mentation's radiance as a deiform energy (*lha*)
deserves special attention. The technical term used is often carelessly
rendered as "god" by imputing to it the popular associations of its Sanskrit equivalent *deva*. But neither the connotations of the Indian term
nor those of its Western counterpart can do justice to what is implied by
the Tibetan term in this context. What is intimated by this term is
neither a construct within an enclosed sphere of subjectivity nor a postulate in an allegedly objective realm of essences. Rather it is a pointer to a
dynamic quality of a psychic force termed mentation or mind which
remains elusive and irreducible to any material dimension. Thus Klong-
chen rab-'byams-pa succinctly stated that "any deiform energy is one's
own mentation,"[34] and sMin-gling Lo-chen Dharmaśrī (1654–1717)
elaborated as follows:

By knowing that this deiform energy is precisely mentation's play and creativity, one becomes convinced that yonder, where mentation has been relinquished, there is no gestalt quality of a deiform energy, and that thither, where the gestalt quality of a deiform energy has been relinquished, there is no mentation. Mentation and the gestalt quality of a deiform energy are indivisible.[35]

Long before these authors, Rong-zom Chos-kyi bzang-po (eleventh century) distinguished between a higher-order deiform energy and a deiform energy as a "quantized" feature of this higher-order reality, pertaining to or characterizing mentation in its predichotomic operations.[36] The use of the prefix "pre-" in the term *predichotomic* does not mean that the predichotomic level in any way precedes or antedates the dichotomic one. We know that Being's expanse or "sea" of energy is never at rest but ceaselessly operative in its "quantization" and that its "quantized" packages may then be studied in their own right. In terms of cognition this means that Being's originary awareness is ever active in its intending operations, but the incipient dichotomic trend has not yet congealed into the rigid dichotomy of a concrete subject and object. This observation re-occurs with mKhan-po Yon-dga' (nineteenth century), whose concise account, because of the wealth of information it contains, can only be paraphrased:

Being's meaning-rich potential, a real deiform energy, is the system's self-existent and endogenous originary awareness. A thematized, representational deiform energy manifests as Being's impression on the experiencer who feels it in such a way that his live body is the center of a milieu, an orientational point from which spatiotemporal coordinates organize and structure the milieu and also house the psychic strivings that initiate the organization and structure of the milieu.[37]

From all that has been said so far about what the Tibetans understood by the word *lha*, clearly this term is essentially an indicator of direction, a stimulus for an intended effect and, although vague in outline, is nevertheless most precise with respect to its dynamic features. Thus while the dichotomies geared to rational thinking elucidate quantity and set up a world that is coarse and rough, opaque and impure, the predichotomic, in its pure and transparent symbol-rich lighting-up in deiform energies, introduces quality and focuses on value whereby it opens the way to a holistic experience of reality that includes the human individual, who is simultaneously source and agent of this movement. Indeed sGam-po-pa is quite explicit on this theme:

> The gestalt quality of a deiform energy is the object pole in the intentional structure of thought. That which sets up this intended object is the intending subject pole in the act of mentation. By coming to know that subject and object do not exist as a duality, one will understand that all the granular entities which are supposed to make up our reality have no essence in themselves. This is what is meant by seeing reality.[38]

The emphasis on quality—a holistic notion comprising both form (referred to as gestalt) and feeling (referred to as happiness or pleasure)— and on value, the basic link between ourselves and our reality, indicates the recognition of a different, higher-order level in the hierarchical organization of the individual and introduces a more instrumental approach to self-realization and self-cognition. Actually, the so-called developing phase has always been understood as an instrumental approach in that everything implied by this code term—attitudes, gestures, and actions—is inseparably expressive of and made possible by the biological structures of the body, whereby it also serves as the medium through which a person may come to appreciate his situatedness. This is, a person's bodily existence is both the expression, the self-actualization process, of that person's psychic organization dynamics and the expressed, the concrete actualization of it. Thus it is *in* one's bodily existence that one perceives and feels, that is, experiences happiness as its optimization dynamics. The *Hevajratantra* (II, ii, 35–36) states:

> If there were not the concrete reality of the body, from where
>   would happiness come?
> One could not speak about happiness.
> Happiness permeates the world of the living
> In the manner of being the permeating and the permeated;
> Just as the fragrance in a flower
> Would not be known in the absence of a concrete flower,
> So also, if the experience of shape and so on, were not a
>   tangibly felt experience,
> There would be no access to the experience of happiness.

This active, instrumental approach, which initiates the symbolic recreation of ourselves and our world by opening up dynamic perspectives

where felt images and imaged feelings of the forces working around and
through us play a significant role, was summarized by sGam-po-pa as
follows:

> The definition of the developing phase/transformative experience
> involves three modes: (1) setting up the complexity of mentation
> and one's live body as a deiform energy; (2) setting up the com-
> plexity of one's live body and mentation as a deiform energy; and
> (3) setting up the complexity of mentation and language as a
> deiform energy.
>
> Here, setting up the complexity of one's live body and menta-
> tion as a deiform energy means the experience of this complexity
> as the radiancy of the gestalt quality of a deiform energy when the
> ordinary materiality, in terms of flesh and blood associated with
> one's body, is no longer mentation's objective reference. Setting
> up the complexity of mentation and one's live body as a deiform
> energy means that one knows that even this gestalt quality of a
> deiform energy, as mentation's lighting-up, is not something tan-
> gibly objectifiable, but is like a magic show or like the rainbow in
> the sky. Setting up the complexity of mentation and language as a
> deiform energy means that one knows that, although the gestalt
> quality of a deiform energy is said to be like a magic show, such a
> statement is but a name, a symbol, a label, a metaphorical expres-
> sion, and as such has no grounding.[39]

Lastly, in this context, Padma dkar-po (1526–1592) may be mentioned. He gave an individual interpretation of each of the two terms in
the compound term bskyed-rim. His words are:

> bskyed-pa means to set up a deiform energy in conformity with the
> ontogenesis of living beings; and rim-pa means to refine and trans-
> mute this very process step by step.
>
> Or, bskyed-pa means a deiform energy; and rim-pa means the
> expansion of its circle of influence and so on.
>
> Or, bskyed-pa is the system's dynamics in being both the center
> of a milieu and the organizing principle of this milieu; and rim-pa is
> the instrumental approach taken by experience within one's bodily
> existence.
>
> It also means "configuration" (dkyil-'khor), where dkyil refers to
> the energetic center and 'khor to the act of engaging in it.[40]

This lengthy discussion of the technical term bskyed-rim, based on
the writings of various representative authors in the richly diversified

tradition of Buddhism in Tibet, is meant to highlight the significance that this experiential process has for a person's psychic development while discouraging him from taking it as an end in itself. The developing phase is a preliminary procedure that facilitates a holistic experience of the system's self-organization and self-renewal (autopoiesis) in which the broken symmetry and lost unity are rediscovered and restored in a new, higher-order level, which is deeply appreciated. The various processes involved do not so much constitute a linear progression, even though our language tends to conjure up such an idea, but may, in view of a living being's multilevel organization, be conceived of as a kind of ascent. The image that comes immediately to mind is that of a ladder. Thus it has been stated in the *Pañcakrama* (II, 2):

> For those who are firmly established in the techniques of the
>   developing phase and who
> Aspire for the fulfilling phase,
> The procedures in the developing phase have been laid out by
>   the completely awakened ones
> Like the rungs of a ladder.

Like all metaphorical expressions, the metaphor of the ladder leaves out more than it reveals. The developing phase attempts to activate the individual's latent potential, which is already present in utter completeness. To the extent that this potential is experienced as an evolutionary thrust toward the system's optimization, transcending the opposites of samsara and nirvana by comprising them, it is referred to as fulfilling phase. Of this evolutionary thrust the *Hevajratantra* (II, iv, 32–34) declares:

> This is samsara,
> This is nirvana.
> Elsewhere than in samsara
> Nirvana is not understood.
> Samsara is shapes, and sounds and so on.
> Samsara is feeling and the other psychic operations.
> Samsara is the sensory functions.
> Samsara is irritation and the other emotional pollutants.
> But all these particulars are nirvana.
> They have assumed the shape of samsara
> Because of the individual's confusion about them.
> But when the individual is no longer confused, samsara is
>   experienced as pure and hence
> Samsara turns into nirvana.

This idea of complementarity, which embraces the opposites of samsara and nirvana as well as the experiencer's psychic dispositions of being confused and not being confused, reflects an even higher level than those commonly referred to as samsara and nirvana. But what does "higher" or "lower" mean? In a person's self-realization it is apparently not so much a matter of higher or lower levels but of a balanced, harmonious blending of the vibrations and rhythms associated with the life of the mind that cuts across all levels. This blending is the way of the individual's self-renewal and self-actualization, which begins when the individual has become aware of Being's abidingness as being the immediacy of existence in which all opposites contain each other and which is the intensity and intensification of life itself.

As previously noted, whenever the term *way* is used in the context of lived through experience, it is a metaphor for the total system's unfoldment, in which appropriate activity (*thabs*) is coupled with and expressive of the system's appreciative discernment (*shes-rab*), both processes being mutually enhancing. In the developing phase, a transformative experience, the system's appropriate activity is engaged in a clean-up operation to the effect that one's addiction to and preoccupation with the quantitative, the opacity or impurity of the phenomenal world in its thematized version, is purged of its obscuring tactics and a qualitative assessment is initiated. This qualitative assessment is referred to by the code term *three thrones*. One such throne is the one commonly classified in terms of the five psychophysical groupings and their underlying force fields, which also admit of both a physical and psychical interpretation; another throne is the individual's perceptual apparatus—the sensory cognitions, seeing, hearing, smelling, tasting, and their sensory bases, eye, ear, nose, tongue, together with their time- and space-binding operations; and the third throne is the body as an animate organism "on" and "in" which the above-mentioned fields of sensation are spread out and which, as a sensory organ itself, most immediately actualizes volitional strivings and tendencies. Though one speaks of "three thrones," this numerical accounting is not meant to refer to three separate and unrelated sets of entities but to an intimate linkage of three hierarchically organized levels such that, while each level has its own self-organizing dynamics, in the total person they are fully coordinated. Hence the code term "three thrones" can be resolved and paraphrased as "an organism's triune value-oriented setting."

With respect to the fulfilling phase (*rdzogs-rim*), the holistic experience of the individuation process, far from being a static end-state, is the system's appreciative discernment that provides the access to a systemic originary awareness (*lhan-cig-skyes-pa'i ye-shes*), so much more so as it is itself the manifest creative dynamics of the total system's resonance with itself. Specifically, as Klong-chen rab-'byams-pa pointed out:

Appreciative discernment is, as the creative dynamics of the total system's resonance with itself, a cognitive process in which the rising of a content and its releasement in the totality do not constitute a duality. Although in its excited state it may be aware of an object, it does not follow it up by way of exteriorization, but remains an undivided projective glow.[41]

This systemic awareness accessed by the appreciative discernment of the fulfilling phase is, in a sense, the whole system itself in its cognitive dynamics. On a more modest scale the total system is our live body, which we have seen to constitute a cognitive system, as well as being a sensory organ, in the sense that presenting (not re-presenting) Being, it is both part of Being and the whole of it, as a wave is both part of the ocean and the whole of it. Thus systemic awareness is a higher-dimensional reality that reaches into what seems to be its projection: our live body. The *Hevajratantra* (I, i, 12) expresses this idea as follows:

This super originary awareness resides in the body,
Thoroughly divested of dichotomic trends.
Although as that which encompasses all concrete realities,
It resides in the body, it is not of the body.

Characteristically, process-oriented thinking cannot but conceive of this higher-dimensional reality, which in terms of its cognitive character is variously spoken of as a "super originary awareness" (*ye-shes chen-po*)[42] or, in connection with the developing phase, as a "systemic originary awareness" (*lhan-cig-skyes-pa'i ye-shes*), constituting a complex self-organizing process of unfoldment. This process has been described in terms of three phases: (1) a starting point as the system's totality in its capacity of being its own evolutionary incentive; (2) a way as the system's unfoldment, which can be described rationally but must be experienced and "felt" in order to be known;[43] and (3) a goal in which the system becomes increasingly more complex and self-reflexive. All this is reflected in the problematic term *lhan-cig-skyes-pa'i ye-shes*, here rendered as "systemic originary awareness" in order to capture something of its holistic aspect. Specifically, the term *ye-shes* refers to the system's originary awareness and its cognitive operations—"originary" in that this cognitiveness has been there since its beginning, which has had no beginning (*ye*). More precisely, this cognitive operation is a function of the total system's excitation (*rig-pa*), which is also the system's radiance (*gsal-ba*) and open-dimensionality (*stong-pa*). The system in its totality, referred to by the descriptive term *systemic*, presents a triune character that has been explicated by the Sixth Zhwa-dmar Karma-pa Chos-kyi dbang-phyug (1584–1630):

> It is not the case that apart from the system's open-dimensionality there is excitation and radiance, or that apart from radiance there is open-dimensionality and excitation, or that apart from excitation there is radiance and open-dimensionality. It is mentation alone that so emerges open-dimensional, radiant, and excitatory. Although it emerges in these three aspects, they emerge together (*lhan-cig-skyes-pa*) as a triune indivisibility. Since it is the totality's open-dimensionality that emerges as excitation and radiance, and since it is the totality's excitation that emerges as open-dimensionality and radiance, and since it is the totality's radiance that emerges as open-dimensionality and excitation, each facet in this triad comes in a triune manner. This is what is meant by "systemic."[44]

The author went on to say that when the system has become self-reflexive, one speaks of "systemic originary awareness" (*lhan-cig-skyes-pa'i ye-shes*), but as long as it does not become self-reflexive, one speaks of "a systemic lack of cognitive excitability" (*lhan-cig-skyes-pa'i ma-rig-pa*). These two activities do not occur sequentially but merely point to the inner dynamics of the system in its instability phase, where the kind of activity that dominates—originary awareness or lack of cognitive excitability—introduces a directedness, a vector indicating the direction in which the new system organization may be expected to move.

A profound and detailed explication of the term *systemic*, which describes what is pure process, was offered by Dwags-po Paṇ-chen bKra-shis rnam-rgyal (1512/13–1597).[45] With reference to the way as manifested in the fulfilling phase and with an appreciation for the dynamics involved, he highlighted the "systemic" pleasure and happiness (*lhan-cig-skyes-pa'i bde-ba*) that goes with the system's self-reflexiveness or systemic awareness. This pleasure is felt as fluctuations in intensity of kinesthetic flow patterns by means of which the system strives for its optimization. Because these flow patterns occur within the live body, the metaphors used to describe them contain an element of the physical and physiological. To a certain extent these flow patterns resemble the buildup of the physiological state of sexual excitement climaxing in orgasm. But this is not the whole story, and bKra-shis rnam-rgyal, like many others, warned against mistaking a mere illustration for the real stuff. Of course the reductionist and literalist will not be impressed by such cautionary words; his incomprehension of the nature of metaphorical diction, born out of his fear of his emotions and imagination, blinds him to anything that is not allegedly "objective," in this case the physiological.

As the total system's unfoldment, the way comprises both the developing phase, as appropriate activity for the unfoldment, and the fulfilling phase, as appreciative discernment of the unfoldment, such that the former allows the latter to come into its own right. Klong-chen rab-'byams-pa stated:

> Since appreciative discernment will not come into existence in
> the absence of appropriate activity,
> First of all, look for its foundation by means of various
> appropriate activities.

He went on to explicate the meaning of this statement by saying:

> Just as a sprout grows out of the combination of many causes and
> conditions, so also the emergence of this originary awareness that
> is the totality's sheer lucency does not occur just by virtue of its
> being within ourselves. We have to do something about it by
> resorting to appropriate activities.[46]

For this reason the developing phase is of primary importance in initiating the individual's actual engagement in the process of self-renewal and self-actualization. The total system's thrust toward optimization, the impetus itself, has been referred to in various ways. From an ontological, not ontic, point of view it is called "Being's abidingness"; from the viewpoint of its dynamics, "the thrust toward optimization"; and in view of its experiential character, "the concern with limpid clearness and consummate perspicacity." In the human context it is concretely operative as the individual's quest for a holistic understanding of himself commensurate with his holistic feeling of happiness. In other words, the way is the direct outcome of the felt thrust toward optimization. The above-noted sequence was indicated by 'Jigs-med gling-pa, who, after a lengthy discussion of preliminaries, began the account of this way of self-renewal with the words:[47]

> The way has two aspects: developing phase and fulfilling phase.
> First the developing phase is going to be explicated in analogy
> with the four kinds of ontogenesis[48]

> In order to cleanse and transmute the tendencies and
> propensities operative in them.
>
> The procedure itself is a kind of recapitulation of the four onto-
> genetic patterns, respectively, within the context of the three-
> phase evolution[49] of the world referred to as samsara, whereby the
> holistic triune hierarchical order is restored to its original purity.

Several points in this summary account need elucidation. The phrase
"tendencies and propensities" refers to an ensemble of built-in programs,
self-perpetuating but modifiable psychic patterns that include what we
usually consider to be the physical aspect of a person. A rather clumsy
but exact rendering of what the Tibetan term means is "experientially
initiated potentialities of experience."[50] In the context of a person's
physical, bodily existence, the body as an experienced phenomenon is
not so much something represented by objectifying thought, which deals
with it as a potential corpse, but as something apprehended in the immediacy of its lived concreteness. However, its presentational immediacy or
gestalt quality is constantly subverted by representational, objectifying,
and quantifying thinking, which "disengages itself from the experiencer
and prescinds from his existentiality" (Schrag 1969, p. 113). The point
that needs emphasizing, to avoid any misconceptions about the transmutation to be effected, is that while we are biologically normalized in
presenting a self-perpetuating species, mentally we can creatively trans-
form ourselves through the symbolic re-creation of our reality.

Though relatively flexible, these programs have been recognized by
the Buddhist thinkers, especially those who focused on experience and
its unfoldment, as providing the conditions for a movement within experience that develops into objectifying and, by implication, subjectifying,
representational thinking within a context of an objectifiable environment. This movement was further recognized as having a veiling rather
than revealing effect because of the implicit assumption that, with respect to the concrete individual, body and mind are determinable entities that somehow stand to the inquiring subject, postulated as a self
and often identified with the mind, in the relation of "ownership"—the
subject "has a body" (lus-can) and "has a mind" (sems-can). Against this
naive assumption the Buddhist thinkers, specifically those of the rDzogs-
chen tradition, noted that the two qualifications of "having a body" and
"having a mind" are descriptive of a symmetry-breaking process such that
the initial, undifferentiated core, variously termed "thrust toward optimization" or "concern with limpid clearness and consummate perspicacity," in its dynamics is permutated and enfolded in these conspicuous

"quantized" aspects. With the idea of a holomovement in mind, Klong-chen rab-'byams-pa spoke of this quantization as follows:

> The total system's excitation as its thrust toward optimization is termed "having a body" (*lus-can*) when it is enfolded in the net of the body; it is termed "having a mind" (*sems-can*) when it is enfolded in the net of mentation with its eight perceptual patterns; it is termed "having a veil" (*sgrib-pa-can*) when it is enfolded in karmic actions with their subliminal programs; it is termed "having darkness" (*mun-pa-can*) when it is enfolded in its stepped-down version of excitation. These and other descriptions apply to it when it abides in the individual's phase transitions.[51]

The phrases "having a body" and "having a mind" are somewhat self-explicatory, whereas the expression "having a veil" refers to the system's inner dynamics whereby its thrust toward optimization has become shrouded in emotional autopollution and by thematizing mentation which also fragments the original unity by the welter of its fictions so that a person misses the forest for the trees.[52] Similarly, the expression "having darkness" refers to the resulting murky state, which, because of its lack of cognitive excitation, is felt as a "blackout" of the system's original lucency. It nonetheless is tacitly admitted to be retrievable.

IN-DEPTH APPRAISALS AND PHASE TRANSITIONS

The symbolic re-creation of the world, which is initiated by the developing phase as a transformative experience, sketches the coevolution of a living system and its biosphere as the unfurling of a space-time continuum generated by the system itself. In this experiential process we can recognize an intimate correlation between in-depth appraisals and phase transitions[53] such that the latter appear to be related to morphological structuration and the former to morphogenetic dynamics within a holistically acting, multilevel reality, with each level exhibiting a clearly defined domain of phenomena.

From among the various phase transitions, three are of particular significance in this context: the dying phase, the re-organization phase, and the renewal phase. Each phase has its own autopoietic dynamics, which, from the viewpoint of its cognitive activity, constitutes one of three in-depth appraisals and, from the viewpoint of its cognitive domain, constitutes one of the three realms of desires, aesthetic forms, and formlessness.

The in-depth appraisals, which probe and lay bare the system's innermost core, effect a linking backward to the origin —a process that restores the broken symmetry and lost unity—and also provides for the possibility of sensing the dynamics of the system's evolution at its origin while, with the dissolution of old structures (death), paving the way for the emergence of new structures (birth) via the domain of increased instability. Though designated "in-depth appraisals" because their experience is similar to what occurs in concentration, pertaining to the lower-order commonly accepted reality, they are basically systemic, time- and space-binding events. That is, the temporal span from the past into the future, concentrated in the experiencer, is suggested by the apparent sequence of these appraisals, while their being spatially concentrated within the experiencer is suggested by the world-spanning lighting-up in-depth appraisal, through which the cognitive principle operative in each appraisal relates the world to the experiencer and the experiencer to the whole world.

Within this triadic scheme, which nevertheless presents an unbroken unity, the first in-depth appraisal, which figuratively marks the origin of the ensuing holomovent of the symbolic re-creation of man and world with all the symmetry breaks taking place, as well as the restoration of the broken symmetry and lost unity, is termed the "Being-in-its-being-ness in-depth appraisal." It was described by bsTan-pa'i nyi-ma as follows:

> First one has to disengage one's mind from its habitually disruptive, symmetry-breaking activity and not chase after its deceptive fictions, and then to allow the mind as the system's pure excitation, an utter openness that cannot be expressed in words, to rest for a while in its own dynamics, as yet undisturbed by thematic stirrings. This putting the mind in neutral is a tuning-in to a super-openness, which is also known as the "diamond-like" or "openness in-depth appraisal." Since it does away with the extremist view that assumes the existence of some static eternalistic principle, and cleans up and restores to their original purity the program for the realm of formlessness as well as the death phase so that they turn into a meaning-rich gestalt experience, this in-depth appraisal is assured in view of Being's open-dimensional facticity, which cannot be fathomed by thematizing thought, in its character of cognitive excitation. [54]

The specification of the Being-in-its-beingness in-depth appraisal as a dynamic openness, the system's facticity, vibrant in its excitation, implicitly points to the system's other feature of being a sheer lucency and radiance, its actuality, which as an in-depth appraisal is called a "world-spanning lighting-up in-depth appraisal." That is, while the "Being-in-its-beingness in-depth appraisal" describes what is felt to be Being's pure potential, the "world-spanning lighting-up in-depth appraisal" describes how this pure potential comes to presence as a luminous horizon of meaning, which manifests as a kind of disposition toward another and is felt as compassion that, because of its world-spanning character, is as yet not confined to a specific object. Nevertheless, it already addresses itself to a possible domain of activity. This in-depth appraisal was described by the same author as follows:

> The world-spanning lighting-up in-depth appraisal is an as yet feeble imaginative cultivation of a magic-trance-like, unobjectified compassion for the sentient beings who do not understand that Being's originary awareness holistically abides in them, in view of the fact that it has surged from Being's dynamic reach and range that is an openness and radiance. It is a tuning-in to the magic of compassion and is also called a "hero's march" or "non-partiality in-depth appraisal." Since it does away with the extremist view which assumes the existence of a static nihility and radically transforms the program for the realm of aesthetic forms as well as the phase transition such that they come fully into play as the gestalt experience of a world-horizon of meaning, this in-depth appraisal is assured in view of it being the effulgence of Being's cognitive excitation as the unimpeded actualization possibility of the system's resonance.[55]

Within the framework of this world-spanning lighting-up in-depth appraisal, the stabilization of specific structures, shaped by systemic conditions in their interplay, is about to occur. This systemic event is referred to as the "causal momentum in-depth appraisal" and was described by the above author as follows:

> When out of Being's dynamic reach and range, as yet undisrupted by thematic stirrings, compassion has effected a projection of what becomes its operational domain, then if the experiencer can keep his mind in the facticity of pure experience in its perceptible mode of such gnosemes as HŪM and HRĪḤ, hovering brilliantly in the

expanse of an empty sky, this is what is meant by the causal momentum in-depth appraisal. It is the experiencer's encounter with Being through the image of its originary awareness having assumed personalistic traits or his establishing a dialogue with Being through subtle gnosemic nuclei.[56] It is also termed a "magic-like" or "attributeless in-depth appraisal." Since it cleans up the grime of the reductionistic belief in a self as well as the program for the realm of desires and brings to maturity the renewal phase (birth) in the gestalt experience of an ideal norm felt and envisaged as a deiform energy, this in-depth appraisal is assured by the systemic excitation's creativity making itself known in an objectively cognitive context.

Thus to sum up, the interplay of the three in-depth appraisals is such that the Being-in-its-beingness in-depth appraisal as such makes the system's auto-excitation, which experiences itself as a meaning-rich gestalt, and the two other gestalt experiences of a world-horizon of meaning and of ideal norms, which are the joint effects of the dynamics of Being's meaning-rich gestalt, the way of its own unfoldment.[57]

As the outcome of the interplay between the Being-in-its-beingness in-depth appraisal experienced as the dissolution of old structures into their origin, which is pure (*dag*) potential, and the world-spanning lighting-up in-depth appraisal experienced as the luminous presencing of this pure potential in a world-horizon of meaning and as the phase of reorganization with all possibilities completely (*rdzogs*) present, the emerging structure that will be experienced as the maturation (*smin-byed*) of a new dynamic regime is a gestalt acting as an ideal norm within the experiencer's life-world, which is both the potential for and the guiding image of cultural design. As such it is also the energizing force of a forward thrust that dynamically links the physical (samsaric) and spiritual (nirvanic) dimensions of the experiencer's existence.

Being creatively forged, as it were, as what moves in between (*bar*) these two dimensions—the lower (*mar*) and upper (*yar*) levels of the system's hierarchical organization—this new structure, from the viewpoint of the whole system, is a globally stable but never static structure, so much more so as it operates in coordination with the two other dimensions; from the viewpoint of the experiencer, it is a guiding image that quite literally "leads" and provides a sense of direction for the experiencer's development, which because of its holistic character is not a mere zigzagging between the two dimensions "below" and "above" but a movement that overcomes every kind of duality. Therefore, after having spoken of the phase of restoring samsara to its original purity, 'Jigs-med gling-pa continued:

> Through the image of a deiform energy whose posturing
>   corresponds to the ease associated with nirvana,
> This goal is already completely present in the ground.
> Since both the purity of samsara and the completeness of
>   nirvana contribute to the maturation into the fulfilling phase,
> The triune operation of purity, completeness, and maturation is
>   of greatest importance. [58]

Note also that the guiding image "speaks" and resonates in the experiencer, who responds by attempting to speak in the "language of the system" (*sngags*), which is gnosemic. Any of its gnosemes is experienced in the sense of being felt as simultaneously audible and visible. This observation of sound being felt as the system's expression that is halfway between its tangibly physical and intangibly mental aspects lends added significance to Suzanne K. Langer's (1967, 1972) contention that language developed around feelings and emotions, not things. Gnosemic language comes as utterance that "asserts nothing and demonstrates nothing, but which nonetheless initiates everything by making it possible for us to speak at all" (Fallico 1962, p.64). This "initiating everything" is indicated by the specification of this in-depth appraisal as causal momentum in the sense that it reintroduces an awareness of value and meaning by providing the guiding image for human culture, of which art is the oldest and finest expression. Buddhist art in particular is utterance, not representation.

Lastly, the measure of the new structure's stability is directly related to the intensity of its radiance and dependability.

The interrelationship between what is "cleaned up" by the three in-depth appraisals and what is "restored" by the clean-up operation is graphically presented in Figures 1 and 2.

Being-in-its-beingness as pure potential and the world-spanning lighting-up of this pure potential together energize, as it were, the causal momentum to specifically enact the symbolic re-creation of one's self and one's world. This re-creation is tantamount to the reinstatement of a sense of quality in one's life. Quality, however, cannot be quantified but only appreciated and, as noted, appreciative discernment as a holistic process is characteristic of the fulfilling phase, which, as a higher-order reality, reaches into the developing phase, a lower-order reality, and

The clean-up operation (In-depth appraisal)		What is being cleaned up		The outcome of the clean-up operation
Being-in-its-beingness (*de-bzhin-nyid*)		Death (*'chi-srid*)		The gestalt quality of meaning (*chos-sku*)
World-spanning (*kun-tu snang-ba*)		In between (*bar-srid*)		World-horizon (*longs-sku*)
Causal momentum (*rgyu*)		Birth (*skye-srid*)		Guiding image (*sprul-sku*)

FIGURE 1:   Process-oriented presentation

which, through its selectively appropriate activity, imparts meaning to what one does. Inasmuch as appreciative discernment and appropriate activity are intimately intertwined and inasmuch as the felt and appreciated quality in what one does is still imaged in the presentational vividness of the flow of intense happiness along the developing lines of the live body, even this aspect of the fulfilling phase is considered to be of the nature of the developing phase. The implication of the distinction between a fulfilling phase as such and a fulfilling phase as *implicate order*—to use a term coined by British physicist David Bohm[59]—is that, from a system point of view, the fulfilling phase as such, being the whole system or the totality of Being, has exact symmetry, while the fulfilling phase as the implicate order in the developing phase has approximate symmetry.

However complex the developing phase may appear with its initiation of visions and its symbolic re-creation of one's self and one's world, none of its "contents" serve as ends in themselves, simply because the developing phase is the total system, the whole of Being, in operation—a gigantic experiment in autopoiesis.

'Jigs-med gling-pa expressed this idea in the following words:

> All appropriate activities, to the extent that
> They have manifested as developing phase aspects due to their being
> Projections of compassion in its operation as a world-spanning lighting-up in-depth appraisal,
> Are as such the projective glow of an appreciative discernment, as yet undisturbed by thematic stirrings, in its operation as the Being-in-its-beingness in-depth appraisal.
> This is what is meant by the unerring, superb way of appropriate activities.

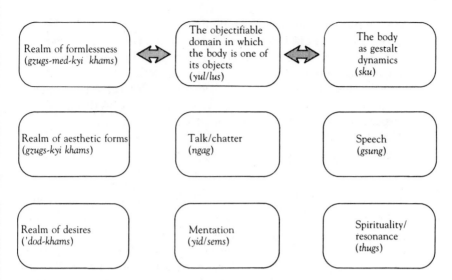

FIGURE 2: Structure-oriented presentation

> The developing phase presents the profound paradox of there
> being a presence (a world-spanning lighting-up) which yet is
> nothing (the openness of Being-in-its-beingness),
> Having never been established as something essential ever since
> Being's lighting-up has occurred.
> It is also the unity of appropriate activity and appreciative
> discernment, and
> The way in which all phases that characterize the developing
> phase are linked together.[60]

Buddhist thinkers have customarily presented their process-oriented thinking, as already indicated by the emphasis on a "way" as the going itself, schematically in terms of what can easily be construed as a linear, teleological (goal-seeking) approach—a starting-point (gzhi), a way (lam), and a goal ('bras-bu). But this concretistic and basically static world view is superseded by a more dynamic conception of what constitutes the logical arrangement of processes operating in the system—the initial vision (lta-ba), the cultivation of the vision as a creative reaching out (sgom-pa), the mutual interaction between the live system and its environment (spyod-pa), and the complexity of the evolving self-realization ('bras-bu) that itself serves as a new beginning. This difference between a static and dynamic conception was succinctly stated by Klong-chen rab-'byams-pa:

The customary intellectual-spiritual pursuits claim the triad of gestalt experiences to be the "goal"; but in this rDzogs-chen teaching, this triad is claimed to be the lighting-up of the way. The
experience of Being's meaning-rich gestalt is the lighting-up of the
way because as long as there is meaning (chos) there is a mind
dealing with it and this is a way (lam), and as long as there is the
experience of a gestalt (sku), this, too, is the lighting-up of the
way, because there is the live-body (lus, as the prototype of the
gestalt). Hence this experiencing is not some dead-end state
(mthar-thug).[61]

In a similar vein g·Yung-ston rdo-rje dpal bzang-po (1284–1365)
stated:

Although there are these four facets: a vision, its cultivation, the
interaction of the experiencer with the environment envisaged,
and the climaxing of this process, the experiencing of these four
facets as an undivided whole is termed "making the goal the way."
It is specific to the gSang-sngags (Guhyamantra) Mahāyoga.[62]

We have now come full circle. What the developing phase, with the
fulfilling phase as its appreciative, higher-order organizing principle, has
created is nothing but that from which it has started—the whole or
Being's abidingness.

To sum up, if we conceive of the developing phase as a description of
the system's self-organization in the direction of its optimization expressed in terms of the commensurateness of blissfulness, radiance, and
undividedness, the idea of safeguards that are presumably built-in comes
to mind. Actually, this idea of safeguards was fully developed by rDza
dPal-sprul O-rgyan 'Jigs-med chos-kyi dbang-po (1808–?),[63] and reiter-
ated by his erstwhile disciple mKhan-po Yon-dga'.[64]

There are four safeguards of the system's life-force (srog-sdom gzer),
which are named after the functions they perform and are distributed
over the various aspects of the developing phase as a whole, with its
logical arrangement of processes operating in the experiencer. The unity
of appropriate activity and appreciative discernment is the initial vision
that, far from being merely receptive, is already actively designing a
course of action in the light of its open-dimensional, appreciative awareness. This vision, which expresses the invariance of Being's meaning-
rich potential that it posits by "seeing" in terms of the complementarity
of open-dimensionality and compassion, is its own safeguard (dgongs-pa
mi-'gyur-ba'i gzer).

The three in-depth appraisals, in their lighting-up and providing the momentum for the system's (man's) development, initiate a symmetry break through which the experiencer begins to reflect on the world he has seen. It is the first attempt to distinguish different things, which at this stage are still mutable—forces or energies that may be formulated and shaped in any way we (as the whole system) please—and as such is the imaginative cultivation of the vision as a creative reaching out to these formulated energies—popularly believed to be "gods" who are somehow "out there" and turned into an eternal principle by subsequent speculation, which is at the root of all forms of theism. In the cultivation of the vision these energies are recognized as "projections" of one's own mind, and in this awareness these very projections serve as a safeguard of the in-depth appraisals (*ting-'dzin lha'i gzer*).

The "paradox of there being a presence which yet is nothing," by virtue of being a presencing that has as yet no boundaries and thus is truly a world-spanning lighting-up, is part of the cultivation of the vision reaching out to and becoming deeply involved in this presence. But to the extent that this presence is ceaselessly sparkling and glowing in energy-rich manifestations—the deiform energies as incomparable figures who communicate something of the mystery of Being to the experiencer as part of the presence and as partners in the evolving communication—this becoming involved is referred to as the mutual interaction of the experiencer with his environment. These incomparable figures who "speak" in gnosemes present a hierarchical organization within themselves in so far as they consist of a mentation level dominated by the in-depth appraisal of Being and of a mentation level dominated by Being's originary awareness. This qualified mentation is still of an undivided character and, with reference to the experiencer of these figures who images himself as a mentation process that is ready to "play the game" by following its rules, stipulates a basic connectedness of dynamic phenomena. The "language" of communication in the interaction of the incomparable figures with the experiencer is the gnosemic utterance that paradoxically says nothing and yet a great deal because it speaks and gives voice to the whole. Utterance as the plenitude of meaning, the very dynamics of the whole, is its own safeguard (*snying-po sngags-kyi gzer*) against getting lost in the everyday chatter or talk that means nothing and merely conceals an utter emptiness and hollowness.

The "way in which all phases that characterize the developing phase are linked together" is the goal that, in view of the fact that the developing phase is a linking backward to the origin, is a new beginning in the sense that the system now optimally "acts itself out." It is not a question of *what* it does but of *how* it goes about acting itself out. This "how" manifests in fluctuations exhibiting various colors and hues expressive of the simultaneously felt and perceived quality of these higher-order actional fluctuations, which themselves are gnosemically in-formed. Thus white in its brilliance is felt as quiet, calm, and soothing; yellow in its smoothness as rich and enriching; red in its brightness as forceful and passionate; green in its darkness as stern and unrelenting; and blue in its luster and radiance as lofty, deep, infinite, and invariant. This value-rich activity of the whole system in its fluctuations, reflecting and coping with the exigencies of a live situation, the contextualized experiencer, is its built-in safeguard ('phro-'du phrin-las-kyi gzer).

In the life of a concrete individual the developing phase aims at regaining the initial, undivided wholeness, a dynamic openness, by re-enacting the system's unfolding in a qualitative context while safeguarding the emergent quality from being transformed into quantity.

IMAGINATION AND THE SYMBOLIC RECREATION OF THE WORLD

In the presentation of holistic existential imagination through which the symbolic re-creation of one's self and one's world corresponding to a restructuring of a new level of life is enacted—primarily as a way to greater freedom—two trends are detectable. Specifically, where the person involved in this process is concerned, these trends reflect the total system's basic complementarity, referred to as "appropriate activity" and "appreciative discernment," of which one or the other can be selected for an analytical presentation and even be given a prominent place in the practical execution of the program. Ultimately, however, both must regain their unity in what has been their original complementarity.

On the basis of these two trends presenting a difference without separation, the indigenous texts that discuss them are classified as father-tantras (pha-rgyud) and mother-tantras (ma-rgyud). The word tantra (rgyud) is used in this combination as a term for a literary form, not in its basic connotation of existenz, the dynamic grounding of the organizing notions in experience, weaving the fabric of one's life. Moreover, the terms father and mother already suggest the intimacy the experiencer senses to exist between himself and the forces that operate around and in himself and that he "images" in figures closest to him; at the same time these terms point to an even more profound aspect of the dynamics that pervade the whole universe. To the components in complementarity dynamics the Tibetan texts apply the terms yab and yum, respectively, and to the complementarity itself, the term *yab-yum*. We may match this subtlety of diction by speaking of the masculine and feminine and the male-female.

Traditionally the masculine has been associated with operational devices, aiming at fixation and stability and standing for explicitness and attention to details. By contrast, the feminine has been associated with sensing, feeling, and appreciating the ongoing process as it becomes ever more alive in gaining intensity and meaning.[65] Long before the idea of a universal connectedness gained ground in modern thought, the Buddhist thinkers had recognized that each of us is the interplay of the fundamental forces of the universe whose "origin" is certainly not found in the violence of the "big bang" of which cosmologists are so fond but is more akin to the "inflationary nothing universe" model recently proposed by American physicist Alan H. Guth.[66] Leaving aside the idea of an origin, which after all has only a logical meaning, the Buddhist idea of universal connectedness stresses the mutual setting of the conditions for the evolution of world and mankind.

In a sense the symbolic re-creation of oneself and one's world recapitulates the evolution of the universe itself. With the unfolding of the original undivided whole—a nothingness that as pure potential is seething with possibilities to become actualized—through its holomovement, which in the language of mathematical field theory may be likened to the total system's phase transition from its "true vacuum" to a "false vacuum," step-wise symmetry breaks occur. This is indicated by the triad of in-depth appraisals, each one, however, weaving a new net of time- and space-binding that the individual experiences and formulates in terms of contextualities. The "critical" phase is reached in the causal momentum in-depth appraisal where the system discloses itself as a spontaneity in its first utterance—the gnoseme. This remember, is not a talking *about* but the immediacy of a felt image that is simultaneously an imaged feeling. It constitutively enters the realized presence that is the "world"—the whole and yet nothing. The immediate consequence of this symmetry break is the simultaneity of the physical and the psychic evolution in the universe as world and mankind. Thus, not only are matter and mind complementary, influencing each other through a feedback link between them, so also are the individual's finitude, the impure and opaque (*ma-dag*) materially bound "false vacuum," and his transcendence, the pure and symbolic (*dag*) materially unbound "true vacuum." In this sense our self-transcendence, through which we open up to the infinite, is made possible by symmetry-breaking processes.

The first utterance, which initiates the symbolic re-creation process, is the gnoseme E, disclosing the total system's openness experienced by the individual to be like the vast sky or the infinite expanse of space. The Tibetan term *nam-mkha'* connotes both "sky" and "space" and has always been understood as a cognitive force, not as an inert container. Thus sensed space in its immediate quality of a wide-open sky is the design of Being's dynamic nothingness made manifest in an immediately felt, all-embracing actuality. Being the whole and yet only part of it, we and our world cannot escape Being and, figuratively speaking, remain shackled to it. Klong-chen rab-'byams-pa expressed this idea in the following words:

> Space, as manifest design of Being's nothingness,
> Shackles all that is without exception in its iron grip.
> Just as space as a shackle shackles the world and what is in it,
> So the self-manifesting entities of reality stay shackled in
>   Being's super originary openness.[67]

In the course of being uttered the gnoseme *E* assumes shape and color, having both abstract and sensuous qualities and implications. Its shape derives from the form of the Sanskrit letter *e* in the Devanagari script and therefore is that of an equilateral triangle with the base pointing upward and the vertex facing downward. In its abstract aspect of a triangle it still has a sensuous quality that is its deep blue color and thus identical with the color of Being's openness, compared by virtue of its fieldlike character to the expanse of the sky.

This color is an intangible nothing, that still is the stimulating presence of infinity that beckons one's mind into ever expanding distances:

> But as we readily follow an agreeable object that flies from us, we love to contemplate blue, not because it advances to us, but because it draws us after it.
>
> (Wie wir einen angenehmen Gegenstand, der vor uns flieht, gern verfolgen, so sehen wir das Blaue gern an, nicht weil es auf uns dringt, sondern weil es uns nach sich zieht.)[68]

In these words Johann Wolfgang von Goethe has captured the very nature of this color. Blue is a color whose abundance we note in sky and sea. Its jubilant intensity and vibrancy seen in a clear sky are gladdening and heartening; its somber darkness and suspense convey awesomeness and nobility that, when agitated, may well be expressive of a fierce mood.

Further, the abstract aspect of the triangle evokes the idea of Being as a self-emancipating process in three interrelated accessing modes. Its base symbolizes the openness accessing as the ground of and incentive to this movement. Its sides symbolize the attribute-free and bias-free accessing modes as the way and the climaxing of the whole process.[69] In its sensuous aspect this triangle is referred to by what at the first glance seems to be a vulgarism, but on closer inspection turns out to be a highly symbolical phrase. We should always remember that our language may be quite adequate for expressing ordinary things but is quite inadequate for other purposes. Having originated in the context of one's physical reality, which is never some clear-cut "nothing-but-physical," but always interlaced with the speaker's feelings, his imagination and understanding, his creative urge and capabilities, it carries with it, but is not restricted to it, an irreducible core of literalness. It can open up and link the individual to the higher-order spiritual dimension, just as it can reduce him to and hold him captive in the lower-order psychophysical and psychosocial dimension. Thus in the tantalizingly ambiguous phrase "indestructibility/diamond mistress cleft,"[70] apart from conveying a sense of indivisibility, irreducibility, inexhaustibility and also of preciousness and valuableness, "indestructibility/diamond" indicates Being's field character or spatiality where its actional aspect becomes located and is being worked out. "Mistress," with its implied sense of youthfulness, indicates a joyous exuberance discerned as bliss supreme, and "cleft" indicates the creative source from what is to become originates. Instead of this seeming vulgarism, aimed at interesting those who are still under the power of their desires and passions[71] and who, as we would nowadays say, think of nothing but sex, the less compromising phrase "space/sky mystery of the feminine"[72] is used. This diction calls to mind the poet's words:

> Sovereign mistress of the world!
> Let me in the azure
> Tent of Heaven, in light unfurled
> Here thy Mystery measure!
>
> (Höchste Herrscherin der Welt!
> Lasse mich im blauen,
> Ausgespannten Himmelszelt
> Dein Geheimnis schauen!)
>
> —Goethe, *Faust II*

In this sensuous context the triangle with its base facing upward symbolizes an ever expanding unfolding of the individual's capabilities in his progress to nirvana, while the vertex facing downward symbolizes the fact that any growth originates here in samsara such that the dynamics of the process holistically resides in both samsara and nirvana. Here the outside color of this triangle is white to indicate the pure symbol-rich quality of the fundamental forces of the universe, of which space is of primary importance as it opens up the possibility for the other, latently present, forces to emerge and then to jointly establish the physical and not-quite-so-physical universe. The inside color is red to indicate the arousal of desire in others.[73] This symbolism has been expressed poetically in the words:

> The eternal Feminine leadeth us
> Upward and on.
>
> (Das Ewig-Weibliche
> Zieht uns hinan.)
>
> —Goethe, *Faust II*

In painting this theme is illustrated in Titian's famous *Venus and the Organ Player* and before him by an unknown artist of about 1420 in the painting of Venus and a troop of ardent admirers on a marriage tray.[74] The sensuous aspect of this triangular gnoseme *E*, in whichever ways it may be referred to, the one always including the other, is of particular importance for the symbolic re-creation of ourselves and our world because it already implies a contextualized experiencer, installed in a world that is *his* life-world, one not yet determined by the quantifying objectifications of thematic thought but still in a process of a qualitatively felt developing. More important, it reflects the simultaneity of physical and psychic organizations such that the without or the physical and the within or the physical-cum-psychic owe their organization to the ubiquity of a universal, systemic connectedness by way of homologous dynamics. From this unified perspective, matter is not just a waste product in the spiritualization—a euphemism for sterilization—of the universe but an indispensable factor in the working of the underlying principle of complementarity. Thus not only are matter and mind complementary, so also are the without and the within, which display a further symmetry break into a live body (*lus*), the matter system in and from which mentation (*sems*) and its higher-order dynamics, the total system's cognitive excitability (*rig-pa*), operate.[75]

This idea of a universal connectedness that, as already indicated, unfolds in the coevolution of the without and the within, pointing to a symmetry break that makes the various stages of their evolution in the direction of a coordinate hierarchy possible, has been axiomatic to Buddhist thinking. With reference to the fundamental forces (*'byung-ba*) operating "out there" in the universe and "in here" as the individual's live body, which in this context are already a unique "quantization" of the totality's field character and hence termed *small* (*chung-ba*), Klong-chen rab-'byams-pa said:

> The "external" (*phyi*) fundamental forces such as solidification/ earth and cohesion/water and so on serve as the foundation (*rten*) of the "internal" (*nang*) fundamental forces, and since they, the external and the internal, are connected in a semantic context hierarchy of the "founding" (*rten*) and the "founded" (*brten-pa*), there are thus two aspects to the fundamental forces, and there is no "sentient being" (*sems-can*) or "Buddha" (*sangs-rgyas*) who is not "founded" on these two.[76]

He went on to explicate the difference between a sentient being and a Buddha as presenting a symmetry break such that a sentient being expresses and is the expression of the grosser, matter-dominated aspect of the fundamental forces, while a Buddha expresses and is the expression of the subtler, radiation-dominated aspect of the same fundamental forces.

In the symbolic re-creation of the world, which is thereby readied to become a place in which one can feel at home, its organizing principle is operative in two different directions, although the starting point is the same. The system's dynamic openness, which in terms of the immediacy of its experience is referred to as space/sky openness or space/sky mystery, remains the primary fundamental force, which even in this "quantized" phase does not lose its connectedness with the higher-order reality of which it is, to be more exact, a "false vacuum." From this openness there emerge, by a process that may be called the system's autovariations in its gnosemic potential, activated by the experiencer's utterance of these very gnosemes, the other fundamental forces and their respective "auto- poietic levels." After all, the world is not only full of colors but also of sounds, as so beautifully expressed by Joseph Freiherr von Eichendorff in his small poem "Divining Rod" (Wünschelrute):

> There is a song asleep in all things
> Which are dreaming on and on,
> And the world starts singing
> If only you sound the magic word.

> (Schläft ein Lied in allen Dingen,
> Die da träumen fort und fort,
> Und die Welt hebt an zu singen,
> Triffst du nur das Zauberwort.)

The sequence of the manifestation of the fundamental forces, seen and heard in their gnosemic activity, is as follows: motility/wind (*rlung-YAM*), heat/fire (*me-RAM*), cohesion/water (*chu-BAM*), and solidification/earth (*sa-LAM*).

This sequence of the fundamental forces in shaping the universe, including the human being, is presented in the *Pañcakrama* (I, 19–22), a work belonging to the group of texts classified as father-tantras, which deal primarily with the developing phase and emphasize appropriate activity in the sense of planning and designing. In the *Hevajratantra* (I, viii, 1–2), a work presenting a mother-tantra that deals with the fulfilling phase as already present in the developing phase and that emphasizes appreciative discernment, the starting point, too, is the system's dynamic openness, referred to as its "mystery" or "the mistress cleft," but the sequence of the manifestation of the fundamental forces is in the reverse order.

This latter movement, which may be seen as restoring the lost unity and harmony by dissolving all contrasts and dissonances and by appreciating the flow of energy throughout the system, is an enfoldment and linking backward to the origin, while appropriate activity is a movement of unfoldment and the establishment of more or less rigid structures that break the original unity. This is visually diagrammed in Figure 3.

There is a further dimension to the sequence of the manifestation of the fundamental forces that we feel operating in us, simply because they have structured and continue structuring us and our environment. Above all, the world in which we live, as the Buddhists knew long ago, is an "appreciated world" (a term coined by Sir Geoffrey Vickers, 1968, 1970). However, we experience and appreciate our world from the viewpoint of and by virtue of our being embodied beings. None of us can escape his or her body, which is therefore always present for experience as the center from and around which visions, actions, and interests are organized. Further, the embodied experiencer's comprehension and organization of his world occurs in the context of his or her sexuality. There is no point in going into the reductionist clichés of the mushrooming theories about the nature of masculinity and femininity, as little can be learned from them. They merely point to what everyone already knows but is reluctant to admit—that sexuality is a mode of world comprehension and cannot be effaced from the embodied experiencer.

In this context of the embodied experiencer as a sexual being, the different sequences in which the fundamental forces appear become significant. In the *Hevajratantra*, emphasizing the felt appreciation of life's dynamics and by implication the dissolution of old structures, the sequence starts from what is felt as solidification or rigidification, termed

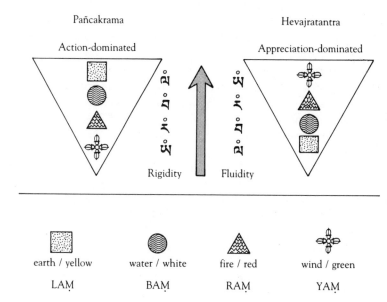

FIGURE 3

earth by virtue of its effect, and then proceeds through fluidity, wetness, and/or cohesion, termed *water*, warmth or heat, termed *fire*, and motility, driftage, and/or turbulence, termed *wind*, to an all-encompassing openness or *space*, itself a fundamental force but one that encompasses the other four forces, which through symmetry breaks, seem to fan out from this undivided force whose quality is felt as bliss supreme.

There are two complementary aspects to this process as it occurs in the embodied experiencer. The first one manifests and expresses itself in the animate organism, the embodied experiencer, as sexuality and is manifested, expressed by the sexuality of that particular animate organism. It therefore manifests in what the literalist will consider an explicit description of the sexual act as it passes from foreplay to climax. However, both the literalist and reductionist overlook the fact that sexuality is a manner of existence and therefore not just a classificatory concept or a particular procedure. As a manner of existence it is also, as noted before, a mode of world comprehension that is never static knowledge but an ongoing organization of information. Hence sexuality plays a significant role in self-reflection, self-transcendence, and self-realization. This certainly is intended by the following passage from the *Hevajratantra* (I, x, 38–40), of which a paraphrase, incorporating the interpretation of Dam-pa bsod-nams rgyal-mtshan (1312–1375) of the Sa-skya tradition,

in particular, and that of Dwags-po Paṇ-chen bKra-shis rnam-rgyal
(1512/13–1587) of the dKar-brgyud tradition, may be given here:

> The joining of *bola* and *kakkola* (the scepter or penis as appropriate
> activity and the lotus or vagina as appreciative discernment) estab-
> lishes a mutual contact between appropriate activity and apprecia-
> tive discernment. Out of the first moment of joy which is the
> comprehension of it as firmness, the individual's biophysical com-
> ponent termed "earth" is born in the manner of a magic projection
> of the individual's systemic reality.
>
> Then when the individual's concern with psychic fulfillment
> has taken on the character of a seminal fluid, the individual's
> biophysical component termed "water" comes into existence,
> while
>
> From the tossing and turning of the scepter and the lotus
> warmth is generated which presents the individual's biophysical
> component termed "fire";
>
> The subtle vibration and movement of the concern with psy-
> chic fulfillment at this moment, which is like the calm before the
> storm, is well known as the individual's biophysical component
> termed "wind."
>
> The feeling of bliss that emerges from this moment is said to be
> the individual's biophysical component termed "space" which is
> not reducible to color or shape since it has no form whatsoever. In
> this way the individual's systemic reality has surrounded itself with
> five fundamental forces.
>
> Since this feeling of bliss has come from the fundamental
> forces constituting the physical reality of the individual, and in
> view of the fact that it is a transitory experience and has been
> brought about by the joining of the sexual organs, it is not the
> higher order systemic bliss. It is merely a pointer to it.[77]

In other words, this "feeling at one's best," which, as it occurs at the
moment of orgasm, may be conceived of as an extreme achievement of
satisfaction involving the whole person, yet it remains organismic and,
taken as an end in itself, it will initiate repeat performances that inevita-
bly fall short of holistically effecting the symbolic re-creation of ourselves
and our world. The second aspect is the process of dying, not as a process
that can be observed from the outside, but as one that the individual
must go through and, in so doing, senses it as the dissolution of old
structures such that, for example, the firmness of the body loses its live-
body solidity.

By contrast with the above account, the *Pañcakrama*, emphasizing designing and structuration, lets the unfoldment proceed from the open-dimensionality of the system. This sequence of the manifestation of the fundamental forces indicates the various stages of the system's mentation (*sems*), specifically in its motility-mentation complexity, in search of a possible embodiment (*lus*). Although we may speak here of "mentation," we must not assume that what is so termed can in any way be considered as "consciousness" or "mind" in the generally accepted sense of these terms, even if it already has all the distinct possibilities for eventually developing into it. Rather it is the evolving system's self-organization dynamics, which, as such, pertains to a comparatively small "quantized" pattern of excitation within the totality and gives rise to relatively stable, autopoietic, and conceptually separable projections into a three-dimensional reality. Its unfoldment into the individual's "body" was described by Sangs-rgyas gling-pa (1340–1396) as follows:

The intrinsic inner glow of the pentad of originary awareness modes, which make up the system's super-diaphanous quality of being a meaning-rich field, radiates outward as five hues. With respect to these hues, mentation arises by a slight trend in the direction of their subjectively appropriating what is their prospective external reference. However, mentation is as yet not found as anything anywhere, rather there is only Being's abidingness as a fundamental force termed "space." The dynamics of this prevailing radiance in all its freshness in which there is nothing that could be given the predicate of being this or that, breaks forth in a variety of manifestations, and this is termed its "motility." Because of the radiance involved one speaks of it as mentation, and because of the movement involved one speaks of it as motility. If one tries to analyze this phenomenon, one does not find anything, neither does one find radiance nor motility as something. Since through the dynamics of this subjectifying motility operation, which fails to recognize the fact that radiance/mentation and motility are indivisible, warmth is generated, this phenomenon constitutes the fundamental force termed "fire." It is as when a person does some heavy work and begins to sweat and feel hot. Through this warmth the fundamental force termed "earth" is generated. The vapor that arises when the warmth of fire hits the earth is the fundamental force termed "water." Thus, once the trend to subjectively appropriate the dynamics of the totality's originary awareness has become noticeable, the five external fundamental forces come into operation. Each of them has its autopoietic dynamics and through

it assumes a distinct pattern. When these fundamental forces combine, the subtle radiation "stuff" in them operates in a co-ordinate
manner and thereby the live-body is established.[78]

In brief, the evolution of the subjective "I"—I appropriate, grasp,
single out, and so on—occurs through a symmetry break and everything
that follows is determined by this first step. Nonetheless, from the viewpoint of the holomovement, the initial symmetry break does not violate
the principle of a universal connectedness or the inseparability of dynamic phenomena, as is clearly pointed out by the reference to the subtle
radiation, which, having come to the fore in the original symmetry
break, continues to be operative in the fundamental forces. With respect
to the individual, the overall effect was described by Edmund Husserl
(1923/24, 1950, p. 60) as follows:

> My organism is the only one in which I experience in an absolutely
> immediate manner, the embodiment of a psychic life (viz., a sens-
> ing, objectivating, feeling, and so forth, which is my own life, or
> which is "expressed" in corporeal form, in changing corporeal,
> animate events). This occurs in such a way that I at once perceive
> not only the thing, animate organism, and its corporeal conduct,
> but also at the same time my psychic life; and, finally, both of
> them at once: the self-embodying of the latter (the psychic life) in
> the former (my organism), and the self-expressing of the one in
> the other.[79]

Following an old tradition already found in the *Majjhimanikāya* of
the Pāli Canon, Klong-chen rab-'byams-pa called this "mentation-in-
search-of-a-body" *dri-za* (Pāli *gandhabba*), literally meaning "scent-eater."
This term may well reflect a very early phase in the evolution of the
brain—the so-called reptilian brain, including the olfactory system,
which still plays an important role in oral and genital functions such as
feeding and mating, and the so-called paleomammalian brain or limbic
system, which brings emotional preferences into play. Related to this
early phase is the designation of the female's contribution to reproduction as "blood" (*khrag*) or "estrus" (*rdul*), the latter still playing a role in
the sexual cycle of all female mammals except the primates who, in the
evolution of their brains, have largely circumvented these older layers
and emphasized visual and auditory functions. Although these old terms
may seem thoroughly antiquated, in light of what we now know about
sexual reproduction, their persistence shows that language does not keep
pace with a rapidly increasing knowledge and also that possibly more is

involved in sexual reproduction than what science so far has been able to account for.

The embodying process starts from the motility aspect of the motility-mentation complex, which "fans" the latent desire in its prospective parents whom it has selected ("having sniffed up their scent") for becoming embodied and who are ready for conception, which takes place in and through the mingling of the father's semen with the mother's estrus. The emotional preference that already comes into play at this early stage is indicated by the mentation-to-be-embodied showing its affection to the father if it is going to be a girl and to the mother if it is going to be a boy. Through this "fanning" the smoldering desire turns into a blaze ("fire") of an ardent attachment ('dod-chags) such that ardor ('dod) as the motivating force (rgyu) is modified by attachment (chags) as the concomitant force (rkyen) to the effect that ardor establishes the mutually effective attraction ("water"), and attachment turns into the "behavioral" modes of looking and smiling at each other, holding each other's hands and so on, and, finally, in the intimacy of an embrace and the sexual act, the solidity ("earth") of the body is effected.[80]

In the context of its search for a body mentation is, through its motility, already embedded in the framework of the fundamental forces of the universe as a whole. Hence mentation is not an epiphenomenon, nor does it stand outside the evolutionary process; rather it is in it as its organizing principle on a specific level. The indigenous texts speak of either four or five fundamental forces, of which four are particularly instrumental in setting up the physical-material, while the fifth is an openness that reaches into the physical-material, making structuration possible without ever being limited to the resulting structure. Note also that this embodying openness is the genus- and species-specific potential in interaction with the other four fundamental forces. Figures 4 and 5 attempt to clarify the complexity of the evolutionary process. Figure 4 illustrates man's cosmic connectedness,[81] while Figure 5 illustrates man's enworlded existential connectedness.[82]

In the structuration and interpretation of what is to become our "world" as viewed from both a cosmic and existential perspective, mentation as the organizing principle of the cosmo-ontological system plays a decisive role. Elaborating this theme by piecing together and paraphrasing Klong-chen rab-'byams-pa's presentations, we can say that the motility-mentation complex operates from and through the higher order reality of four fundamental forces as the organizing principle in the lower-order reality of the same four fundamental forces, which on this level constitute the genetic information of what is to become the "macrosystem," which itself presents a network of functional relationships. The

Color/light values	External fundamental forces	Internal physical aspect	Arcane psychic aspect
Blue	Space	Orifices in the body	kun-gzhi
White	Cohesion/ water	Blood/lymph and the overall constitution	kun-gzhi'i rnam-par shes-pa
Yellow	Solidity/ earth	Flesh and bones	yid
Red	Heat/ fire	Body warmth	nyon-yid
Green	Motility/ wind	Breath	sgo-lnga'i rnam-par shes-pa

The arrow indicates subliminal structuring.

The technical terms retained for simplicity's sake in Figure 4 are:
kun-gzhi: the genus- and species-specific potential as an approximate symmetry transformation of Being (gzhi) as the exact symmetry limit;
kun-gzhi'i rnam-par shes-pa: the genus- and species-specific potential on its way toward constituting the experiencer's background for perceptual processes;
sgo lnga'i rnam-par shes-pa: the five sense-specific perceptual operations;
yid: the concept-forming perception;
nyon-yid: the affectively toned perception determining the character of the subject's response to the environment.

FIGURE 4

father's part contains the "catalytic" capabilities (rgyu), and the mother's part contains the "synthesizing and modifying" capabilities (rkyen). Each offers something that the other does not have. From this interplay between catalysis and (re-)synthesis, mentation's matter system evolves. Significantly, the texts speak of these lower-order fundamental forces in terms of their radiation-"stuff" aspect (dangs-ma) tempered by some matter-"stuff" (snyigs-ma) admixture, whereby the lower-order reality remains dynamically connected with the higher-order reality.

This distinction between "radiation"-dominated fundamental forces (dangs-ma) and "matter"-dominated fundamental forces (snyigs-ma), whose interplay determines the evolution of the universe as it manifests in a global contextuality of interwoven constituents, has come to the fore in the wake of Being's holomovement, which in its ceaseless creativity gives rise to the experiential situations of samsara and nirvana. Because the fundamental forces as features of the holomovement "originate" as and constitute a creative play in Being's projective glow, which itself as

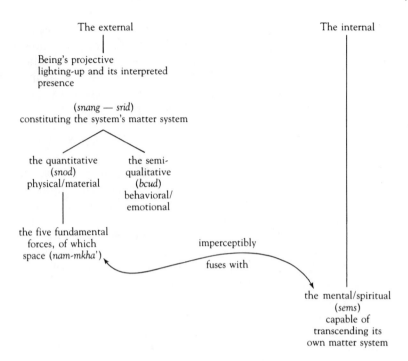

FIGURE 5

the holomovement may be considered an "originary" symmetry break, they derive the name "fundamental forces" ('*byung-ba*) from this occurrence. Within this holomovement a further symmetry break occurs such that "internally" these fundamental forces retain their radiation-dominated character in becoming the pure autoluminescence of an originary awareness (*ye-shes*), while "externally" their matter-dominated character causes the system to go astray into a global, self-perpetuating pattern of contextuality (*bag-chags 'khrul-pa*). In other words, externally the fundamental forces come as the rigidity of structural patterns (*gzugs*) that make up the environment, with its visual, auditory, olfactory, and tactile fields for the experiencer installed in it, and as such they may be considered a kind of "frozen" energy; internally the fundamental forces retain their dynamic character as presenting a kind of vibration-stuff (*dngos*). This vibratory aspect of the fundamental forces serves, as we might say, as the "neural chassis"[83] for mentation (*sems*), on the one hand, and originary awareness (*ye-shes*) or cognitive excitation (*rig-pa*), on the other hand, both in themselves being comparable to standing-wave patterns.[84]

Strictly speaking, the fundamental forces, whether "radiation" dominated or "matter" dominated, are manifestations of the holomovement in its process of becoming shrouded in its own creations, without, however, being permanently affected by them. The projective glow of an otherwise invariant sheer lucency—a symmetry break that is more like an approximate symmetry transformation—is a frolicking that has many ramifications. In the words of Klong-chen rab-'byams-pa:

> Although there is no opacity in the field character of Being, it manifests unobstructedly from the holomovement in any form when it begins stirring. This frolicking of the stepped-down version of original and optimal excitation ushers in mentation; its ornament is the individual's subjectivity manifest in the emotions. Furthermore, frolicking means a capacity or creativity or a ray of light, and as such is merely Being's projective glow; the situation is the same as when a sprout grows from a seed, or when the contours of a face are reflected in a mirror. Ornament means that it is merely an aspect in the culmination of the process, just like a flower is the culmination of the plant's program already present in the seed, or like the engraving on a seal.[85]

This picturesque presentation implies the hierarchical self-organization in which each level has its own organization dynamics and yet operates with the other levels in a coordinated manner. Klong-chen rab-'byams-pa explicitly indicated this triune character in these words:

> The stepped-down version of Being's excitation (ma-rig-pa) does not exist by itself or alone; it abides ornamented by all the programs pertaining to man's embeddedness in his lower order reality, summed up in the term mentation (sems); and it furthermore abides together with objectifying thought, the individual's subjectivity (yid). Their unity is summarily termed the stepped-down version of Being's excitation, and this is precisely what is meant by samsara.[86]

While Klong-chen rab-'byams-pa emphasized the unity in this hierarchy, the *Rig-pa rang-shar* spelled out the evolution of this hierarchy:

> Although in the lighting-up of Being's genuine super-diaphaneity (ka-dag) there is no stepped-down version of its excitation, no mentation, no subjectivity; the stepped-down version of Being's excitation originates the creative dynamics of Being as a spontaneous presence (lhun-grub). From the frolicking of this stepped-

down version of excitation originates mentation; from mentation's ornamentation originates subjectivity; from the subjectivity's object-relatedness originate the five poisons.[88]

Despite the fact that we can differentiate between mentation and excitation and refer to the former as a lower-order reality and to the latter as a higher-order reality, mentation remains an integral aspect of the living system called "man." Again, their connectedness is indicated by Klong-chen rab-'byams-pa in the following words:

Mentation imitates excitation to the extent that the latter is there or not; excitation does not imitate mentation by following it when it is there or returning to itself when mentation is not there. In substance, excitation is not subordinate to mentation; since excitation is Being's creative dynamics, mentation is subordinate to it. If excitation does not stir, mentation with its bifurcating tendencies that split the original unity is unable to operate. It is just like the case with waves which, too, cannot originate when the water does not move.[89]

To illustrate the point he gave a partial quotation from the *Rig-pa rang-shar*, which here may be given in full:

An illustration for the difference between excitation and its stepped-down version is water and its pictorial representation, the latter depending on a variety of conditions. An illustration for the difference between mentation and excitation is water and waves; excitation as water is not subordinate to mentation, the waves.[90]

While the terms *mentation* (*sems*) and *stepped-down version of excitation* (*ma-rig-pa*) are generally used as synonyms in the description of man's embeddedness in the lower order reality that makes up the closed universe of his life-world, the terms *excitation* (*rig-pa*) and *originary awareness* (*ye-shes*), too, are often used to refer to the higher-order reality that is characterized by openness and that, in rDzogs-chen thought, is more of the nature of an approximate symmetry transformation than an exact symmetry limit.[91] The complexity of this holistic rDzogs-chen approach may be resolved by the graphical presentation in Figure 6.

Although cognitive excitation and originary awareness may be used synonymously, a subtle difference in usage is discernible. Cognitive excitation is more specifically used with respect to Being's optimal dynamics, of which originary awareness, with its specific modes, is one of its many functions. As pure cognitive dynamics it manifests and is sensed as a projective glow that generates both mentation and originary awareness modes. This apparent contradiction remains inexplicable when a mechanistic-reductionist approach to a problem's solution is taken and Being is considered to be an equilibrium system. Here we deal with live processes of and in a nonequilibrium system, which, because of its pervasive intelligence, is becoming increasingly self-reflexive by virtue of fluctuations in its excitability. In this process creative, holistic imagination (*sgom-pa*), often vaguely if not misleadingly referred to as meditation, plays a significant role. Bear in mind that there is a tremendous difference between creative, holistic imagination and reconfirmatory imagination based on logical-abstract operations that remain state specific. Again, Klong-chen rab-'byams-pa has most clearly pointed out the difference between genuine creative imagination (*sgom-pa dag-pa*) and egocentric, idiosyncratic rumination (*yid-dpyod*). His words are:

> The gist of holistic imagination is that in it there are no vagaries of the thematizing operations of the mind due to it being Being's sheer lucency...[92]

and

> Not mystified with respect to Being's abidingness, it is free from the extremes of holding it to be something eternally given or to be some nihility . . .[93]

and

> Having missed the gist of what is the profoundness of holistic imagination,
> A stupid person engages in that kind of imagination which is his subjective rumination and thereby deceives his own mind.[94]

For creative, holistic imagination, which, as Klong-chen rab-'byams-pa has intimated, is systemic in the sense of being the dynamic of Being's sheer lucency, the lower-order reality of mentation becomes a challenge to the higher-order reality of originary awareness in one's own self, and through this creative imagination mentation is redeemed from the rigidity into which it has allowed itself to glide off. In creative imagination originary awareness is already at work and is given free reign.

The symbolic re-creation of the outer reality and of the individual

Being (*gzhi*) and its holomovement (*gzhi-snang*)
as

| ka-dag (super-diaphanous) | : | The exact symmetry limit |

| lhun-grub (spontaneous presence) | : | The approximate symmetry transformation or higher-order reality |

| rig-pa (cognitive excitation) | : | Being's nonequilibrium dynamics allowing for fluctuations between higher- and lower-order processes, the latter being a stepped-down version of the former and thus constituting an approximate displacement symmetry transformation |

Figure 6

living in this world by which he is molded and on which he leaves his impression by his very presence is, on the part of the experiencer, a recapitulation of Being's autopoiesis and begins with a first utterance issuing from its higher-order reality level (*don-dam-pa'i sngags*). As such utterance already reflects the system's dynamics as it expresses itself in the complementarity of appropriate activity and appreciative discernment as the formulation of Being's utter openness, which, by virtue of its pervasive originary awareness, implies an intentionality such that it is both act phase and object phase—the object being the original openness. Through the deeply felt understanding of what is as yet an undivided whole, the system is prevented from gliding off into a state marked by stepped-down excitation, and its optimal excitation is preserved. For this reason, utterance has been defined as protecting the individual from becoming subjected to the vicissitudes of samsara and aiding him in his quest for optimization.[95]

On this higher-order reality level, utterance is far from representing a word. In its passage into the lower-order reality, it evolves into the spoken word through its gnosemic components, which are referred to as vowels and consonants and which in themselves already have a gestalt quality whose inner dynamics is provided by Being's originary awareness.[96]

THE IMAGINATIVE RECAPITULATION OF MORPHO- AND ONTOGENETIC PROCESSES

The gestalt that emerges has, as it were, its own life and in its further development expresses itself in deeply moving images. In so doing it initiates a fivefold series of imaginatively and experientially lived through morpho- and ontogenetic processes.[97]

Although these processes operate from the higher-order reality of whose dynamics, referred to as originary awareness modes, they are already an expression in that they express themselves in and are subsequently illustrated by images that belong to the lower order reality. Therefore, by virtue of their being both an expression and the expressed, these images facilitate the accessing to the higher-order reality.[98] Howver, this reality is not something static but is a complex organization in which its originary awareness modes each have a distinct functional quality.

The image of the first imaginatively and experientially lived-through morpho- and ontogenetic process is that of the full moon, which itself has evolved from the gnosemic vowels in what has become Being's first utterance. Its color is white to indicate that what it symbolically expresses is free from any kind of subjectivity (logical-abstract or emotional-pollutant), is without the mist of the mind's divisive tendencies, and is without the grime deposited by the emotions. There is another potent association involved in choosing or giving a prominent place to the image of the moon. The phenomenal world, the lower order reality, has always been felt and seen as being something like the reflection of the moon in clear water, or as Klong-chen rab-'byams-pa expresses it:

> To the extent that there are phenomena, to that extent there is "nothing" (openness);
> Just like the inseparability of water and the moon's reflection in it.[99]

The originary awareness that operates in this sense is the so-called quasi-mirroring originary awareness whose standard definition is given in the *Mahāyānasūtrālaṅkāra* (IX, 68):

> This quasi-mirroring originary awareness is not concerned with an I or mine,
> It is not narrowly circumscribed, always present,
> Not confused about all that can be known,
> But never keen on it.

This definition, however, says nothing about its internal dynamics intimated by the reference to a mirror, which in Buddhist and Eastern thought is generally considered to be a powerful revealer, not merely a passive reflector. This dynamic character is brought out in such works as the *Rig-pa rang-shar* and the *sGra thal-'gyur-ba*. Unlike the *Mahāyāna-sūtrālaṅkāra*, which deals with this awareness and the other related modes in the context of their social implication and applicability, these works deal with the psychic qualities involved. Thus the *Rig-pa rang-shar* states:

> The quasi-mirroring originary awareness operates in the
>   following manner:
> Just like in the disk of a mirror
> Whatever is held up to it seems to get into it,
> So in Being's flawless excitation
> Its awareness is radiating as Being's pure lighting-up.[100]

A more elaborate description appears in the *sGra thal-'gyur-ba*:

> In the quasi-mirroring originary awareness
> The lighting-up aspect of the reflection's shape and color is a
>   total event.
> Because it is white and flawless, it presents a light value
> Which in its lighting-up by itself links itself with what is to
>   become either samsara or nirvana.
> Because the shape of all that is lights up in it,
> It is an auto-excitatory awareness.
> Though radiant, it is "nothing," and because of being
>   "nothing," an utter openness, it is free.
> There are in it no reductionist notions that hold freedom to be
>   some thing,
> It is a totality in being a dynamic ground that need not be
>   posited as a ground and is freedom in and through itself.[101]

Thus the cool whiteness of the full moon, the revealing power of a mirror, as well as Being's dynamic openness "imaging" itself in these images, combine to give this imaginatively experienced morpho- and ontogenetic process a prominent place in the system's autopoiesis. The image for the second imaginatively and experientially lived through morpho- and ontogenetic process is that of the sun, which dispels darkness all around and is beneficial to all living beings. It too is a force such that if the moon opens up possible vistas, the sun fills them with its red-hot light. In terms of awareness this all-encompassing character is expressed by the identity originary awareness or, more precisely, identity as such originary awareness which is defined in the *sGra thal-'gyur-ba* as follows:

Identity-as-such (*mnyam-nyid*) means
Identity with respect to a twofold causal momentum (*rgyu*),
     identity with respect to a threefold modifier (*rkyen*),
Identity with respect to time, and identity with respect to
     dimension.
There is no duality in it, and it has no demarcations.
To abide as an intentionality with the undivided as object phase
     and the non-dividing as act phase
Is what is meant by identity (*mnyam-pa*) and as such
It abides disengaged from distress-laden thought processes.

As-such (*nyid*) means that it cannot be contrived nor found by
     looking for it;
It is there in its own right, devoid of any essence;
As pure experience it is such that in it all dichotomic trends
     have disappeared.

Originary awareness means that with respect to its abidingness
By understanding what it really is in itself
It does not abide in either samsara or nirvana. [102]

     There are a number of difficult key terms in this passage, which have
been elucidated, though in a concise and "encoded" manner, by Klong-
chen rab-'byams-pa. [103] According to him the "twofold causal momentum" refers to the two life-situations in which the concrete individual
finds himself and which are summarily termed *samsara* and *nirvana*. As
long as it makes its presence felt, each such life-situation remains identical with itself. And the so-called identity of samsara and nirvana means
only that both are identical in being a situation; it does not mean that
the one can be equated with the other. The "threefold modifier" indicates the manner in which these life-situations can be understood from
the viewpoint of their identity with themselves. They are, accordingly
and respectively, the deeply felt understanding of each situation as a
lighting-up, an openness or "nothing," as well as the nonduality of this
lighting-up and openness. In other words, the understanding of the situation in its immediacy comes as a restatement of the paradox that there is
a presence and yet nothing. However, through this deeply felt understanding of either life-situation, the experiencer is already actively and
holistically engaged in the situation. In the situation called samsara he
blunders along through the actions initiated by his body (*lus*), speech/
talk (*ngag*), and mind (*yid*)—the three separate "gates" through which
the enworlded individual goes out to meet his enworldedness. In the

situation called nirvana he goes about it in a coherent and coordinated manner reflecting the interpenetrating quality levels of gestalt (*sku*), communication/utterance (*gsung*), and spirituality or resonance (*thugs*). Whether we speak of samsara's identity with itself or nirvana's identity with itself, Being's or the totality's identity with itself is holistically present in each identity such that in samsara's identity with itself it presents an approximate displacement symmetry transformation, while in nirvana's identity with itself it presents an approximate symmetry transformation. "Identity with respect to time" means that in the immediacy of this identity awareness, linear and irreversible time has been suspended, and "identity with respect to dimension" means that all dichotomic trends have been "dispatched to where the experiencer has completely done away with them."

Unlike these two imaginatively and experientially lived-through morpho- and ontogenetic processes, which may be considered as preliminary phases in the total system's self-organization in the strict sense of the word *self* as authentic selfhood (*bdag-nyid chen-po*), not to be confused with the everyday, organismic subject with its limit-cycle behavior and its egological (*bdag, ātman*) preoccupations, the third imaginatively and experientially lived-through morpho- and ontogenetic process is not associated with a distinct image to illustrate its character. Rather this process brings into focus some aspect in the holomovement as it has proceeded so far by the system's quasi-mirroring of itself and "detecting" its identity with itself. It evolves a specificity as a creative design in its becoming increasingly self-reflexive, and any such specificity is not predetermined, even if it occurs within a certain context. So this process is appropriately called "a specificity-initiating, selective mapping originary awareness." It was explicated in the *sGra thal-'gyur-ba* in the following manner:

> The specificity-initiating, selective mapping originary awareness,
>   according to its sensory domains,
> Selectively illumines, step by step, whatever lights up in them.
> That which has been selected, once its lighting-up by itself has
>   become transparently clear,
> Becomes the object for the system's cognitive excitation.
> Specificity-initiating (*so-sor*) means that each specificity
> Comes as an aid to itself which counteracts any other specificity;
> Selective mapping (*rtog-pa*) means to see the specific characteristic
>   of what has been specified;
> It carries with it an increase in clarity of what has been lighting up
>   in the cognitive field by itself.

Originary awareness (*ye-shes*) means that as originary (*ye*) it has
   arisen from a beginning without beginning,
And as awareness (*shes*) it is pure and free from the blemishes of
   emotional pollutants. [104]

These three processes describe the complexity that characterizes the
process of individuation with its endogenous dynamics that corresponds
to the process of embodiment with its endogenous dynamics by way of
homology or holistic connectedness. Moreover, the evolving individuality, as the individual's authentic self, presents itself with a specific
"signature" (*phyag-mtshan*), [105] an emblematic quality that, in a person's
life, becomes a guiding image. To evolve it needs, if we may say so, the
catalytic, innovative incentive of the totality's mirroring itself and the
conservative self-consistency of the totality throughout its totality, the
one imaged as the moon (corresponding on the organismic level to the
seminal fluid), the other imaged as the sun (corresponding on the organismic level to the estrus). The signature in which the totality expresses
and installs itself in its existential context, drawing its sustenance from
the totality as its nourishing ground, corresponds on the organismic level
to the principle of mentation in search of its embodiment and installing
itself in the soil prepared by the mingling of the seminal fluid with the
estrus.

The fourth imaginatively and experientially lived-through morpho-
and ontogenetic process, which on the organismic level corresponds to
the period of gestation in which the fetus develops into a sentient being,
is called the "task-posed and accomplished originary awareness." In this
connection it is important to remember that all these morpho- and
ontogenetic processes are systemic, pertaining to the whole, and hence
the phrase "task-posed and accomplished" must be understood from this
level. As systemic activity this cognitive and morphogenetic process does
not, therefore, imply a sequential, problem-solving, and strictly linear
kind of activity, which proceeds step by step and is never a *fait accompli*,
but constitutes a creative dynamic as Klong-chen rab-'byams-pa has
pointed out: "The manifestation of Being's capabilities is their creative
dynamics." [106]

This systemic awareness was explicated in the *sGra thal-'gyur-ba* as
follows:

The task-posed and accomplished originary awareness is such
   that
Once the stress of having to do something and the strain in
   accomplishing something have slackened and waned by
   themselves,

Everything falls into its place and its intrinsic freedom.
From out of the holomovement, intrinsically free and complete,
Its flawlessness that is aloof from atomistic reductions has
    become an inalienable possession.
It is beyond the domain of thematizing discursiveness,
It just is such that it cannot be split by anything.

Since it is complete in what it is, there are no limits to its
    lighting-up;
Since what has been selected is understood in all its immediacy,
    it is referred to as task-posed (bya-ba), and
Since any such task posed turns out to be an fait accompli (grub-
    pa), there is no necessity for repeating or quitting
What is no longer a matter of desire.

Once the totality that has been there from its beginningless
    beginning (ye)
Has come to the fore by its (re-)cognition of itself as such
    (shes),
The stage where one has done away with the welter of separate
    things has been reached.[107]

The fifth and last imaginatively and experientially lived through morpho- and ontogenetic process corresponds on the organismic level to the birth of a child as a psychophysically embodied being (lus). Here the totality, which in the culmination of its holistic process of self-realization experiences itself as a gestalt (sku), is meaning (chos) through and through and irreducible to any preconceived or predetermined and otherwise postulated "meaning." As the totality's inner dynamics, meaning is its ever widening expanse (dbyings), which coincides and is commensurate with its originary awareness (ye-shes). This holistic awareness is described in the sGra thal-'gyur-ba in the following words, each of its descriptive terms being the encodement of an intricate program:

The dimension of meaning is vast and
Neither an outer circumference nor inner center can be pin-
    pointed;[108]
Hence it is Being's pure meaningfulness as the ground and reason
    for freedom as a holistic process.[109]
Meaning (chos) is that which, in one's engagement with it,
Sets the parameters of the transworldly and the worldly,
While as such it remains Being's intrinsic lucency in its effulgence.

Dimension (*dbyings*) is an opening-up of possibilities,
A self-existent, ultimate abidingness.

Originary awareness (*ye-shes*) means that originary (*ye*) is the abiding authentic self which is such that
Ever since its beginningless beginning it has never existed as some contrived entity,
And awareness (*shes*) means that through this awareness
Being stands free from samsara and nirvana.
This is life's bestowal of meaning on itself, a holistically self-manifesting lighting-up. [110]

With the emergence of meaning, we have once again come full circle. In the immediacy of its experience the dualism of body and mind, the dualism of a lower-order and a higher-order reality, has been transcended and resolved into a unified perspective that is best described as pure process. But meaning as process is precisely that from which what we ordinarily call "consciousness" as self-cognition has started. This "beginning" was cryptically indicated by the quasi-mirroring originary awareness as the first imaginatively and experientially lived through morpho- and ontgenetic process. It is as if the totality—here we can only speak figuratively—is holding up to itself a mirror of its own making, and what it sees is but itself in its totality. This has been stated quite explicitly by Indrabhūti (of unknown date) in his *Jñānasiddhi* (I 49):

In the same manner as a person sees his reflection firmly established in a mirror,
So also Being in its meaning-rich gestalt sees itself present in its mirroring awareness.

Because of Being's totality becoming so revealed in the mirror, its reflection is an invitation to see in a creative manner that expresses the inner dynamics of Being. Such seeing is tantamount to creative imagination, which furthers itself through the images it calls up and develops. These images, apart from being pictures and conventionally agreed-upon signs, are preeminently symbols because in their sensuous quality, they do not lose their connectedness with the concrete situation in which they occur, and because they have around them what Hans Lipps (1938), with reference to the spoken word, has called "the circle of the unexpressed" and "the infinity of the unsaid," which in this situation draws the experiencer into ever widening realms of a deeply felt and sensed meaningfulness. The importance of creative imagination in the process of self-realization as self-cognition and, by implication, in the symbolic re-creation of ourselves and our world has therefore always been recognized by the rDzogs-chen thinkers. They knew that these images not only instigate a probing of the deeper layers of the living system but they also become the vitalizing force in it. Dam-pa bSod-nams rgyal-mtshan has the following to say about the significance of the imagery in the five imaginatively and experientially lived-through morpho- and ontogenetic processes:

> Since creative imagination is easy when these five originary awareness modes are imaginatively dealt with in terms of their sensuous images such as the moon and so on, this is what is meant by making the sensuous images the way to self-realization; since by the conviction that these sensuous images are actually the five originary awareness modes, their pentad is thereby realized, this is what is meant by making conviction the way to self-realization; if one further thinks that this pentad belongs to the level referred to as the one who has been victorious and imagines this level as having this pentad now, this is what is meant by making the goal the way to self-realization; and since through this pentad the prerequisites for self-realization are readied and the intellectual and emotional obscurations have been dispersed, this is what is meant by making revitalization the way to self-realization.[111]

A careful examination of this passage reveals an important feature of live processes: their circularity. In the context of the developing phase as a means to effect the symbolic re-creation of ourselves and our world, circularity not only involves a linking backward to the origin as a new beginning but also shows imagination to be a circular rather than a linear process, such that the cognizing-imaging and the cognized-imaged are related to each other in a manner similar to the correspondence between the initial state of a dynamic system and another state of it as its image. Such a correspondence holds for all states in which a system may find itself, be this an optimally cognitively excited (*rig-pa*) state or a cognitively unexcited (*ma-rig-pa*) state.

The transformation taking place has its root in the system's internal nonequilibrium, which has been intimated by what has been termed Being's cognitive excitation as its self-referential dynamics. This internal nonequilibrium prevents the system from ever coming to a state of rest— or death, but through a sequence of mutatory transitions (the multi-faceted features of the developing phase) drives it to new dynamic regimes. The richness of this formative process, which shapes the intellectual and spiritual horizon of the individual, the way he will see himself and the world, reflects the tremendous wealth of open possibilities to be shaped into new realities, which in turn shape him and his world. In this thoroughly creative process the world is transformed into and re-created as realms of the imagination, often referred to, in mythological language, as "Buddha"-realms, which are somehow believed to be "located" in the four directions of the compass and, in the manner of a sociopolitical organization, to be presided over by the vassals of the central organizing authority—the king who, in being inseparable from his queen, illustrates the principle of complementarity pervading the whole universe. As such these realms reflect, despite the symmetry breaks involved, a new space- and time-binding dynamics. This certainly is the indigenous interpretation of the term *zhing-khams*, rendered in English as "Buddha"-realms:

> One speaks of *zhing*, because it is like a field in the sense that it is the source from which Being's lighting-up as samsara or nirvana spreads, as well as in the sense that it has become the universe as man's cognitive domain. One speaks of *khams*, because in whatever sensuous modes samsara and nirvana manifest, they have the same flavor by virtue of being the expression of man's potential as his optimization thrust.[112]

Although the reference to the optimization thrust may be understood as suggesting the system's self-organization in terms of its time-binding, the first structure that emerges, in terms of its space-binding, is that of a palace or temple, which because of its cosmic scale still participates in the openness of the totality and as such defies any attempt to measure it by the standards of thematizing, representational thought.[113]

Through this structuration Being or the universe has become the "home" of us as living beings. In a narrower sense this home mediates between us and our environing world. By virtue of being a mediator, the palace or temple or home is more of the nature of being an extension of our embodied existence (*lus*), so much more so as the palace gates or, according to other sources, the palace walls are the four immeasurably great catalysts of kindness, compassion, joy, and dynamic balancing out.

There is only *one* temple in the world, and that is the human body.

(Es gibt nur *einen* Tempel in der Welt, und das ist der menschliche Körper.)[114]

In these words Novalis has admirably captured the sentiment of the dignity of the human individual as an embodied being.

CONCLUSION

In his embodiment a human being is, at any moment, a vibrating energy pattern, a set of relationships that reach out to other regions within a larger whole. In mythological-religious language he is a god or goddess, and this deiform energy is more explicitly experienced as having a gestalt quality in which the whole of Being's meaningfulness reverberates. According to the context in which this gestalt experience manifests, it exhibits either a calm, serene, and peaceful quality or a fierce, frantic, and irate quality. These qualities do not imply an alternation but illustrate Being's paradoxical nature of being "nothing," an utter openness, and yet a "radiant" presence, a ceaseless frolicking in various roles. This is explicitly stated in the dGongs-pa zang-thal, a huge collection of works rediscovered in 1366/67 by Rig-'dzin rGod-kyi ldem-'phru-can (1337–1408):

> From the openness aspect of Being's meaning-rich gestalt come the
> peaceful deiform energies;
> From the radiance aspect of Being's meaning-rich gestalt come the
> irate deiform energies.[115]

These transformative energies, whether in their peaceful or fierce aspects, are felt to be steering factors in the overall symbolic re-creation of the world. In this process the human individual figures most prominently, not in the sense of a fixed egological center but as an autopoietic agency that is as much in coevolution with itself as with the world it is re-creating.

PART TWO

EASTERN PRESENTATION

THE TRANSLATION

[Prologue]
[Introduction]
I. Preparation
  A. The General Preparation
    1. The Sense of Disengagement
    2. Taking Refuge
      a. Its Meaning
      b. Its Imaginative Development
    3. Raising One's Mind to a Higher Level
      a. Its Meaning
      b. The Training in It
  B. The Special Preparation
    1. The Elimination of Adverse Conditions
      a. Driving Out Obnoxious Spirits
      b. Closing Loopholes
    2. Effecting Favorable Conditions
      a. The Feeling of Being Spiritually Revitalized
      b. Hallowing the Articles Used in Worship
        (1) Tonic
        (2) Cakes
        (3) Life-stuff
II. The Main Part
  A. Tuning-in to a State of Composure
    1. Tuning-in to a Gestalt Experience Felt as Being's Impression on Us
      a. Retracing the Three In-depth Appraisals
        (1) The In-depth Appraisal of Being-in-its-beingness
        (2) The In-depth Appraisal of a World-spanning Lighting-up
        (3) The In-depth Appraisal of a Causal Momentum
        [A Summary of the In-depth Appraisals]
      b. Setting Up a Dynamic Configuration as the Site for the Forces in Us to Operate and Activating These Very Forces

(1) The Construction of the Palace
    (a) Terracing the Fundamental Forces
    (b) The Erection of the Palace [The Palace Symbols]
    (c) Setting Up the Throne
(2) The Activation of the Deiform Energy
    (a) The Activation Procedure
    (b) The Distinct Features of the Deiform Energy [The Calm Aspect] [The Fierce Aspect]
    (c) Inviting Being's Originary Awareness
        (1) The Invitation
        (2) The Request to Be Seated
    (d) Worship and Praise
        (1) The Greeting
        (2) The Worship
            (a) An External Act
            (b) An Internal Act
                (i) Tonic
                (ii) Cakes
                (iii) Life-stuff
            (c) An Arcane Act
                (i) Coupling
                (ii) Loosening
            (d) A Being-in-its-beingness Act
        (3) The Praise
    (e) The Involvement with the Presence of the Deiform Energy
        (1) The Lucency of Its Observable Features
        (2) The Consolidation of the Proud Feeling of Being an Aspect of the Whole of Being
        (3) Keeping Before One's Mind the Symbols and Understanding Them
        (4) The Holistic Experience of Bliss, Lucency, and Openness
B. Remaining Tuned-in When Reemerging from the State of Composure [Epilogue]

Brackets indicate headings added by the translator.

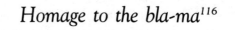

Homage to the bla-ma[116]

[PROLOGUE]

The two realities[117] through which Being's mystery expresses itself reenter their original unity when one sees Being as both appropriate activity and appreciative discernment.

Appropriate activity, the way of rDo-rje-'chang[118] during the developing phase, restrains one's slipping into low-level concretizations and reifications by means of its dynamic impression[119] on us, demonstrating that Being's meaning-rich potential[120] is its very optimization thrust.[121]

Appreciative discernment, not held captive in the thematic horizon of believing that whatever lights up in symbolic images is some concrete reality, sees that the procession of phantomlike images is not found as something in Being's abidingness.[122]

[INTRODUCTION]

The following deals with what must be known by those who aspire to reach both the highest attainments as well as the ordinary achievements[123] in life through the overwhelming experience offered by the existential approach of the Guhyamantra,[124] the unsurpassable method of tuning in to the mystery of Being. Only the most important points will be discussed in an easily intelligible manner so that they may be practiced and experienced. The detailed exposition of the practices and actual experiences, however, must be learned from the texts of the direct transmission and the rediscovered treatises[125] as well as from the works written by the venerable ones of yore; they cannot be understood in just a few words.

Although the potential for the Buddha-experience,[126] embracing the totality of qualities such as the Buddha powers[127] and operating as its own optimization thrust and the experiencer's incentive to gain this experience, has forever existed in every sentient being's Existenz,[128] it is spoken of as one's psychophysical potential or affinity with Being[129] in view of how it has become temporarily ensconced in a sheath of grime.

What must be purified and transmuted is all that which obscures and begrimes the optimization thrust and is associated with samsara, postulated to exist as something though not actually existing as anything. In the wake of a fluctuation within this optimization thrust, its cognitive capacity fails to recognize itself for what it is and strays into a spatiotemporal contextuality that, on the one hand, is prepredicatively linked to the creative dynamics of this thrust and, on the other hand, is gliding into the subject-object dichotomy of ordinary thinking. Although this contextuality is not something really existent, subjectively taking it to be something existent and getting caught up in the thematic-representational fictions that constitute samsara turns this optimization thrust into an obscuring process.

Although, on the whole, there are many transmutation procedures, here the developing phase will be discussed in preference to the fulfilling phase, because a capable person knows the former to be the very foundation of and incentive for his endeavors by virtue of its approximation to the goal. The climax of this transmutation comes about when, through the power of creative imagination as the path, all incidental grime has been removed and original purity restored so that the qualities of the gestaltism of meaningful existence come to the fore as they are already latently present in the foundation.

Therefore, it is of the utmost importance to know what the developing phase is all about. Even if, from having studied the ordinary aspects of the Mahāyāna, with its division into a cause-related and a goal-sustained pursuit, we have an inkling of what starting point, way, and goal mean, the significance of the developing phase and what it entails will not dawn on us if we know nothing about this method, which operates in consonance with the goal. I will not here discuss in detail the division into starting point, way, and goal because, in order to elucidate the overall significance of the developing phase it is only necessary to discuss what has to be transmuted and how the transmutation is effected.

The defining characteristics of the developing phase have been stated by the venerable Kun-dga' snying-po (1092–1158):

> The process of tuning-in to the dynamics of Being by means of the developing phase involves the conceptual specification of the gestalt experience of a formulated, deiform energy, which has four special features: ritual practice, auto-climaxing, substance, and function.
>
> The special feature of its ritual practice ensuring passage from one state to another is the completeness of the ritual details as they relate to the developing phases that have been discussed in the

various Tantras. The special feature of its auto-climaxing, an effect without an antecedent cause, is its capacity to activate the potency of the total system's communicative dynamics. The special feature of its substance is its flowing bliss and utter openness. The special feature of its function is its symbolic character, its holistic character, and its maturation into a unitary presence.

There are three sections in this essay: (I) preparation, (II) main part, and (III) conclusion.

I.   PREPARATION

This consists of (A) a general preparation and (B) a special preparation.

A.   THE GENERAL PREPARATION

Generally, an individual who embarks on an existential approach to life's meaning must have his mind set on the Mahāyāna. The indispensable presupposition for realizing limpid clearness and consummate perspicacity is the willingness to always carry the burden of love and compassion: a love that is convinced that all sentient beings are and have been one's loving parents and a compassion that, like an all-consuming fire, is solely concerned with the welfare of others. If such a presupposition is not present, all intentions and actions will go awry, and however much one may strive to reach the exalted level of limpid clearness and consummate perspicacity in all its wholeness and perfection, one will never be able to reach that exalted level because such a person is neither suited for the Mahāyāna nor the Hīnayāna. Only when one lives with the restrictions and obligations[130] of an ethical individual does one become a valuable member of humanity.[131]

When, through the power of his affinity with Being, someone possesses love, compassion, and an attitude tending toward and sustained by limpid clearness and consummate perspicacity and has received the empowerments within the configurational setting[132] of any spiritually stabilizing force[133] from among the general and specific configurational settings of the Vajrayāna, he will attain spiritual maturity. He will also be marked by the three kinds of restrictions and obligations.[134] Therefore it is most important to set up the primary and secondary rules of the game[135] in oneself, the site of realization. Then one must understand what is meant by inducing a sense of disengagement, taking refuge, which is the cornerstone of the general spiritual pursuits, and raising one's mind to a higher level, which is the basis of the Mahāyāna pursuits.

1.   The Sense of Disengagement

Although we now have a human body, so precious and yet so difficult to find, we should be concerned that death may at any time catch up with us. Convinced that the relationship between our actions and the results we experience holds infallibly, we should realize that in whatever high or low status we may have been born in samsara, we will not escape its frustrations. Although there may be some semblance of happiness in samsara, it is like the sun breaking through the clouds only to disappear again. Pleasure and pain, victory and defeat, are but succeeding each other, and none will last forever. Being fully aware of this truth, we should not for a moment give in to the pleasures of this world. We must change our attitude by thinking that there is nothing else necessary or more beneficial than living a truly meaningful life. Whether or not we put these ideas into words, it is important to imbue our whole being with this change of attitude.

2.   Taking Refuge

a.   Its Meaning

According to the Mahāyāna, the basis of taking refuge is the unique attitude that desires release for sentient beings, who are seen to be like one's aged mother agonizing in the fiery pit of samsara. Where can one take refuge after renouncing teachers who seem to have great power in this world, such as Brahma, Śiva, and Viṣṇu; after renouncing their teachings, which, with their eternalistic claims, positive or negative, are pitfalls on a way that is misleading; after dissociating oneself from their followers, the sectarians and barbarians, and emancipating oneself from the belief that the lord of one's country, its popular gods, totemic serpents, ancestors, and so on can provide refuge?

Generally, one can take refuge in the precious triad of Jewels. In this existential pursuit, in particular, the unique object is the *bla-ma* as the quintessence of the Three Jewels, the *yi-dam* as the Buddha Jewel, and the *ḍākas*[136] and protectors as the Sangha Jewel. In them the well known three Jewels find their completeness and fulfillment. The *bla-ma* is the quintessence of all Jewels together, and his imprinting, which reflects the unity of presence and openness, manifesting as a *yi-dam*, a formulated energy presiding over the configurational setting, is the Buddha as the teacher. Existential communication, as a process comprising an object phase and act phase, is life's message. The audience, constituted by the heroes, *ḍākas* and *ḍākinīs* and so on, are the community. This precious triad forms a single configurational setting. One achieves one's aim in life by knowing that the *bla-ma*, in whom the Three Jewels and three main-springs of authentic existence[137] combine, and to whom one devotes oneself as if he were the unique wish-fulfilling gem, suffices as the sole object of refuge. In the *sDom-byung* it has been stated:

> The *bla-ma* is Buddha; the *bla-ma* is Dharma;
> Also, the *bla-ma* is Sangha.
> The *bla-ma* is glorious rDo-rje-chang.

b.   ITS IMAGINATIVE DEVELOPMENT

In front of oneself, in an open place, one must imagine one's primary *bla-ma* in the form of rDo-rje-'chang, seated on a spacious throne supported by lions, surrounded by the *bla-mas* of one's lineage.[138] In front of him is the *yi-dam*, the deiform energy of one's overriding spiritual aspiration, surrounded by the deiform energies of the configurational setting as specified in the four or six great divisions of Tantra.[139] To his right are the Buddha Jewel, the Buddhas of the three aspects of time or the thousand Buddhas living in this auspicious age; behind him is the Dharma Jewel, the scriptures resounding in their "language".[140] To his left is the Mahāyāna Sangha Jewel, the eight chief Buddha-sons[141] or the crowd of saintly aspirants such as the sixteen spiritual beings[142] of this auspicious age, as well as those who travel the way of the buildup phase and the breakthrough phase[143] in the Mahāyāna and the crowd of saintly persons represented by Śrāvakas and Pratyekabuddhas. At the periphery are the host of spiritual heroes, *ḍākas*, protectors and guardians, like thick clouds filling the sky. Mankind's leaders, caring for us with great love, they possess immeasurable qualities of sensitivity, tenderness, and ability. All sentient beings, oneself included, from one's parents to harmful spirits, extending from earth to heaven, stand before them with folded hands. Then one should say fervently, three times or more, until one feels satisfied, "From now on until I have reached the very core of limpid clearness and consummate perspicacity, I shall depend on you, shall make offerings to you, and shall never take refuge in anybody else but you."

When oneself and all sentient beings merge with these objects of refuge and these in turn with rDo-rje-'chang, the *bla-ma* in the center, and when this experience has settled in the dynamic reach and range into which no subjective notions enter and where all objective references have subsided, this is the real meaning of taking refuge in Being's abidingness. Such taking refuge is the foundation of all spiritual training, the site of accepting all restraints and obligations, the commencement of being an insider concerned with the Buddha-experience, the capacity for guarding oneself against dangers, and the source of the values and qualities that cannot be fathomed by ordinary thought.

Having taken refuge in the *bla-ma*, one holds whatever he "says"[144] to be authoritative; having taken refuge in the Buddha, one does not pay homage to the popular gods of the world; having taken refuge in the Buddha's message, one does not harm others; and having taken refuge in the Sangha, one does not associate with those who have no faith in the message of the Victorious One.

As a rule, one should take refuge six times during the day. Once the mind is set on these Jewels, one should, out of a sense of trust in them, show one's reverence[145] to Buddha statues, the scriptures, and so on, banishing all disrespect.

3.   RAISING ONE'S MIND TO A HIGHER LEVEL

a.   ITS MEANING

Though all sentient beings already have in them the momentum for the realization of the Buddha-experience, which from its very beginning has been pure and translucent in being devoid of any limiting essence, by not recognizing themselves for what they are, they have gone astray into the confines of a subject-object dichotomy, where they now roam about, believing this fiction to be something real. Like one's aged mother, they yearn for happiness but find only frustration; their desires and efforts are thwarted and come to nothing. From a deep sense of compassion, one should strive to set them free from this frustration and install them on the exalted level of unsurpassable limpid clearness and consummate perspicacity, the abiding happiness.

For this purpose I myself must first reach that exalted level. I myself must experience the quick and profound way, arousing and fully appreciating the yi-dam, the special agency in the actualization of this purpose. This is engagement.

Thrice one should boldly articulate in words the intent to raise one's mind to a higher level according to the tradition one follows,[146] while thinking that by means of a positive intention, enhanced by purpose and engagement, one will raise one's mind to this level that is suffused with limpid clearness and consummate perspicacity, free from any turbidness.

Simultaneous with raising one's mind to a higher level, one becomes a Buddha-son; all positive actions become conducive to emancipation; all evil is wiped out in a moment; the slightest good one has done will turn into infinite merits; and the way leading to freedom is actually traveled. The De-bzhin-gshegs-pa'i gsang-ba'i mdo declares:

> If the merits of an attitude imbued with limpid clearness and
>   consummate perspicacity
> Were to assume visible shape,
> This shape would fill the whole sky.
> The attitude itself is even greater.

b.   THE TRAINING IN IT

What has to be learned and practiced is to attract all sentient beings by committing oneself to never dismissing them from one's mind out of the desire to help them and never forgetting one's desire to reach the exalted level of the Buddha-experience. When these two commitments are forgotten, "purpose" and "engagement" are completely eradicated, and the positive root of Mahāyāna is thereby destroyed. Thus these two commitments must be held firmly in mind because there is no other means to realize limpid clearness and consummate perspicacity in its entirety and perfection. For this reason mental discipline is of primary importance for an ethical person. In the process of raising the mind to a higher level, "meaning" and "training" must go together.

B.   THE SPECIAL PREPARATION

1.   The Elimination of Adverse Conditions

This consists of (a) driving out obnoxious spirits and (b) closing loopholes.

a.   Driving Out Obnoxious Spirits[147]

Here the imaginative procedure is as follows: When one has become fully aware that the whole of reality is both presence and openness, one must imaginatively transfigure oneself into a deiform energy, be this rTamchog Heruka or any other spiritually stabilizing force. This transfiguration is felt to come about through Being's very dynamics as the path of spiritual growth, like a bubble surfacing in water. One then utters the following formula over the offering of sacrificial cakes to the obnoxious spirits: "ŌM" eliminates all impurities and nullifies evil and corruption; "ĀH" multiplies and infinitely expands the sacrificial ingredients; "HŪM" induces the understanding that the colors, fragrances, and flavors that these ingredients assume are of a most exquisite quality in keeping with one's devotion. Lastly, "HŌ" removes corruptible blemishes and changes everything back into the nectar of incorruptible originary awareness.[148]

One then imagines these obnoxious spirits to bow before oneself because of the light that bursts forth from the center of one's spirituality, and to listen to one's admonitions. While giving them the admonitions according to the tradition one follows, one should make the offering and then dismiss them. If they do not listen and are about to do mischief, one should imagine fiery weapons and countless replicas of the wrathful Heruka to explode from their germinal points centered in one's heart. These burst forth like shooting stars in numbers countless as atoms, from above, below and in between, pounding the bodies and minds of these obnoxious spirits into dust and incinerating them so that not even their names remain.

b.   Closing Loopholes[149]

This is like locking the door after the thief has been thrown out.

Imaginatively one gathers the scattered weapons and places them, one next to the other, so that they seem to be welded to each other and to fence in the protective tent of one's life-world, whose floor is the earth, whose roof is arches and curtains, and whose walls are made of a circular high fence. The whole resembles our universe encircled by the iron mountain. The tent itself, high in the center, gradually slopes toward the outer edges, covering the fence like a lid. In between the tent and the fence hang curtains fastened by ropes. The top of the arches consists of a demiscepter, and the middle of the fence is encircled with garlands of full scepters. All the scepters used in the construction and decoration of the protective circle are of a deep blue color. In between the large scepters are smaller ones, arranged so that they seem to be welded together. Outside this protective circle a rain of various weapons is imagined to fall, and from the fierce force in the center there rise clouds of lesser wrathful forces. Beyond lie arches of blazing flames, and beyond them, arches of billowing rivers, and beyond these, arches of fierce storms cutting to the bone. Here, where obnoxious spirits and demons cannot enter because any loopholes through which they might slip in have been closed by the protective circle, one must imagine oneself as well as those to be protected together with all one's belongings and attendants to be safely installed. One must then recite the formula of protection according to the tradition one follows. Lastly, through the exercise of one's appreciative discernment which no longer has any objective reference before it, that which is to be protected, he who protects, and the act of protection turn into a protective circle that is reality itself. This is the finest form of protection.

2.   EFFECTING FAVORABLE CONDITIONS

This consists of (a) a feeling of being spiritually revitalized and (b) hallowing the articles used in worship.

a.   THE FEELING OF BEING SPIRITUALLY REVITALIZED[150]

Prompted by one's fervent devotion, one must imagine this revitalization to stem from one's being in tune with the three mainsprings of authentic existence, who in their resonance with the whole are the source of all achievements. This revitalization is felt to be such that the gestalt quality of these mainsprings makes an indelible impression, their message is conveyed in gnosemic nuclei, and their resonance with the whole inscribes itself into one's very finitude. This triad fuses with oneself, one's social status, and one's status symbols, just like snow falling into a lake. One must then utter the formula that goes with this feeling of being revitalized, as laid down in the tradition one follows.

b.   HALLOWING THE ARTICLES USED IN WORSHIP

One must imagine the three gnosemes RAM, YAM, and KHAM to emanate from the spiritual center of the deiform energy that one visualizes oneself as. Fire, leaping up from the RAM, burns away all impurities and contaminations in the articles used in worship; wind, blowing from the YAM, scatters all the fetters of believing in concrete things; water, gushing forth from the KHAM, washes away all the grime of evil tendencies. Then, after composing oneself in this clear openness of Being, which does not exist as something "real" and concrete but is like the sky, one imagines that out of this openness, with a resounding BHRUM, there emerges a large, wide-open, and precious vessel in which from the ŌM there spring flowers and other sensory objects that consist of ethereal material and make up the ordinary external offering, as well as the self-existing psychic material, which is represented by the five sense organs, each perceiving its respective object, and makes up the inner worship. Each offering symbolizes a specific goddess carrying her particular article of worship. Together these goddesses move about like clouds filling the sky.

In addition there is a special offering consisting of (1) tonic,[151] (2) cakes, and (3) life-stuff:[152]

(1)   Tonic

One should imagine a self-originated vessel in the shape of a large and wide-open skullcap,[153] containing five kinds of flesh and five kinds of nectar. These contents are arranged[154] so that in the center is human flesh and feces, in the east bull flesh and semen, in the south dog flesh and brain tissue, in the west horse flesh and estrus, and in the north elephant flesh and urine. In this order these ingredients are to be transformed into the male and female partners in their resounding gnosemic shapes of HRĪH-BAM, HŪM-LAM, TRĀM-MAM, ŌM-MUM, and ĀH-TAM, each couple holding sway over its respective affinity with Being. From where they unite there flows a creative stream in colors of white and red, filling the whole vessel. Finally, these deiform energies dissolve in a diaphanous glow that, becoming absorbed by the articles used in worship, turns into the five modes of originary awareness, each having a most intense color, fragrance, and flavor.

(2) Cakes

One should imagine the sacrificial cakes, laid out on a ceremonial tray or some other precious plate that is as level as the earth, to represent the objects of one's desires, whose qualities one relishes and which, as quantities of nectar, fill the whole of space.

(3) Life-stuff

One should imagine all one's fictions about and addictions to the three world spheres to stream as blood into a large and wide-open vessel in the form of a fresh skull with its hairs still on it. Then one must imagine this ocean of blood, whose very nature is ultimate bliss, not attached to anything particular, to surge in clouds of whatever one desires, engulfing the whole sky.

It is merely a matter of convention and convenience whether, in summary accounts of such experiences,[155] these special preparatory practices are mentioned or only those of taking refuge and raising one's mind to a higher level.

II. THE MAIN PART

In-depth appraisals involve two procedures: (A) tuning-in to a state of composure and (B) remaining tuned-in when re-emerging from this composure.

A. TUNING-IN TO A STATE OF COMPOSURE

Tuning-in has three aspects: (1) tuning-in to a gestalt experience felt as Being's imprint; (2) tuning-in to an information experience felt as Being's communication; (3) and tuning-in to Being's sheer lucency felt as resonance with the whole.

1.   TUNING-IN TO A GESTALT EXPERIENCE FELT AS BEING'S IMPRESSION ON US

The gestalt experience as a tuning-in to being-marked-by-Being, which is the imaged feeling of oneself as a gestalt presence, involves five procedures: (a) retracing three in-depth appraisals, (b) setting up a dynamic configuration as a site for the forces in us to operate and activating these very forces; (c) inviting Being's originary awareness as a guest and having it firmly seated; (d) greeting, honoring, and praising this guest; and (e) attending to the projected presence of the primary deiform energy and one's involvement with it.

a.   RETRACING THE THREE IN-DEPTH APPRAISALS

(1)   The In-depth Appraisal of Being-in-its-beingness[156]

What must be transmuted is the momentary presence of a felt lucency, openness, and undividedness that, as the sheer lucency of Being's meaning-rich gestalt, implies both the death of old and familiar structures and the possibility of new structuration in terms of the familiar. This momentary presencing occurs when, at the time of dying, with the dissolution of the external and internal world, there arise light experiences growing in magnitude and intensity and finally passing into Being's sheer lucency,[157] from which people turn away and revert to the familiar when they fail to understand what this moment holds for them.

The transmutation procedure is such that when one's natural cognitive capacity, experience as such, the abiding presence of the uncontrived and genuine in one's finitude, has firmly settled in its unartificiality, there is the in-depth appraisal of Being-in-its-beingness, which sees the very face of its own meaning-rich potential that cannot be subjectively taken as some existent reality, because what lights up as one's phenomenal world neither goes anywhere nor stays anywhere and also cannot be thematized as anything.

Because its intrinsic character has never been experienced as something existent, it is not *eo ipso* something nonexistent, and because it has never been experienced as something nonexistent, it is not *eo ipso* something existent; it is there as an open-dimensionality that is not tied up with claims of eternal existence and eternal nonexistence. Because it cannot be established as something knowable that can be expressed in words, it is an open-dimensionality devoid of any attributes. Since its facticity cannot be localized within the domain of one's model building, it is an open-dimensionality that is not biased in favor of any one model. This is what is meant by Being's abiding in three releasements.[158]

The outcome of this transmutation process is an originary awareness totally disengaged from thematic limitations, the meaning-rich gestalt quality of the Buddha-experience. Because this in-depth appraisal is in harmony with both what must be transmuted and the outcome of the transmutation, through its imaginative cultivation at the lower level of the triune hierarchical organization of the individual and his life-world the grime of samsara, the tendencies associated with the dying and possibilizing processes as well as the belief in any concretenesss, is transmuted into pure symbols. At the upper level of this organization, through the activation of the capacities that lie in one's affinity with Being as expressed in its meaning-rich gestalt, the climaxing into the holistic experience of nirvana is guaranteed to come into full play. In between these two levels, because the ground has been prepared for Being's sheer lucency to grow in oneself, the maturation of the individual through a process of evolutionary advancement is effected.

(2) The In-depth Appraisal of a World-spanning Lighting-up[159]

What must be transmuted is the psychic factor[160] about to become embodied, complete with all sensory capacities constituted out of a motility and mentation combination at the moment of not recognizing the sheer lucency of Being's meaning-rich gestalt quality, manifesting in the transitional phase between dying and restructuration. It is a fleeting momentary presence, like a dream image, and is referred to as a "scent-eater"[161] in search of satiation in an embodied existence.

The transmutation procedure is the imaginative cultivation of compassion, encompassing all the sentient beings of the six kinds of life-forms, without showing any preference for the one or the other and without making discriminatory distinctions on this basis. It proceeds magiclike and without any subjective claims. It is the sentiment that all sentient beings may be freed from the misery they experience in having to roam powerlessly in their respective stations in samsara through having taken for real what is actually but a magiclike lighting-up of the creative dynamics in the abiding presence of Being-in-its-beingness. From the latter's reach and range this lighting-up has never moved away into the extremes of either samsara or nirvana.

The outcome of this transmutation is a gestalt experience of a world-horizon of meaning whose gestalt qualities are the modes of its magic like originary awareness, glistening in the luster and perfection of signs and symbols spreading everywhere. One imaginatively cultivates this in-depth appraisal, in which both the phase transition of the psychic factor to become embodied and the gestalt experience of a world-horizon of meaning are in consonance. At the lower level of the triune hierarchical organization, the tendencies and propensities of the phase transition constituting the pollution that is samsara, as well as the notion of some partial openness, are transmuted into pure symbols. At the upper level of this organization, because the seed for direct access to the gestalt experience of a world-horizon of meaning has been planted and germinated, its fruition is guaranteed to come into full play. In between these two levels, because the ground has been prepared for compassion to grow within one's being, where compassion is the momentum for Being's originary awareness to become articulated as the gestalt quality of a deiform presence from out of Being's sheer lucency, it will mature into the lived-through fulfilling phase.

(3)   The In-depth Appraisal of a Causal-Momentum[162]

What must be transmuted is the motility-mentation combination at the moment of its entering the particular life-form from among the four possible ones[163] to which it has felt attracted in its search for an embodied existence.

The transmutation procedure brings into play the experiencer's auto-excitatory capacity in which openness and compassion form a unity. This, then, becomes the site for the concern with limpid clearness and consummate perspicacity such that, without being anything in itself, it lights up as a gnosemic ciphering by a life-force that is one's basic resonance with the whole in its formulation as a deiform presence reverberating in such gnosemes as HRĪH or HŪM.[164] This very life-force, which stems from the radiation aspect of the fundamental forces, although very luminous and not undergoing any change, must be imaginatively cultivated as being capable of arising as anything whatsoever.

The outcome of this transmutation is the display of concrete cultural norms that are experienced as having a gestalt quality by those who must be taught and trained from the vantage point of the gestalt quality experience of a world-horizon of meaning. One then cultivates this in-depth appraisal, which is the seed for all configurational settings in that it is in consonance with both the cause-momentum for the emergent

existence of the motility-mentation combination about to enter a particular life-form in the course of this phase transition and the display of
various guiding standards of perfection by those to be taught and trained
by these Buddha-norms having a gestalt quality. At the lower level of the
triune hierarchical organization, the tendencies and propensities for entering a particular life-form, as well as the thematizing thoughts that
crave for a difference between what lights up and what is open, are
transmuted and transformed into pure symbols. At the upper level of this
organization, because the seed for releasement through the Buddha-
norms experience grows, its climaxing is guaranteed to come into full
play. In between these two levels, since the ground has been prepared for
the motility-mentation combination to emerge as a deiform presence of
Being's originary awareness gestalt quality, it will mature into the lived-
through fulfilling phase.

[A Summary of the In-depth Appraisals]

Because these three in-depth appraisals are the foundation for realizing the general features of the developing phase, a deeper understanding
of the deiform energies, whether in a concise or detailed manner, is
indispensable. Therefore, before beginning the imaginative cultivation
of any one or all deiform energies one must utter the following formula:

Ōṃ svabhāvaśuddhāḥ sarvadharmāḥ svabhāvaśuddho 'haṃ

which means "Just as all that is naturally pure, so also I am naturally
pure." This formula refers to the in-depth appraisal of Being-in-its-beingness. Or one may utter this formula:

Ōṃ mahāśūnyatājñānavajrasvabhāvātmako 'haṃ

which sums up all three in-depth appraisals and means that "I am of the
nature of Being's indestructibility as originary awareness and higher-order
openness." Here "higher-order openness" describes the in-depth appraisal
of Being-in-its-beingness, while the rest of the formula describes the
other two in-depth appraisals such that "indestructibility as originary
awareness" is higher-order openness in its unity of bliss supreme and
openness and "I am of the nature of the unity of openness and compassion" describes the in-depth appraisals of a world-spanning lighting-up
and a causal momentum.

b.   Setting Up a Dynamic Configuration
as the Site for the Forces in Us to Operate and
Activating These Very Forces

This involves two systematic undertakings: (1) the construction of a
palace as an operational site and (2) the activation of a deiform energy as
the central operative force.

(1)   The Construction of the Palace

The construction of the palace involves three imaginative procedures: (a) terracing the fundamental forces to serve as a foundation,
(b) erecting a palace to serve as a residence, and (c) setting up the
throne.

(a)   Terracing the Fundamental Forces[165]

What must be transmuted is the terraced configuration of the fundamental forces of the universe, with its axial mountain as it has come into
presence in ordinary consciousness, which is the state of having strayed
into believing in the concreteness of its creations. This is the coming
into presence of the blundering activities of one's mentation in its impure
and opaque mode.[166]
The transmutation procedure, which will be initiated within the
spacious and expansive protective circle previously imagined, proceeds as
follows: From the gnosemic nuclei pertaining to the causal momentum
in-depth appraisal, which are imagined to hover before one in the sky,
the germinal potentialities of the five fundamental forces with the axial
mountain spread out in an orderly manner. From the gnoseme E there
evolves the repository and source of meanings, blue in color, its sharp
angle pointing downward and its broad base upward, its size extending to
the farthest limits. On top of it there evolves from the gnoseme YAM the
motility configuration, cross-shaped and surrounded by clusters of smoke-
like, green-black light rays. On top of it there evolves from the gnoseme
RAM the heat configuration, red in color, triangular in shape, and
surrounded by garlands of tongues of flames. On top of it there evolves
from the gnoseme BAM the cohesion configuration, white in color, its
globular periphery surrounded by white light rays. On top of it there
evolves from the gnoseme LAM the solidity configuration, golden in

color, quadrangular in shape, and surrounded by yellow light rays. On top of it there evolves from the gnoseme *SUM* the axial mountain, with four terraces, each consisting of one of the four precious materials.[167]

The outcome of this transmutation is the autopresencing of a nonerrant originary awareness belonging to the higher-order reality. Its commensurate cognitive domain is Being's meaning-rich field as its super-releasement, symbolized by the Diamond-Mistress cleft[168] and the diaphanous space vortices of the female consorts of the male regents in this higher-order contextuality as her impressive presence.

(b)   *The Erection of the Palace*

What must be transmuted is the compulsive and dissociative tendency to take as concrete entities the social milieux and countries in which sentient beings move around and go about their daily business, as well as the houses and cottages in which they dwell.

The transmutation procedure consists in the construction of a palace from the light into which the gnoseme *BHRUM*, glistening in five colors, breaks up when, bursting forth from the causal momentum in-depth appraisal, it melts into five distinct hues and falls on top of the axial mountain. The terracing of the fundamental forces together with their configurational patterning within the protective circle need not be made more lucent than the fences and the tent of this protective circle as they have been imagined previously. However, from a fence that is made of scepters and that surrounds the outer edges of the earthlike basis, made of a scepter, like the iron mountain surrounding our world system, there flare up masses of fire in various colors and of infinite size. Inside this fence made of scepters, the level ground is surrounded by eight great cremation grounds.

Inside this whole pattern, on top of the pistil of a thousand-petaled lotus flower made up of the same precious material of which the essence of the universe is constituted, there rests a bright and radiant sun disc, identical in size with the pistil. On this disc, on a ground which is formed by the deep blue quadrangular center of a double scepter, there rests the quadrangular palace. Its walls are made of vertical plates of five kinds of jewels, shining inside and outside in the colors of these jewels, starting with the color of the principal affinity with Being in the center. At the bottom of the outer wall are buttresses with red pedestals on which the sixteen goddesses of worship stand,[169] holding in their hands the respective articles used in worship and turning their faces toward the resident in the palace. The upper edges of the walls are lined with yellow tiles encrusted with jewels protruding in the shape of lotus flowers. Resting atop these tiles are roofbeams supported by small pillars or posts, and on top of these rests a crowning beam whose ends are formed by fabulous creatures from whose mouths hang jewel garlands and jewel curtains. From the top of the crowning beam there slopes a tiled roof reaching to the outer borders of the pedestals, and underneath, on the inside, are tiles of white jewels, looking like inverted jugs with garlands whose ends reach the lower part of the crowning beam. Along the roof lie three or four tiers of jewel planks, extending to its base, known as railings or balustrades.

Inside the palace, on top of the capitals of eight pillars rest rafters made of decorated wooden boards. An exception are the pillars for the roof window, which is made up of twenty-eight beams. The uppermost part is bedecked with jewels, and at the four corners of the roof window, on the spires of the roofing supported by pillars of wooden posts, is a carving decoration made from diamonds and other costly jewels. Directly in the center of the walls are four gates with turrets. On each of the four supports of these turrets, with their two upper and two lower corners extending to the buttresses, are placed eight markerlike steps leading up to the crossbeam capital. Their order is as follows: an ornamental arrangement of raised golden scepters on a blue ground;[170] an ornamental arrangement of lotus leaves made of red jewels;[171] a square box with relief work consisting of various jewels, located between the capitals and the pillars;[172] lattice work of white jewels;[173] a network of tiles;[174] lattice and half-lattice work made from jewels;[175] shingles;[176] the roofing, as explained above.[177]

On top of the roof there is a white baldachin over a male and female deer made of gold and holding between them a golden wheel.

Although a palace would generally be like this one, in some configurations where the operating force is of a fierce kind, the palace is described as having been built in the manner of a blazing cremation ground in consideration of the unruly character of those who have to be taught and trained. In this case one must imagine the palace walls to have been constructed from dry, wet, and rotting skulls; the pillars from the great gods of popular belief; the rafters from the eight great serpent demons; the roof from the twenty-eight lunar mansions; the windows from the eight planets together with sun and moon; the lattice and half-lattice work from snakes and skulls; the markerlike steps from garlands of chopped-off fingers, skulls, the five sense-organs, sun and moon; the parapet from the bones of the spine; and on top of the roof made from the hollow skull of Mahādeva, the pointed top ornament with its awnings and draperies, is made from skin. The ground outside and inside this

palace is dotted with cremation grounds and oceans of blood, and inside
and outside, everywhere, terrifying fires are burning and fierce storms are
raging.

When one imaginatively builds such a palace, one should ponder
over these symbols and what it all means; if one does not understand
these symbols, what is imaginatively to be developed takes on an autonomous character. But if one does understand these symbols, the creative
imagination of the palace and the deiform energy in it may be made the
way toward spiritual maturity by those of low intelligence who do not as
yet feel and understand Being's abidingness as that which imparts meaning to their life by its thrust toward limpid clearness in which the qualities of the Buddha-experience as well as its resonating concern, unfathomable by ordinary thought, and its optimization activity are gath-
ered. If one does not know it in this manner, one is fettered by one's
tendencies and propensities, which take on a life of their own, and one
cannot break away from samsara. One becomes a god of the world of
desires or a Rudra.[178]

[The Palace Symbols]

The meaning of the palace symbols is as follows:

Its quadrangular shape is the symbol of Being's meaning-rich field,
which remains identical with itself everywhere.[179]

Its four gates are the four immeasurably great catalysts, which lead to
the citadel of bliss supreme.[180]

The eight markerlike steps, as far as they aid progress on the way, are
the symbols for entering the nondual pursuit after having traversed the
other eight ways.[181]

The four markerlike steps, to the extent that they pertain to one's
goal realization, are symbols of the four ways and means[182] to gather the
interest of those who are to be taught.

All of them, whether they form a set of eight or of four, have eight or
four banisters, respectively, which are the symbols of the qualities as they
are holistically present in the philosophical systems[183] pertaining to the
eight or four spiritual pursuits.

The wheel is the symbol of the ceaseless rotation of the Buddha
message.[184]

The buttresses are the symbols of the application of the four kinds of
inspection.[185]

The four posts as the marker-like steps are the symbols of the four
eliminations.[186]

The four windows are the symbols of the four bases of success.[187]

The walls made of five layers of jewels are the symbols of the five psychic controlling powers.[188]

The tiles, the banisters connecting the short pillars, the shingles, the balustrades, and the roof window are the symbols of the five psychic strengths.[189]

The ornaments consisting of jewel nets, lattice work, flower garlands, silk scarfs attached to the pillars, mirror, moon, and yaktail are the symbols of the seven constituents of limpid clearness and consummate perspicacity.[190]

The eight pillars are the symbols of the eight constituents of the noble way.[191]

The eight capitals are the symbols of the eight releasements.[192]

The four beams are the symbols of the four intrepidities.[193]

The twenty-eight rafters inside the palace are the symbols of the eighteen aspects of openness[194] and the ten operations of self-transcendence.[195]

The roof beam is the symbol of the qualities and capabilities[196] in the Buddha-experience, which are unfathomable by ordinary thought.

The four casings of the roof window are the symbols of the four analytical comprehensions.[197]

The top ornament on the spire is the symbol of all configurational patterns which have become a whirling mass in the vortex of Being's originary awareness as a function of its auto-excitation.[198]

The baldachin is the symbol of the protection extended to living beings by the Buddha-system's super-compassion.[199]

The banners hanging down from the baldachin are the symbols of a higher-order compassion.[200]

The rays of light that spread everywhere are the symbols of the gyration of the inexhaustible beauty of Being's gestalt quality, communication, and spiritual resonance.[201]

The lighting up of the radiation aspect of the fundamental forces in unobscured lucency is the symbol of the creativity in originary awareness.[202]

The double scepter of the foundation of the whole universe is the symbol of Being's originary awareness of its utter openness.[203]

The twelve fence posts are the symbols of the twelve members of universal connectedness.[204]

The throne in the shape of the sun is the symbol of Being's meaning-rich potential, a sheer lucency in itself and in its actuality.[205]

The garland of lotus flowers encircling the sun is the symbol of Being's meaning-rich potential uncontaminated by any flaws.[206]

The eight cremation grounds are the symbols of the eight perceptual patterns[207] and the pointers to their magic-like presence as illustrated by eight similes.[208]

The fence made of scepters is the symbol of Being's originary awareness undisturbed by divisive concepts.[209]

The masses of fire are the symbols of the burning of the deadening forces[210] and the emotional pollutants by the fire of originary awareness.[211]

Though it is important to understand each symbol as being both the revealing and the revealed, the beginner may not be able to understand them all in one session. He may, however, conceive of all these properties of a palace as presenting the dynamic qualities of the Buddha-experience, described in terms of the elimination of intellectual and emotional obscurations and the felt understanding of Being's meaningfulness, unfathomable by ordinary thinking, as well as being the pointers to them. Such thinking comes close to an understanding of the symbols.

The outcome of this transmutation is the autopresencing of the real 'Og-min realm,[212] Being's abidingness within ourselves, the mystery that is the supreme joy of life, the citadel of ultimate freedom, nirvana—all of this symbolized by a palace. Furthermore, the terracing of the fundamental forces of the universe with its axial mountain may be imaged as presenting the bilateral chreods, the five focal points, and the central flow pattern[213] in the emerging worldstructure; the basis of this imaged configuration is a crosslike shape with lotus flower and sun from which the motility and information input move through the center of the chreods and focal points. To the extent that mentation in its triune aspect of lucency, openness, and bliss fuses with them, this process constitutes the construction of the palace. By properly developing this imaginative process, the triad of chreods, information input, and motility is made pliable and yielding. Thereby the ground is prepared for the originary awareness pertaining to the fulfilling phase to grow within one's being, and the maturation of the process of an evolutionary advancement is brought about.

(c)   Setting Up the Throne

What must be transmuted are the tendencies and propensities latent in the procreative fluids of the prospective father and mother in the case of womb-born living beings about to embody and take birth in any social milieu, or with the heat and moisture origination of other life-forms.

The transmutation procedure is to imagine, in the center of the palace, a throne made of a red lotus flower on top of which there rest, one above the other, a red disc of the sun and a white disc of the full moon, equal in size with the center of the lotus flower. This applies only to the central and primary deiform energy who takes his seat on it, while the thrones of the surrounding energies are to be known according to each one's character. In the case of the fierce deiform energy, its throne is made up of Rudra, a rotting corpse, and sundry animate beings.

The outcome of this transmutation is the Buddha-experience in the form of a guiding image that, wherever and in whichever social milieu it may manifest, is not vitiated by evil and defects; and because of the natural diaphaneity of its spiritual resonance with the whole, it is the ultimacy of Being's originary awareness in its sheer lucency in which appropriate activity and appreciative discernment form a unity.

The special significance of this imaginative process lies in the fact that, when one travels higher paths, the ground is prepared for realizing the invariance of bliss supreme. This spiritual maturation is brought about by one's reliance on the inner forces felt and imaged such that the lotus flower is the network of chreods and focal points; the sun is the inner heat symbolized as the gnosemic short A, stationed in the perineum; the moon is the gnosemic HAM,[214] stationed in the cerebrum; and their union is the feeling of bliss flowing down from above due to the heat rising from below and melting the rigidity of one's ego.

(2)   The Activation of a Deiform Energy

This has two sections: (a) the activation procedure and (b) the special features of the deiform energy.

(a)   The Activation Procedure

Many activation procedures have been compiled in the rediscovered texts of the early transmission of Buddhism in Tibet. Among these the expanded version comprises procedures that ensure passage from one state to another by way of five experientially and imaginatively lived-through morpho- and ontogenetic processes, a medium version comprises four such processes, and a condensed version only three imaginative procedures.[215]

What must be transmuted by this activation procedure is that moment when the consciousness principle in its embodying phase transition immerses itself in the mixture of the white and red procreative fluids as materialization potentials in its mother's womb. This is imaged as follows: When this consciousness principle in its embodying phase transition has implanted itself in the midst of the father's semen and the mother's estrus and gradually becomes fully developed in body and shape, it presents itself as the germinal capacity of a gnoseme in the causal momentum in-depth appraisal, which settles down on its throne formed by the sun, symbolizing the mother's estrus, and the moon, symbolizing the father's semen.

The transmutation procedure consists in the transformation of what has become the remarkable fusion of the male and female procreational fluids together with the mentation of the being-to-be once this consciousness principle in its phase transition has installed itself in what is now becoming the white and red materialization potential. This consciousness principle constitutes a germinal capacity that will grow into the particular signature[216] of the deiform energy to which one feels drawn. This germinal capacity is felt to pulsate in rays of light that, on the one hand, as functions of the four fundamental forces, initiate the evolution of the physical body inside the womb—its psychophysical aggregates, their operational potential, and their operational fields—and that, on the other hand, initiate the evolution of the full presence of the organism's gestalt quality as it unfolds out of the signature. This is what is meant by the transmutation of the tendencies and propensities that are operative throughout the period from conception to birth in those living beings who are born from a womb.

This activation procedure also applies to the transmutation of the tendencies and propensities operative in the animate beings of the other life-forms. In the case of beings born from an egg, the procedure is as follows: The germinal capacity, the scent-eating mentation, transformed into a signature, implants itself in the midst of the male and female procreational fluids inside the womb. When the pulsating in rays of light has come to an end, this signature, as a globule dissolving into a pure luminosity, transmutes the tendencies and propensities that are operative in those beings to be hatched from an egg.

In the case of beings originating from heat and moisture the procedure is as follows: The throne formed by the sun as heat and the moon as moisture, together with the germinal capacity as the signature, constitute the motility-mentation combination in its phase transition. The triad comprising the motility-mentation combination, the pulsating in rays of light, and the full presence of a gestalt quality transmutes what is to become the physical body of those beings to originate from heat and moisture.

In the case of supernatural beings, the procedure is as follows: The deiform energy's throne is its very birthplace, the germinal capacity as its signature is the motility-mentation combination in the phase transition, and the pulsating in rays of light is the nourishing of the status and physical appearance by an intense craving for and an identification with them. The full presence of a gestalt quality is the momentary bodily existence that becomes transmuted through this procedure.

To sum up these transmutation procedures: to have this germinal capacity, which is a cause momentum as it hovers before one in the sky, settled upon its throne is the activation procedure of Being's communicative dynamics through its gnosemic utterance. The effulgence of infinite rays of light from any signature to which one feels drawn, and which is marked by the gnoseme in its germinal capacity as its dynamic core, invites the Buddhas to appear before one in the sky. Their dissolution in the manner of rays of light in the signature, together with its germinal capacity, is the activation procedure of Being's resonance dynamics through its signature. The full-fledged gestalt of a *yi-dam* such as rDo-rje 'dzin-pa,[217] as the climax of the metamorphosis of the signature with its germinal capacity, replete with all marks, lucent and rich in symbolic meaning, is the activation procedure of Being's gestalt dynamics in its holistic presence.

The Buddha-activities are the outcome of this transmutation readying themselves in the time span between conception and birth for the moment to manifest in gestalts of guiding images and cultural norms in order to meet the needs of those to be taught and trained.

When it comes to higher ways and levels, the fitting together of sun and moon, resting on a throne formed by a lotus flower, is felt through the network of experiential focal points in the central chreod as a rising warmth and downward flowing bliss. The felt presence of a germinal capacity and its signature marks the submergence of the motility-mentation combination into the chreod termed *avadhūti*.[218] The transformative pulsating is the feeling of bliss and utter openness in their unity arising from the bliss flowing through the organism. The experience of a full-fledged gestalt dynamics is the maturation into the fulfilling phase, which may make its presence felt in any gestalt quality that the deiform energy of Being's systemic[219] originary awareness may assume out of the unity of bliss and openness.

Summary accounts of such experiences contain many references to developing phases in which the throne is imaged but not the palace and in which no elaborate symbolic re-creation of one's world is called for, because there the lucid understanding of the symbols in a single moment is of primary importance. However, the various contexts in which these statements occur cannot be reduced to a single level of interpretation. One should note, therefore, that the elaborate version of a developing phase with its palace and so on is not always necessary.

(b)   The Distinct Features of the Formulated Energy

Because the imaginative development of a yi-dam as detailed in accounts of such experiences cannot be reduced to and dealt with from a single point of view, it will not be fully elaborated here. We shall give only a general survey of the symbolic meanings of the deiform energies that are to be imaginatively developed in their calm and fierce presences.

[The Calm Aspect]

A single face indicates the singularity of Being's meaning-rich gestalt experience.[220]

Three faces indicate the three releasements[221] or the experience of Being as having three gestalts.[222]

Two hands indicate appropriate activity as a higher order compassion[223] and appreciative discernment as Being's openness.

Four hands indicate four originary awareness modes[224] or the four catalysts of loving kindness, compassionate sympathy, participatory joy, and a dynamic balancing out.[225]

Six hands indicate five originary awareness modes, with the endogenous originary awareness mode as the sixth.

[Four legs indicate the four bases of success.[226]

The color white of the yi-dam's gestalt indicates that he is not defiled by any defects.

The color yellow indicates that his capabilities have expanded fully.

The color red indicates his attachment to the world through his resonance with it.

The color green indicates his unimpeded optimal activities.

The colors blue and black indicate the invariance of Being's meaning-rich potential.

With respect to his emblems, which are experienced as signatures, the scepter indicates that Being is not something constructed.

The wheel indicates that the pollutants are being eradicated.

The jewel indicates the unfolding of capabilities.

The lotus flower indicates that he is undefiled by defects.

The cross-legged posture indicates the identity of samsara and nirvana or the fact that Being cannot be localized in any of these extremes.

Because the yi-dam's calm and quiet bearing is enhanced in beauty by nine sensuous-sensory sentiments,[227] he is pleasing to look at, all the more so as there is nothing incongruous about him. Of these nine sentiments, five relate to the properties of the "stuff" of which the yi-dam is made. The plumpness of his shape points to birth transmuted; the well proportionateness of his shape, in which the parts are discernible and yet flow harmoniously into one another, points to illness transmuted; the tautness of his shape, never slackening, as well as his tall and straight stature, point to death transmuted; the smoothness and youthfulness of his shape point to old age transmuted.

Of the remaining four properties of the *yi-dam*'s shape that relate to his appearance, his clear and radiant complexion is due to his being adorned by auspicious marks that are like flowers and in their symmetry arrangement are like the fruits; his brightness and brilliance is due to his sensory operational fields being holistically present; his natural beauty is due to his luster and pleasantness; and his splendor is due to his wielding authority with those to be taught and trained.

As a symbol of being free from every kind of affliction by the pollutants, the *yi-dam* wears a white silken scarf, an upper garment with gold stripes, and a checkered lower garment fastened with a multicolored cord. As a symbol that everything positive is fully present, the hair on his head is plaited into a tuft. Jewel and flower ornaments indicate the greatness of the fact that sensuous and sensual pleasures, without having to be given up, are ornaments of originary awareness modes such that the jewel ornaments indicate the seven features of the way to limpid clearness and consummate perspicacity;[228] the jewel necklace, attentive inspection; the head ornament, critical investigation of the ideas that constitute our reality; the bracelets, sustained effort; the earrings, serenity through refinement and clarification of the vision; the shoulder ornaments, an in-depth appraisal of the vision; the pearl necklace, the dynamic balancing out; and the flower garland, joy.

[The Fierce Aspect]

The symbols of the *yi-dam*'s fierce presence are generally as follows:
Because his originary awareness, unattached and unobstructed, ranges over the three aspects of time, he has one or many heads with three eyes in each; further, through the quaternity of gestalt quality, communicativeness, responsive resonance, and originary awareness, he is sensitive to everything that can be known. Of his two pairs of legs, one pair has the right leg stretched, indicating that he does not stay in the extreme of nirvanic quiescence, and the left leg bent, indicating that he does not stay in the extreme of limited samsaric possibilities. The other pair of legs, expressing appropriate activity and appreciative discernment, tramples on a male demon, being the quintessence of the nihility

extreme and the preoccupation with subjectiveness, and on a female demon, being the quintessence of the eternity extreme and the preoccupation with objectiveness.

To indicate that the six transcending functions are complete in him, he wears six bone ornaments: the necklace signifies generosity; the bracelets, self-discipline; the ear ornaments, patient acceptance; the round crown ornament, strenuousness; the waistband, concentration; and the silken raiment, appreciative discernment.

His distorted angry face, be it one or many faces, indicates that all wrong viewpoints have been refuted. To crush the four deadening powers represented by the psychophysical aggregates, the pollutants, the Lord of Death, and overevaluated notions, he bares his four fangs in as many faces as he may have. His figure is smeared with ashes because the jasminelike white concern with limpid clearness and consummate perspicacity has assumed the gestalt quality of bliss supreme. On his forehead he wears a mark of blood because the three poisons[229] have been drained. Because he serves the living beings through his expertise, he has whiskerlike strands on his cheeks. To indicate that his originary awareness has defeated jealousy and is cleansed of the fifty gnosemes operative in the *ro-ma* and *rkyang-ma*[230] chreods within the live body as well as of the fifty operators effecting the dichotomy within mentation, he wears a necklace of fifty dripping heads. Because spiritual darkness has been vanquished by the ten powers of his sensitive awareness, he wears an elephant's hide as his upper garment; and as a symbol of the defeat of the six defects—desire, anger, arrogance, low-level intelligence, opinionatedness, and hesitancy—he wears a tiger's skin as his lower garment. These garments may also be understood as symbols of irritation-aversion having been overcome. As a symbol of the pollutants having been eradicated, he wears a waistband made of human skin; as a symbol of desire having been defeated by the concern with limpid clearness and consummate perspicacity, he wears a silken cord as his sash; and as a symbol of arrogance having been defeated, he wears a head ornament of five dry skulls that symbolize the five originary awareness modes pertaining to the five affinities with Being as the Buddha-experience. Because the optimal activities stemming from his greatness are spontaneously executed, he wears a crown ornament of jewels. To eradicate vulgar ways of living, he displays sentiments of fierceness on a large scale. Possessing the nine sentiments of fierceness as they are expressed in the dance of the regents of the five affinities with Being together with their four consorts[231]—any one such sentiment displayed by him at any time as circumstances demand—he shows that he is the unity of these nine deiform energies: the sentiment of seduction and allurement is present as Vairocana, prowess as Ratnasambhava, hideousness as Akṣobhya, merriment and laughter as Amitābha, stentorian shouting as Amoghasiddhi, frightening shrieks as Māmakī, compassion as Tārā, wonder as Pāṇḍaravāsinī, and serenity and peacefulness as Buddhalocanā. Because inner calm and wider perspective have formed a unity, he joins scepter and lotus. Because openness and compassion are not separated from each other, the gestalt quality and the live body are also joined in union. Because unfaltering joyfulness has a single flavor in that state where no thematizing obtains, he and his consort join their mouths in an act of deep kissing. Because his appreciative discernment, which understands the non-ontic status of what is called "world," burns away the horrible features of the three world spheres, he stands in the midst of the wildly leaping flames of the five originary awareness modes.]

The "stuff" of which this deiform energy is made is as follows: From the perspective of the lower order commonly accepted reality, his concern for the welfare of living beings, displayed through his inclination to engage in an extraordinary kind of compassion,[232] constitutes his appropriate activity, which is the presencing aspect of Being's originary awareness as its invariant supreme bliss. This is to be imaginatively developed by means of the felt image of him as the male consort. From the perspective of the higher order reality, the open-dimensional aspect of Being's dynamic field, an utter openness and appreciative discernment, is spoken of as the female consort, and by thinking of her as a felt image, this is made the way of imaginative development.[233] For this openness serves as the ground and the reason for the emergence of the whole of one's reality, comprising the transmutation processes leading toward the quiescence of all that pertains to nirvana, as well as the external world with all its contents—the colors, sounds, fragrances, flavors, and so on—that go by the name of samsara. And because all this, apart from its intrinsic open-dimensionality, has never been experienced as anything existing or as having in it even so much as an atom of concreteness, it may arise as anything whatsoever with nothing to obstruct it in one way or another, just like a magic show. It thereby makes its presence felt in what seems to be the cause and effect relationship and seems to undergo origination and cessation, decrease and increase, transmigration and transfiguration.

Further, (1) the truth of this utter openness appearing as the cause-and-effect relationship in its ceaseless presencing out of the creativity of Being's openness—a truth that cannot be denied once one has seen the onset of Being's presencing from its openness, and (2) the truth of this universal connectedness as not contradicting this openness together form a unity such that one will never attain real nirvana by rejecting one feature in this complementarity and merely pursuing the other. Hence one must develop this process of self-regeneration by means of the felt image of the male and female consorts in close embrace, exemplifying the unity of appropriate activity and appreciative discernment, which cannot be broken apart and reduced to either aspect alone.

The female consort, as exalted as her male consort, has these characteristics:

[Her single face indicates that the whole of reality has but one flavor in Being's beingness.

Her two hands indicate that she exercises both appropriate activity and appreciative discernment.

She is ablaze in a luster like the fire that consumes the world when its end has come to indicate that her whole nature is of a desire that surpasses all desires and her originary awareness encompasses the entire animate and inanimate world.

She is highly agitated to indicate that she overcomes all divisive trends.

She rolls her three eyes in a red glare to indicate that her direct experience of bliss supreme, purged of the three physiological determinants of *rajas*, *tamas*, and *sattva*,[234] shakes up all that can be known.

She wears her hair loose to indicate that her originary awareness fans out from Being's fieldlike expanse without falling to one side or the other, and she is nude to indicate that all obscurations[235] have been removed.

To indicate that she is wise in administering her expertise, she holds up to her consort's mouth a skull symbolizing bliss supreme and containing the blood of the four deadening powers, which have been vanquished by this bliss supreme.

To indicate that the limits sets by thematic proliferations have been abolished, she threateningly wags her raised forefinger of the hand holding a scepter, in all directions.

Because she looks at samsara as never having had any validity as such and at the living beings who move about in it, likewise, as not having anything substantial about them, she has her monthly discharge of the subtle aspect of the *rajas* oozing out.

Her bent right leg indicates that because of bliss supreme manifesting as appropriate activity, she does not stay in samsara, and her stretched left leg indicates that because of her gestalt quality that is the openness of appreciative discernment, she does not stay in a quietistic nirvana.

The symbolic meaning of her being in union with her male consort is the same as that explicated in the passage on the male in union with the female consort. However, there are two aspects to this unity: the one, which has been complete from its very beginning and relates to the symbol character of the male consort, is such that once appropriate activity reflects Being's originary awareness it is also appreciative discernment; the other one, which must never be discarded and relates to the female consort, is such that once appreciative discernment reflects Being as such it is also appropriate activity.]

The five emblems symbolizing the five originary awareness modes are as follows: The wheel on the crown of her head indicates the originary awareness mode of Being's meaning-rich potential; her bone necklace, the originary awareness mode of Being's identity with itself; her ear ornaments, the originary awareness mode that is specificity-initiating; her bracelets, the originary awareness mode that is quasi-mirroring; and the sash, the originary awareness mode that optimally executes its tasks.

[The rows of bells hanging on her shawl and anklets indicate either the twelve features of the principle of universal connectedness or the twelve divisions in the Buddhist scriptures.[236] When one refers to six emblems, the six transcending functions are meant, because appropriate activity plays the decisive role; when one refers to five emblems, the five originary awareness modes are meant, because appreciative discernment plays the decisive role. According to other texts, they refer to Being's five great aspects of openness[237] and the six aspects of Being's in-formation dynamics[238] so that the implication is that appropriate activity is marked by appreciative discernment and appreciative discernment by appropriate activity.

The five dry skulls are symbols of the Buddha-experience as it pertains to its five affinities with Being.

The shoulder ornament of fifty dry skulls is in its symbolic meaning similar to the one discussed in connection with the fifty gnosemes and the fifty operators in mentation. However, there is the following difference: these skulls and heads are both dry and dripping wet. Moistened by the water of bliss supreme as appropriate activity, the heads are dripping wet. Dried out by the heat of the open-dimensional appreciative discernment reflecting the fire of originary awareness, the skulls are dry.

To manifest her originary awareness, which is everlasting and not subject to change and old age, she is an image of fresh youthfulness. To indicate that her own aim as well as that of others is firmly realized, her two nipples stand erect.

To point out that Being's meaning-rich potential is difficult to understand and cannot be fathomed by rational thought alone, her waist is very slim.

To show that her concern with limpid clearness and consummate perspicacity provides a firm ground for her endeavors, her hips are broad and well rounded.

To show that merits and cognitions have been well built up, her thighs are thick.

To show that she possesses all qualities in highest perfection, her pubic region is highly arched in the shape of a tortoise.

To show that she will grant the very best through every means possible to the living beings, all aspects of her shape are pure and exquisite.] Here a brief account of the symbolic meanings of her emblems will be given:

A five-pointed scepter symbolizes the five originary awareness modes.

A cutlass symbolizes the cutting off of the divisive trends.

A skull symbolizes an undivided originary awareness and the preservation of bliss supreme. This skull filled with blood indicates that ultimate originary awareness has defeated the four deadening powers, whereby samsara has been brought under control.

A sword symbolizes the eradication of birth and death.

A trident symbolizes the eradication of the three poisons.

The manifestations of the yi-dam's entourage are not something different or separable from the principal figure in the configuration, of whom they are mere transformations that manifest according to the needs of those to be taught and trained. So also the palaces inhabited by these deiform energies have emerged solely from the creativity in the triad of bliss, lucency, and openness, as the fantastic show staged by the principal figure's originary awareness. All that is thus staged seems to appear like a rainbow in a clear sky or like the reflection of stars in the clear water of a lake. Because they have no reality value of their own but merely illustrate the principle of universal connectedness, the very meaning of Being, it is very important to keep this fact before one's mind. Although it is necessary to develop by creative imagination each and every gestalt, its colors, and its signatures as emblems, and also to keep before one's mind each and every symbol that points to their deeper meaning, the beginner may not be able to do so if he is not yet ready to fuse his mentation with the developing phase.[239] Therefore, it is very important that he focus his interest and devotion on the idea that when he has had a glimpse of the lucent presence of a deiform energy, be it only for a little while, all this is the wondrous symbolism and expertise pointing to the originary awareness pervasive of the meaning-rich gestalt of the Buddhas, their capabilities that cannot be fathomed by rational thought alone, their immeasurable resonance with Being, and their optimizing activities. Such an attitude comes close to a vision and understanding of the symbols.

Through such creative imagination, on the level from which one starts, this transmutation procedure deals with the following stages in an individual's life: his being born, his growing into manhood; and plagued by desires, looking around for a suitable match, taking a wife; developing his physical, vocal, and mental capabilities step by step; and finally mastering the duties that go with his standing in society. The outcome of this transmutation is to be born as the embodiment of a cultural ideal, to undergo hardships in search of limpid clearness and consummate perspicacity after having left home, to leave this phase behind and go directly to the vitalizing source, to defeat the deadening powers, to develop concentration as a solid basis for one's thinking, and to gain the originary awareness that is sensitive to all aspects of reality. On the next higher level, where the problem too is that of realizing in oneself the gestalt experience of being a deiform energy consisting of bliss, openness, and originary awareness, the maturation process involves making the jump into such a gestalt experience from one's triune state of pleasure, motility, and mentation by resorting to either of two felt images[240] with the desire for realizing the highest achievement in one's life, familiarizing oneself more and more with Being's endogenous originary awareness, and thereby laying the foundation for the speedy realization of the highest achievement in one's life.

The feeling of being revitalized involves the following:

What must be transmuted are the tendencies and propensities of manhood once the capacities in what are an ordinary person's body, speech, and mind have become fully developed.

The transmutation procedure consists in imagining oneself as a configurational assemblage of commitments such that inside one's head, in the so-called *dung-khang* palace[241] in the brain, on a throne in the shape of a wheel, the white, brilliantly shining gnoseme ŌM symbolizes Being's indestructibility in its gestalt quality; inside one's throat, on a throne in the shape of a red lotus flower with eight petals, the red, brilliantly shining gnoseme ĀH symbolizes Being's indestructibility as communicativeness; and inside one's heart, on a throne of sun and moon, the blue, brilliantly shining gnoseme HŪM symbolizes Being's indestructibility as its resonance with itself.

Some texts state that deiform energies may be imagined as being adorned with these gnosemes. However, where this is not the case, it is sufficient to imagine these gnosemes alone. The reason is that inasmuch as these gnosemes are the felt image of the impact of Being's originary awareness, and because the three aspects of Being's indestructibility are the quintessence of the six originary awareness modes, they turn into the respective felt images and there is no need to imagine these deiform energies in concrete shapes with a face and hands.

The outcome of this transmutation is the realization of being in possession of Being's mystery, which, unfathomable by rational thought, is the triune indestructibility of the gestalt dynamics, communicativeness, and sense-bestowing resonance of all Buddhas.

c.   Inviting Being's Originary Awareness

What must be transmuted are the tendencies and propensities to become equal in intellectual capabilities with one's peers, past and present.

The transmutation procedure consists of (1) inviting the circle of originary awareness modes and (2) requesting them to be seated.

(1)   The Invitation

One imagines that from the gnoseme HŪM in the heart of oneself, conceived of as presenting a circle of commitments,[242] red rays of light in the shape of hooks burst forth and latch on to the spirituality centers of the three mainsprings, of authentic existence. When called upon, these mainsprings who are the quintessence of all guises that the gestalt experience of Being's meaningfulness may assume, come forth from their respective realms of residence, encompassing the whole of space, in a playlike display of sensuous forms, without parting from their original gestalt quality.

(2)   The Request to Be Seated

Together with the words of invitation as laid down in the tradition one follows, one requests this circle of originary awareness modes[243] to be seated amidst the circle of commitments, like water poured into water so that no duality obtains and only one flavor prevails.

The general formula covering every phase consists of the following gnosemes: DZAḤ, HŪM, BAM, and HŌḤ. By the DZAḤ, the originary awareness circle is invited into the commitment circle; by the HŪM, both circles submerge into non-duality; by the BAM, the originary awareness circle is held fast and not allowed to depart; and by the HŌḤ, it is made to stay on happily.

The outcome of this transmutation is that at the time of the Buddha-experience, all the Buddha-processes and the originary awareness modes become a single act of sense bestowal.

d.   Worship and Praise

What must be transmuted are the tendencies and propensities that compel an ordinary person to amass wealth and gain honor and fame in order to indulge in sensual pleasures to his heart's content.

The transmutation procedure consists of (1) greeting, (2) worshipping, and (3) praising.

(1)   The Greeting

Greeting is the awareness that the intermingling of the configurational assemblage of commitments with the configurational assemblage of originary awareness modes, like water poured into water, is the unique configuration in which Being's meaning-rich field has become inseparable from its originary awareness. However, one may also imagine that such greetings, as gestures of respect, occur in a manner reminiscent of the Nirmāṇaratidevas,[244] who enjoy the pleasures of their own creation. That is, from the spirituality center of the principal figure in this configurational setting, who is none other than oneself as authentic subject, phantom-like figures, similar to the principal one, leap forth, like a second flame from the first.

Uttering the words of greeting according to the texts of the tradition one follows, this triad made up of the crowd of deiform energies of the configuration constituting the object to be greeted, the meeting with them so that they and one's understanding form an inseparable bond constituting the meaning and purpose of the act of greeting, and the act of greeting itself, be it only by way of a gesture inspired by a sincere delight in their outstanding qualities, is what is meant by the buildup of merits and knowledge.

(2)   The Worship

Worshiping comprises four aspects: (a) an external act, (b) an internal act, (c) an arcane act, and (d) an act of Being-in-its-beingness.

(a)   The External Act

The act of worship, which is common to both the external and internal acts, is to imagine that from the spirituality center of the princi-

pal figure as the authentic subject in this drama there come forth countless goddesses of sensory delights. As if each of the goddesses worshiped
one another by way of external and internal acts, they move like clouds,
completely filling the imaginary realms as well as the ordinary spheres of
human activities, surpassing the limits of rational thought. Simultaneously with uttering the words of worship according to the texts of
one's tradition, these goddesses, carrying their respective articles of worship, offer these articles to the individual senses: a clear, cool, and sweet
drink as a general offering; clean water for cooling hands and feet; color-
ful flowers from fields and ponds to be worn on the head; perfumed
incense corresponding to Being's intrinsic fragrance for the nose; glitter-
ing jewels and burning oil lamps for the eyes; cool water sprinkled with
sandal and saffron powder for the mind; tasty food for the tongue; and
melodious sounds from musical instruments that are blown, shaken, and
beaten for the ears. At the conclusion of the act of worship, these
goddesses disappear and dissolve in the very senses they have worshiped
and regaled.

(b) The Internal Act

The internal act of worship includes the offering of (i) tonic, (ii)
cakes, and (iii) life-stuff.

(i) Tonic

All that is summed up by samsara and nirvana has been from its very
beginning the pure quality that is the essence of a genuine, self-originated elixir.[245] This is intimated by eight basics as they pertain to each of
the three hierarchically organized levels (the external, the internal, and
the arcane)[246] or by four basics as they pertain to the external and the
internal with respect to the five kinds of elixir.[247] The eight basics each
have one hundred twenty-five branches, altogether totaling one thousand branches. The stuff in them is the elixir, so called because it is the
solvent—derived from the felt understanding that all that is points to the
identity of Being with itself so that there is nothing to accept or reject—
that removes the deadening power of dichotomic thought with its belief
in duality as incontrovertible. When this elixir has been consecrated into
the stuff of which the five affinities with Being and their originary awareness modes are made, in accordance with the formula laid down in the
texts of one's tradition, one scoops up a drop from the ocean of this elixir

with one's thumb and ring-finger joined so as to form a casket, its lid matching its base like the sun and moon, and lets it drip into the mouth of the assembled deiform energies, imagining them all to become satiated with the flavor of bliss supreme.

(ii)   Cakes

One imagines that the cakes prepared from the wondrous ingredients we live by, such as food and drink, have been piled up in huge quantities in a keg as vast and spacious as Being's meaning-rich field. These cakes, which are the elixir of originary awareness modes, provide the essential nutrients for indulging in the pleasures of the senses. When one offers these cakes to the deiform energies of the configuration, with the appropriate words for the occasion, they take them using their scepter-shaped tongue as a ladle of light, eat them, and feel delighted. The meaning is that the foods, which are the five objects of the senses, and the drinks, which are the five perceptions of these objects, frolic together in a swirl of sheer lucency.

(iii)   Life-stuff[248]

The root of frustration is blood as the craving for and being attached to the spurious. To drown this frustration in a swirl of bliss supreme, where no attachment obtains, is the purpose of offering this vital stuff, which is such that in it samsara has remained in its original freedom as the dimension of unoriginatedness, to the deiform energies of the configuration. While making this offering of an ocean of blood that is samsara, one should imagine the deiform energies to eat and drink it so that nothing whatsoever is left over.

(c)   The Arcane Act

The arcane offering has two aspects: (i) coupling and (ii) loosening.

(i)   Coupling

Being's lighting-up as the owner of a cognitive domain and as constituting appropriate activity is what is meant by the male principle. Being's openness as this cognitive domain and as constituting appreciative discernment is what is meant by the female principle. Their inseparable unity[249] is what is meant by the statement that all and everything has been a superoriginary coupling. The flavor of bliss supreme deriving from this coupling satiates all configurations. This is intimated by the image of the male and female joining in a kiss and enjoying the rapture of their most intimate union. Where one imagines only a single goddess, she enjoys this rapture in union with the trident into which the lord of the affinity with Being or her hidden male consort has transformed himself. Concentrating on this originary awareness, which is bliss supreme, as it gradually reaches its fullest intensity in a special feeling of flowing bliss, streaming down from above and rising from below and becoming ever more stable, there grows in oneself a sense of pride in being inseparable from the love of these deiform energies.

(ii)   Loosening

What must be cut loose is the externalizing dichotomic trend into a rigid separation between subject and object that is still subtly operative in one's self conceived of as a deiform energy. Because this dichotomic trend throws one into samsara, it is the enemy who obstructs the deeply felt understanding of an originary awareness in which no duality obtains. How is this loosening effected? It is done by the sharp sword of this very originary awareness, which stands apart from the trend into the subject-object dichotomy. First, it cuts loose this dichotomy, which is operative in one's Existenz, together with the addiction to it, and casts it into Being's fieldlike continuum in which there is no origination of anything whatsoever into something. This is what is meant by the statement that all and everything has been a superoriginary freedom.[250] Then, from this dynamic reach and range of Being, there arises a higher-order compassion for the sake of protecting the sentient beings in the ten higher realms against the unbearable frustration that is the result of accumulating evil deeds. Through the deeply felt understanding that in oneself all that must be cut loose is but a magic show or a veil before one's eyes, never having been experienced as something really existing, the dichotomic trend is cut loose, and the whole crowd of thought constructions subsides in Being's meaning-rich field. One should think of this procedure as an act of worship in which samsara and nirvana form a swirl that has the same flavor throughout.

(d)   *The Being-in-its-beingness Act*

The Being-in-its-beingness worship is the most sublime of all forms of worship because in it the object of worship, the subject performing the worship, and the very act of worship no longer have any external or internal reference. It keeps before the mind and understands that whatever lights up and is interpreted in terms of samsara and nirvana has been pure as such from the very beginning and has been spontaneously present, in its symbolic character, as the ultimate configuration of the Victorious One.

(3)   *The Praise*

Praising means that at the end of the act of worship, one feels a deep trust in the deiform energies of the configuration and continues thinking of their qualities in the following manner: Although Being's meaning-rich field, which as bliss supreme, encompassing all that can be known spanning the three aspects of time and manifesting in all the modes of samsara and nirvana, is dissociated from all thematic proliferations, it first takes shape as a meaning-rich gestalt with its two originary awareness modes that are sensitive to the things of the world as they are in themselves and to their interconnectedness[251] without attachment or hindrance. Out of a concern for the welfare of the countless sentient beings and in the course of its frolicking in two sensuous gestalts that have never parted from Being's meaning-rich gestalt, it assumes many peaceful and fierce appearances, possessing the most exquisite characteristics and marks. Its communicativeness possesses the sixty modulations of voice, harmonious and ringing. Its resonance, nonthematic and nondivisive, is forever in a state of delight because it is bliss supreme. Its capabilities, involving renunciation and understanding, cannot be fathomed by rational thought. Its optimizing activity, not involving any efforts but proceeding spontaneously, manifests wherever and whenever sentient beings are to be taught and trained. By keeping the gestures and the greatness of this existential value before one's mind, one puts them into words of praise. One should utter such praise with the awareness that the object of praise and the praising subject are such that they cannot be added to nor subtracted from one another.

The outcome of this transmutation procedure is such that, when one has this Buddha-experience, one is for ever the sense-bestowing process through acts of worship requiring no efforts and has become the unsurpassable focus for being greeted and worshiped by the whole of what constitutes samsara and nirvana.

e. THE INVOLVEMENT WITH THE PRESENCE OF A DEIFORM ENERGY

This involves four felt qualities: (1) the lucency of its observable features; (2) the consolidation of the proud feeling of being an aspect of the whole of Being; (3) keeping before one's mind the symbols and understanding them; and (4) the holistic experience of bliss, lucency, and openness.

(1) *The Lucency of Its Observable Features*

This is to envision the whole gestalt as bathed in light in a single moment and keep it before the mind's eye, or, beginning from the top of the head and working down to the lotus throne, to envision in detail the gestalt and its ornaments, one by one, as bathed in light. At the conclusion, when everything is in a single moment envisioned as being bathed in light, one must focus one's mind fully on it, as if this presence were a reflection in a clear, glistening, and mud-free lake that has not been stirred up by a storm. Whether one begins with a complete or a piece-meal envisioning depends on one's temperament. There is no fixed rule.

(2) *The Consolidation of the Proud Feeling of Being an Aspect of the Whole of Being*

This is the proud feeling of being any such deiform energy as which the Buddha-experience, devoid of any defects and replete with capabilities and qualities, is to be imaginatively developed, and which comes first as the apprehendable, pride-suffused notion of "I am." But when this proud feeling in all its brilliance is experienced by a mind unconcerned with trying to appropriate it in a subjective way[252] the developing and the fulfilling phases form a unity.

What must be transmuted is the common, impure, and opaque presence of the world and the egotistically inordinate attachment to it.

The transmutation procedure involves, first, envisioning the observable features of the deiform energy as bathed in light and keeping before one's mind and understanding their symbolic meanings and second, changing the objective concreteness of the external world into a luminous, purely symbolic presence and the subjective, egocentric attachment to this world into a purely symbolic feeling of pride and self-esteem through attending to what this proud feeling of being a part of the whole of Being means.

(3)   Keeping Before One's Mind the Symbols and Understanding Them

In the present context this may be done in the manner explicated in the section on the activation of a deiform energy. From the viewpoint of genuine experience, the qualities of the deiform energies, as well as the stuff of which they are made, have been symbolic in character from the very beginning because they are already spontaneously present in the Buddha-experience. Hence one must know that these deiform energies, evoked through in-depth appraisals, as well as their qualities and the stuff of which they are made, are also symbolic in character. Also, when one evokes these symbols according to the accounts of such deeply felt experiences, one must keep them before one's mind in order to understand them. In the present context of becoming involved with the presence of a deiform energy, one must approach the symbols with a deep sense of devotion, and when each symbol has become ever more consolidated within, one must immerse oneself in an in-depth appraisal of this developing phase by linking the previously discussed phases of envisioning the observable qualities bathed in light with the consolidated, nonegological feeling of pride and self-esteem.

(4) The Holistic Experience of Bliss, Lucency, and Openness

It is important to learn how to assess the developing phase, which is lucent, symbolic, and consolidating, through an appreciative discernment that is dissociated from the divisive tendencies with their involvement in a static reality and that knows that the stuff of which this phase is made is open-dimensional, though its actual presence lights up like the reflection of the moon in water or a rainbow in the sky, having no substancelike or qualitylike characteristics. By sealing the developing phase with the fulfilling phase, Being's marvelous activity comes into full play, bringing to the fore all configurations as meaning-rich gestalt experiences. Thus the developing phase which has been cultivated as a re-creation of the world in symbolic terms by the intellect, transforms the accumulation of merits into the accumulation of holistic and uncontrived originary awareness modes. Because the two accumulations of merits and cognitions, the two gestalt qualities of Being, the two real-

ities, and the duality of appropriate activity and appreciative discernment, are restored to their original unity by this procedure, this quick
way presented by the existential approach must be known as being particularly profound.

If, without knowing what it is actually about, one were to busy
oneself with the developing phase alone in terms of substance and quality, even though one might have the experience of a luminous presence
and a certain sense of self-esteem, this experience would never become
the way toward limpid clearness and consummate perspicacity. Rather it
would be only a clever device for holding one fettered in samsara. By
attributing an autonomous existence to the calm and peaceful energies
when creatively imagining them, one would become a god in the realm
of aesthetic forms, while by attributing an autonomous existence to the
fierce energies when creatively imagining them, one would become a
demoness or a Rudra, as has been related in the histories and introduc-
tions to the Mantrayāna works. One must not become slack in maintain-
ing the lucency of the envisioned forms, the understanding of their
symbolic character, and the consolidation into a nonegological feeling of
pride and self-esteem that go with the developing phase. But if one
should grow tired of exercising this creative imagination, one should
begin intonations.[253]

[EPILOGUE][254]

B. REMAINING TUNED-IN WHEN REEMERGING FROM THE STATE OF COMPOSURE

When one reemerges from Being's sheer lucency into which one has
immersed oneself and experiences oneself as the gestalt quality of a
deiform energy in all its magic, one must know that the visible and
audible in one's environing world is the frolicking of Being's originary
awareness in the guise of deiform energies and their communication in
the context of one's three affinities with Being.[255] One must also understand that walking, sitting, and other voluntary and involuntary movements are gestures of a deiform energy; that the consumption of food and
drink is an internal sacred rite; and that the participation in the

frolicking of the world's many sensuous delights, without reserve or anticipation, is the traveling of one's way with a friend.

This immersing oneself into and reemerging out of Being's sheer lucency is said to be like making the passage from deep sleep into dreaming and from lying down to getting up again.

CONCLUDING REMARKS

In the process of the symbolic re-creation of ourselves and our world, initiated and effected by the so-called developing phase, which pertains to that aspect of Buddhist thought and level of human growth where the individual has broken away from a mechanistic perspective of himself and his world and increasingly attempts to tune in to the forces working in and around him, the principle of complementarity plays a decisive role. This principle is summed up in the idea of the inseparability of appropriate activity and appreciative discernment, each facet expressing in its own way the underlying dynamics of a single reality, in this case the reality of the human individual.

The first stirring of this principle is noticed when, having outgrown our childhood phase, we set out on the long and often arduous road to adulthood and spiritual maturity. The initial step in this direction is taken from the level, referred to as Mahāyoga, on which the developing phase becomes distinctly operative. In the overall development of the human individual this phase is, in a very special sense, tied in with appropriate activity, which basically means the activation of one's inner potential whereby physical and spiritual meaning fuse into a single life-sustaining and life-enhancing dynamics. The emphasis on appropriate activity points to the fact that knowing, in the vital sense of self-cognition, is ultimately possible only by means of doing. "In the beginning was the Deed" (Im Anfang war die Tat!)—Goethe's insight is more than a mere restatement of Romantic idealism, which, in its theoretical presentation by Johann Gottlieb Fichte, (1762–1814) displays certain similarities with the idealistic trends in Buddhist philosophy whose reductionism one attempted to overcome by an existential-experiential approach to the problem of becoming truly human.

Appropriate activity in the sense of activating one's inner potential is, on the basis of its being a facet in the principle of complementarity, already touched by appreciative discernment, which aims at integration, unity (not to be confused with a meaningless "The One"), and a deeply felt understanding of life's meaning, which, by virtue of its internal dynamics, gives direction and meaning to the activity that is necessary and hence "appropriate." The emphasis on appropriate activity is therefore not an invitation to act blindly. Rather all activity, if deemed appropriate, must be performed in the light of appreciative discernment whose luster, seemingly deriving from a higher-order reality, is in this interaction made even more brilliant. Thus, while appropriate activity is the quintessence of the developing phase, appreciative discernment is the life of the fulfilling phase. Though complementary to each other in what is a unitary process, language, because of its inability to express complexity, presents complementarity in a linear arrangement and creates the impression that its two facets are separable and constitute a sequence—first this, then that.

There have always been people who did not and still do not realize the trap that language sets and, once they have fallen into it, keeps them firmly imprisoned. In the dGongs-pa zang-thal (Vol. 2, pp. 530f.) we are told that a person, having first called up the image of a formulated energy expressive and symbolic of the system's primary concern with experiencing its originary awareness, proceeds to render it null and void. Though he may claim that this emptying or rendering a felt presence null and void is the fulfilling phase, his procedure is merely an annihilation phase that does not come close to what the fulfilling phase is actually all about. Even more outspoken was Saraha, who, using the literally and reductionistically used synonyms compassion and emptiness for appropriate activity and appreciative discernment, respectively, declared:

> He who meditates on emptiness divested of compassion
> Is a person who does not find the unexcelled way;
> If he should concentrate merely on compassion
> He will stay on in samsara and not achieve releasement. [256]

Translated into today's language, this scathing aphorism unequivocally states that the activist, whatever his motives, will not get out of the mess he has made of his life and that of others; and the meditation freak, locked up in the cage of his private fancies, will not get anywhere because he has no way to go.

The key element in the implementation of the principle of complementarity, which starts with the activation of one's inner potential, is "understanding." This is never a merely rationalistic game of reducing whatever one encounters, be this of an external or internal order, to some stale triviality. Rather, as a searching and creative process, it is a multifaceted opening up to a rich world of symbolic significance bathed in supernal light and suffused with the warmth of feeling. Paraphrasing Klong-chen rab-'byams-pa's terse statement, we may say that:

> Understanding is the intensity with which the system's originary awareness is experiencing itself in recognizing (1) its cognitive domain, populated by animate and inanimate objects, as a field continuum from which meaning constantly grows; (2) the living beings in their coming into existence and their passing away as presenting dynamic gestalt qualities; (3) the phenomenal world as Being's lighting-up in the sense that Being's sheer lucency manifests forever in a projective luminosity; (4) the presencing of images in shapes of finitude and the releasement from finitude as not constituting separable events nor involving a dubious dualism; and (5) appreciative discernment as the total system's excitation on its way toward self-realization.[257]

Above all, understanding is a kind of "seeing" that goes far beyond what we ordinarily call seeing and is more in line with what William Blake expressed by saying: "If the doors of perception were cleansed everything would appear to man as it is, infinite." This synonymity of understanding and seeing is stated in *Rig-pa rang-shar* (pp. 558f.) to be such that:

> The quintessence or pure facticity of understanding is seeing.
> This seeing as the system's function or actuality is as follows:
> In the swirling center of the wide-open sky
> The undivided illumination of the system's cognitive domain is,
> In view of the fact that two lamps never cease shining,
> The system's self-originated, self-rising lighting-up.
> Such seeing is what is meant by superb understanding.[258]

What we encounter in this process of seeing and understanding, rolled into a single operation, are primarily symbols. Unlike signs, symbols do not point to something else and alien. The paradox about them is that they may be seen, perceived, apprehended "out there," but refer to an "in here," an interiority that has neither a within nor a without. They have their own self-organizing dynamics in evolving as formulated energies that the primitive mind, unaware of their origin and evolution, concretizes into independent gods and goddesses. At a time when the Western world was still in the clutches of darkest superstition, the Ti-

betan woman teacher Ma-gcig Lab-kyi sgron-ma (1055–1145) stated
that we tend to speak of our mind's projections in terms of gods and
goddesses when things go well with us and of demons and ogres when
things do not go so well. Instead of succumbing to the fallacy of mis-
placed concreteness by lack of understanding, the visualization of the
formulated energies as symbolically significant is primarily an aid or
appropriate activity to becoming aware of the possibilities that we can
become and live through meaningfully by appreciative discernment.

These formulated energies in their symbolic significance are visualized as presenting a gestalt quality, which as quality is pure potential
but as a gestalt suggests a corporeal schema that has originated and taken
form out of the depth of the primordial field-continuum of Being in its
genus- and species-specific potential as the carrier of Being's implicit
meanings and encoded programs. Inasmuch as this genus- and species-
specific potential constitutes a symmetry break in the original unity and
initiates further symmetry breaks, its programs evolve through homologous dynamics into our world and our organismic existence in which the
original openness enframes itself as an organizing principle called mentation or mind. Hence "the well-known fundamental biogenetic law, 'On-
togeny recapitulates phylogeny,' is not only valid in the realm of physical
structure, but extends also into the realm of consciousness, or spiritual
structure!" (Jantsch, 1975, p.151). With respect to the enworlded experiencer, the emerging and evolving gestalt as a structured nothingness,
through its symbolic significance, draws attention to and centers the
experiencer's body in the open-dimensional field-continuum of Being.
This gestalt, being both the expression and the expressed of the process
of embodiment, may be visualized and by implication felt as being either
predominantly male or predominantly female but never as the one or the
other exclusively—a further example of the principle of complementarity
in operation. Most important, the gestalt quality not only arises from the
depth of our inner potential but, as a true symbol, puts us into touch with
this inexhaustible source of what may become our spiritually enhanced
existence. The perceived gestalt quality of our being embodied is only
one of the many symbols our inner potential creates in making itself
explicit through what on the part of the experiencer is his or her understanding of the symbols. It should be sufficiently clear that in the symbolic re-creation of ourselves and our world, understanding is not predetermined, and the symbols that it deciphers are merely prefigured by
the totality of our endowments, capabilities, and dispositions. The symbols therefore cannot actually be equated with specific, fixed meanings
without reducing them to meaningless counters. Rather what to the
literalist seems to be an equation is only a suggestion, a possible inter-

pretation. The visualization of the gestalt quality of our embodied exis-tence, which we cannot simply dispose of, is part of the larger dimension of understanding this ever present reality. In the structuration by under-standing, the visualized gestalt in the richness of its qualities may assume distinct features; hence there is never one gestalt or gestalt quality fixed once and for all but an infinite variety expressing the infinite possibilities of our inner potential. Consequently, there are many developing phases and, as our author has stated explicitly, the one he presents is merely an overview and invitation to the experiencer to probe deeper. Though he is not an original thinker but merely an epitomizer, his succinct presenta-tion constitutes a valuable contribution to the rich world of ideas devel-oped by other process-oriented thinkers, who often were and are still found among artists and poets as well, and whose works, in whatever language these may have been written, as David Michael Levin (1985, p. 220) observed:

> ask us to focus on the way we in-habit and experience our bodily nature, and do so, moreover, with but one goal: the nurturing of our capacity for feeling and perceiving in more open, more spon-taneous, more creative and meaningful ways.

More and more it is now felt that the split between fact, one-sidedly overvalued as "objective" because quantifiable and measurable, and val-ue, equally one-sidedly dismissed as merely "subjective" because non-quantifiable and nonmeasurable, can no longer be maintained without endangering our very existence. We should not forget that the word *fact* is derived from the Latin *factum*, which means "something that has been made" and hence denotes an artifact that is becoming increasingly dys-functional. The rediscovery as well as the recovery of the lost sense of value must be effected by a renewed, that is, creativity-oriented, ap-proach to what Being's potential in us may hold for us in our attempts to become more fully human. With this emphasis on creativity as auto-poiesis and self-cognition through self-transcendence, any cheap imita-tion of already stereotyped patterns of ritual behavior and/or insipid affectation of some pseudospirituality is made impracticable. The spir-itual is neither on the side of the sensuous and sensual nor on the side of the nonsensuous and nonsensual because it is not some *thing* or *factum* to be pinpointed and turned into some other dysfunctional artifact. Rather the spiritual playfully manifests through the sensuous as well as the non-sensuous so that both, the one complementing and giving meaning to the other, serve to ensure an extraordinary happiness. In the context of the symbolic re-creation of ourselves and our world through a restructuring of what is already there on the basis of the "feel" of the forces in and around us by entering into a dialogue with them, it may not be out of place to quote Martin Heidegger:

> What is needed is neither abolition of the sensuous nor abolition of the nonsensuous. On the contrary, what must be cast aside is the misinterpretation, the deprecation, of the sensuous, as well as the extravagant elevation of the supersensuous. A path must be cleared for a new interpretation of the sensuous on the basis of a new hierarchy of the sensuous and nonsensuous. The new hierarchy does not simply wish to reverse matters within the old structural order, now reverencing the sensuous and scorning the nonsensuous. It does not wish to put what was at the very bottom on the very top. A new hierarchy and new valuation mean that the ordering *structure* must be changed. To that extent, overturning Platonism must become a twisting free of it.[259]

The first real step in this "twisting free" of *all* prevailing ideologies (philosophical, religious, social, political, and what not)—not merely Platonism—is the developing phase, so aptly discussed in terms of a cleanup operation, which every sensible person knows not to be an end in itself but an effective means to make what is and has already been there shine more brightly. In this sense, then, the developing phase— with its rich world of symbols that, apart from their intrinsic significance, act as guiding images—may well have something to say to us in our capacity of being human beings in search of our humanity.

NOTES

1. Tibetan titles of indigenous works usually consist of two parts: one specifying the topic under consideration and the other presenting it in vivid symbols. Here the topic is the developing phase in the individual's attempt to regain the lost unity of the human and the divine through ritual procedures involving both appropriate activity (*thabs*), as a means to rouse the latent potential, and appreciative discernment (*shes-rab*), as a growing sense of wholeness. The burgeoning potential and its ripening into full maturity are both symbolized by an ear of corn. From the perspective of the individual still on the way to retrieve the lost unity, this endeavor is experienced as a process of bringing one's ordinary reality into union (*zung-'jug*) with one's higher-order reality. From the perspective of the fully matured individual, these two realities are experienced as having always remained inseparable (*dbyer-med*).

Both perspectives are presented in the *Bla-ma dgongs-'dus*. There (Vol. 5, p. 749) we read:

> If one does not make appropriate activity and appreciative discernment team up, the existential approach to the mystery of Being will go astray.

and on p. 667 we are told:

> Appropriate activity and appreciative discernment are inseparable.

2. An excellent presentation of the problem of translating has been given by K. R. Norman in his article "On Translating from Pāli." His statements concerning translations from Pāli apply as well to translations from Tibetan, taking into account that the Tibetan sentence structure is associative in character, rather than logical-deductive. Norman's article is a "must" for every would-be translator.

3. *Chos-dbyings*, p. 106. Much the same sentiment is expressed by Nietzsche's Zarathustra (1954, p. 307):

> It was only reluctantly that I ever inquired about the way: that always offended my taste. I preferred to question and try out the ways themselves .

. .. "This is *my* way; where is yours?"—Thus I answered those who asked me "the way." For *the* way—that does not exist.

4. To facilitate an understanding of what is to follow, the nine pursuits may be diagrammed as follows:

The spiritual pursuits		The follower's intellectual acumen
Śrāvakayāna		
Pratyekabuddhayāna	}	low level
Bodhisattvayāna		
Kriyātantra		
Caryātantra	}	medium level
Yogatantra		

Mahāyoga or Anuttarayoga

The new (*gsar-ma*) tradition (bKa'-brgyu-pa, Sa-skya-pa, dGe-lugs-pa)		The old (*rnying-ma*) tradition
Father-Tantra	Mahā	
Mother-Tantra	Anu }	high level
Non-dual Tantra	Ati	

rDzogs-chen Ati

sems-sde		
klong-sde	}	superhigh level
man-ngag-sde		

This last subdivision is specific to rDzogs-chen teaching of the rNying-ma tradition, and its internal subtle gradation is indicative of an ever deepening probing of pure experience. None of these designations can be rendered adequately, and until an exhaustive study has been made, they are best considered as proper names. Probably, the most detailed presentation of all the above-mentioned pursuits is offered by Klong-chen rab-'byams-pa in his *Grub-mtha' mdzod*.

5. The terms *fore-structure* and *fore-conception* are English renderings of Martin Heidegger's *Vor-Struktur* and *Vorgriff*. They indicate that in any act of understanding or interpretation, there is a tendency to legislate in advance what we are setting out to discover. In Heidegger's words (1962, p. 191): "In every case . . . interpretation is grounded in *something we have in advance*—in a *fore-having.*" And "The interpretation has already decided for a definite way of conceiving it, either with finality or with reservations; it is grounded in *something we grasp in advance*—in a *fore-conception.*"

6. The term *thub-pa* is of singular importance. Unless used as an ordinary verb, it occurs in the compound of *Śākya thub-pa*, the Tibetan rendering of *Śākyamuni* "the sage of the Śākya clan," by which term the historical Buddha is designated. It also occurs in the compound *dka'-thub*, which is the Tibetan equivalent for the Sanskrit term *tapas*, usually rendered in English as "penance," "self-mortification," or "austere practices." None of these connotations apply to the Tibetan term. The Tibetan *thub-pa* expresses the most elementary experience of possibility, the "I can"—the historical Buddha *could* do what others could not; he *could* (*thub*) do what was difficult (*dka'*) to do. This emphasis on the "I can" and, by implication, also on the "I cannot" is clearly brought out by Rong-zom Chos-kyi bzang-po (*Selected Writings*, pp. 83, 92).

7. *Theg-mchog* I, p. 97, and *Chos-dbyings*, pp. 104–105 in particular.

8. Such is the explanation given in the *rDor-rje sems-dpa' thugs-kyi me-long* (in *Ati*, Vol. 1, p. 235) and the *gSang-ba snying-po*, fol. 2b.

9. This term refers to the quality of a whole whose nature is not reducible to any of the parts that we may abstract from it. The Buddhist idea of the gestalt quality (*sku*), which is both the expression and the expressed of an originary awareness process (*ye-shes*) such that neither can be added to nor subtracted from the other (*'du-'bral med-pa*), comes close to Martin Heidegger's "internal experience" of the body (1979, p.99), in which feeling plays a prominent role. According to him (1979, p. 99), this kind of feeling is "that basic mode of *Dasein* by force of which and in accordance with which we are always already lifted beyond ourselves into being as a whole."

As David Michael Levin (1985, p. 49) explicates:

> What gives feeling its truth-disclosive nature, then, is that it is inherently directed toward an experience which is global and holistic. Our 'felt body' therefore *contests and counterbalances* the objective 'natural' body which we come to know only much later, and only through the influences of analytical science.

Buddhist texts speak of a "deeply felt understanding" (*nyams-rtogs*).

10. It is the merit of the phenomenology-oriented philosophers such as Edmund Husserl, Maurice Merleau-Ponty, and Martin Heidegger to have drawn attention to the presence of the "body" in a human being's enworldedness. Special mention should be made of David Michael Levin's innovative work *The Body's Recollection of Being*, quoted above.

11. The terms *autopoiesis* and *autopoietic*, invented by Humberto Maturana during a conversation with his friend José Bulnes, express what Erich Jantsch (1980, p. 10) described as the "fundamental complementarity of structure and function, that flexibility and plasticity due to dynamic relations, through which self-organization becomes possible." This concept is of great value not only in the domains of the biological and cognitive sciences but also in the attempts to arrive at a deeper understanding of Buddhist process thinking, concerned as it is with the individual's self-realization or authenticity of being.

12. Arturo B. Fallico (1962, p. 95).

13. Herbert Guenther (1981, pp. 195–208).

14. Concerning these two realities in Buddhist thought, see p. 125, n. 117.

15. Concerning the neologisms autopoiesis and autopoietic see p. 111, n. 2.

16. Tib. *bde-(bar) gshegs-(pa'i) snying-po*. On this term see in particular my *Matrix of Mystery*, p. 228, n. 55.

17. Tib. *snang-ba*. I have avoided the usual rendering of this term (on the basis of its Sanskrit equivalent *ābhāsa*) by "appearance," because of the ambiguity that attaches to this word in philosophical literature. Thus, for instance, for Hegel the problem is ontological; his "appearances" of the spirit constitute stages in the development or history of consciousness. For Husserl the problem is epistemological; his "appearances" are the slanted views (*Abschattungen*) through which an identical thing makes its appearance. The Buddhist term is descriptive of a process: *snang-ba* is *not* a correlate to an unknowable thing-in-itself, nor can it be identified with semblance (*Schein*). It is more akin to the early Greek terms *phainetai* and *phainomenon*, both of which imply a lighting-up process prefiguring the so-called phenomenal.

18. See David Bohm, *Wholeness and the Implicate Order*. Concerning the implicate order the author said (p. 149): "This order is not to be understood solely in terms of a regular arrangement of *objects* (for example in rows) or as a regular arrangement of *events* (for example in a series). Rather, a *total order* is contained, in some *implicit* sense, in each region of space and time." Illustrating the meaning of this implicate order in its becoming explicate, he went on to say: "Thus, in a television broadcast, the visual image is translated into a time order, which is 'carried' by the radio wave . . . . The function of the receiver is then to *explicate* this order, that is to 'unfold' it in the form of a new visual image." On a larger scale the holomovement (the term implying the unfoldment of the whole) acts as the carrier of the implicate order (p. 151): "To generalize so as to emphasize undivided wholeness, we shall say that what 'carries' an implicate order is *the holomovement*, which is an unbroken and undivided totality. In certain cases, we can abstract particular aspects of the holomovement (for example light, electrons, sound, and so on), but more generally, all forms of the holomovement merge and are inseparable."

19. The above is a summary of *Zab-yang* II, p. 441.

20. *Yid-bzhin*, pp. 641f. The rendering given here differs in some instances from the one given in *Matrix of Mystery*, pp. 33f. In the present context I have attempted to bring out Klong-chen rab-'byams-pa's hermeneutical way of thinking even more clearly. He is unique in the history of Buddhist thought in that he presented his ideas in a poetic, highly evocative, and aesthetically appealing style that has nothing in common with the labored versification and dry-as-dust pedantry that have often dominated Buddhist scholasticism. Further, in his presentation the key notions are set, one after another, in precisely the order in which the topics to which they refer occur and are associated in immediate experience. It should never be forgotten that Klong-chen rab-'byams-pa's writings, in particular, and many of those who followed in his footsteps are not so much an assemblage of preestablished meanings but a challenge to the reader.

This challenge can only be met by an openness to possibilities on the part of the interpreter, not by a stale reductionism. It is nonsensical to attempt to draw a clear line between a translation, hailed as being "objective," and an interpretation, denounced as merely "subjective." Each and every translation is already an interpretation, because the translator works on a text from a fore-structure of understanding or fore-conception, which, as Martin Heidegger (*Being and Time*, p. 191) has pointed out, "has already decided for a definite way of conceiving it, either with finality or with reservation." The deplorable, if not deceitful, attitude of the objectivist is that he attempts to conceal this fore-structure.

21. Tib. *ye-shes*. The rendering of this term by "originary awareness" is prompted by the consideration that the neologism "originary," formed after the German *ursprünglich*, is best suited to convey the meaning of *ye-shes* as being the preconceptual, areflective matrix of lived-through experience that makes possible all reflective (reflexive, self-reflexive) and conceptual thought. It does not denote a specifiable temporal onset; rather it refers to the possibilizing source of thoughts and meanings. See also Calvin O. Schrag, *Radical Reflection and the Origin of the Human Sciences*.

22. Tib. *bdag*. According to Rong-zom Chos-kyi bzang-po (*Rong-'grel*, fol. 80ab), this term is synonymous with *byang-chub-kyi sems*, the individual's concern with limpid clearness and consummate perspicacity, which is felt to be the evolutionary force (*bde-gshegs-snying-po*) that gives meaning to his life and, by implication, with *sangs-rgyas*, the dissipative unfoldment of the whole. Rong-zom Chos-kyi bzang-po's interpretation continues with Klong-chen rab-'byams-pa (*Tshig-don*, p. 221) and has been taken over verbatim by mkhan-po Yon-dga' (*Nyi-zla'i sgron-me*, p. 160). In the Buddhist context this term, which is the Tibetan rendering for the Sanskrit word *ātman*, points to Being's (or any living system's) autopoietic (self-referential) function and its dissipative self-organization. Moreover, the Buddhist critique of the Brahmanical and popular Buddhist conception of a self (*ātman/bdag*) shows that the attempt to achieve a totally independent mind or isolated subject remains without foundation. The Buddhist idea of a self is based on the distinction between a self that is authentic—that is its *own self*, and an unauthentic it-self, which is largely they-determined.

23. The idea of identity must not be confused with the notion of equation. Samsara and nirvana are identical in being identity transformations of Being. Each such transformation can be given a (static) "state → image" interpretation; the image (samsara, nirvana) of a state (Being) is just that state itself, while dynamically it is a transformation.

24. Tib. *stong gsal rig-pa*. On these key notions in rDzogs-chen thinking, see my *Matrix of Mystery*, p. 255 n. 24.

25. Tib. *dkyil-'khor*. For details see my *Matrix of Mystery*, *s.v.*

26. *Yid-bzhin*, p. 654.

27. *Ibid*. p. 664.

28. *Ibid*. p. 665.

29. On this term *sku*, used here in the plural, see n. 9.

30. In his *Sems-nyid ngal-gso* and his autocommentary on it (p. 771), Klong-

chen rab-'byams-pa discussed the functions of the developing and fulfilling phases to the effect that the developing phase undermines the naive belief in the concrete reality of the phenomenal, and the fulfilling phase the yearning for and addiction to its magic- or trancelike, apparitional character. See also my *Kindly Bent to Ease Us*, Vol. 1, p. 162. Klong-chen rab-'byams-pa's words were repeated by 'Jigs-med gling-pa (*rNam-mkhyen shing-rta*, p. 403).

31. *Chos-dbyings*, p.261.
32. *Ibid.*
33. sGam-po-pa, *Collected Works*, Vol. Nya, fol. 8a.
34. *Klong-'grel*, p. 436.
35. Lo-chen Dharmaśrī, *Collected Works*, Vol. 16, p. 300.
36. Rong-zom Chos-kyi bzang-po, *bKa'-'bum*, p. 505.
37. *Nyi-ma'i 'od-zer*, p. 54. These ideas were repeated by Mi-pham 'jam-dbyangs rnam-rgyal rgya-mtsho (1846–1912), using the same terminology without adding any further information, in his *Mun-sel*, fol. 45a–f.
38. sGam-po-pa, *Collected Works*, Vol. Ki, fol. 19a.
39. *Ibid.* Vol. Nya, fol. 8b.
40. *bSre-'pho'i gzhung-'grel*, fol. 75b. See also fol. 195b.
41. *Zab-yang* I, p. 457.
42. The qualification of originary awareness by "super" (*chen-po*) is meant to emphasize its holistic time- and space-binding activity. See Rong-zom Chos-kyi bzang-po (*bKa'-'bum*, pp. 380, 384).
43. Johann Wolfgang von Goethe expressed this idea in the famous dictum (*Faust*, Part I):"If you do not feel it, you will not get it" (Wenn ihr's nicht fühlt, ihr werdet's nicht erjagen). For more recent expressions of the same sentiment, see the references on p. 113, n. 9.
44. *Phyag-chen lhan-cig skyes-sbyor-gyi zab-khrid*, pp. 494f.
45. *Kye'i rdo-rje 'grel-pa nyi-ma'i 'od-zer*, pp. 263f.
46. *Yid-bzhin*, p. 674.
47. *rNam-mkhyen shing-rta*, p. 265.
48. Traditionally known as the four kinds of birth. See p. 142, n. 163
49. This refers to the hierarchically organized world with the realm of form-lessness at the top, the realm of aesthetic forms in the middle, and the realm of desires at the bottom.
50. Klong-chen rab-'byams-pa spoke of three such programs (*bag-chags*), which together account for the movement in experience that marks the deviation from its optimal dynamics. His words (*Yid-bzhin*, pp. 92f.) follow:

> Whatever makes its presence felt as a going astray is the working of
> · three programs:
> The program for the experiencer's environing domain is the world in
>   which he is installed as well as
> The sensory impressions such as color-shape and so on depending on it.
> The program for the experiencer's cognitive existence is the set of eight

perceptual patterns as well as his actions, judged to be either good or bad and depending on his psychic apparatus.

The program for the body as lived is the corporeal shape the six kinds of living beings assume, including the limbs suited to the overall shape.

The eight perceptual patterns are the psychic background (in the sense of Martin Heidegger's "fore-structure"), the emotionally toned interpretative perception, the interpretative perception itself, and the five sense-specific perceptions,

51. *Grub-mtha'*, p. 378.

52. See also *Theg-mchog* II, p. 64; *Grub-mtha'*, p. 378; and *Chos-dbyings*, pp. 315f., 320.

53. Tib. *bar-(ma-)do*. So far the best presentation of the various phase transitions is by Detlef-I. Lauf, *Geheimlehren tibetischer Totenbücher*. The English translation *Secret Doctrines of the Tibetan Books of the Dead* by Graham Parkes does not come up to the standard of the German original. Figures 1 and 2 show the complementarity of stochastic (time-dependent) and deterministic factors in these phase transitions.

54. *Zin-bris*, fol. 31a. See also p. 138, n. 156.

55. *Ibid.* fol. 31b. See also p. 141, n. 159.

56. The key term here is *ye-shes sems-dpa'*. On its hermeneutical interpretation see p. 156, n. 242. By giving personalistic traits to the forces working in and through us, an intimate relationship between ourselves and the world is established, whereby we are enabled to enter into a dialogue with it.

57. *Zin-bris*, fol. 31b f. See also p. 142, n. 162.

58. *rNam-mkhyen shing-rta*, pp. 265f.

59. On this term see above p. 114, n. 18.

60. *rNam-mkhyen shing-rta*, pp. 291f.

61. *Theg-mchog* II, p. 367.

62. *gSal-byed me-long*, fol. 84b.

63. *Collected Works*, Vol. 4, pp. 479ff.

64. *Nyi-ma'i 'od-zer*, pp. 185ff. Both of these authors have given lengthy accounts of the forty vital points associated with the four safeguards, which, however, lie outside the scope of the present discussion.

65. It may not be out of place to highlight the tremendous difference that exists between the Buddhist idea of the complementarity of the two pervasive principles of appropriate action (*thabs*) and appreciative discernment (*shes-rab*), the one imaged as male and the other as female, and the rigid dualism of the two "ground principles," as Plato called them. He defined the one as the rational, formal principle or *lógos*, which he identified with the masculine, and the other as the emotional, aesthetic principle or *éros*, which he identified with the feminine. Because of his misogyny, he then went on to brand the female principle as evil and the male principle as good. This misconception has had devastat-

ing consequences for the intellectual, emotional, and spiritual life of Western man.

The Buddhist conception of complementarity has been beautifully summed up by Advayavajra (*Premapañcaka*, "Five Verses on Love," in *Advayavajrasaṃgraha*, p. 58) but translated into Tibetan under the title *Thabs dang shes-rab brtse-ba lnga-pa* (Skt. *Prajñopāyadayāpañcaka*, "Five Verses on Love Between Appropriate Action and Appreciative Discernment") and found in the Tibetan *bsTan-'-gyur*, Vol. mi, foll. 149b-150a, Peking ed. Vol. 68, p. 286):

> Being's lighting-up is the beloved groom, who lives only because of his
>   loving bride;
> If he were not, Being's openness, the loving bride, would be as dead.
> If ever the blooming bride, Being's openness, whose beauty is without
>   compare,
> Were to be alone, the loving groom would be paralyzed.
> Therefore, this conjugal pair apprehensively approached the teacher
>   supreme
> Who through his genuine affection aroused in them a native love.
> Ah! such was the expertise and wisdom of the teacher supreme
> That this couple became unsurpassed in their inseparability that does
>   not admit of any objectifying reference.
> Replete with all characteristic qualities, but devoid of the twice-four
>   extremes,
> They were the quintessence of all being, without having an essence of
>   their own.

The "twice-four extremes" are gain and loss, happiness and sorrow, fame and disgrace, praise and blame.

66. *Science News 123*, 12 February, 1983, pp. 108–109. This theory was initially developed to provide an explanation of the widely held "big bang" theory, which, among other difficulties, failed to solve the problem of what caused the big bang. According to Guth's theory, empty space itself exploded under the repulsive power of the quantum vacuum. A good overview of Guth's theory in relation to other cosmological theories has been given by Paul Davies in *Superforce*, pp. 192ff.

67. *gNas-lugs*, p. 58.

68. *Goethe Farbenlehre* (selection by Johannes Pawlik, Köln: DuMont Buchverlag, 3rd ed., 1980), section 781. There is still another aspect to this color, noted by Goethe in section 779 and corresponding to the Buddhist idea of *stong-nyid* (*śūnyatā*) as "dynamic nothingness." His words are:

> Diese Farbe macht für das Auge eine sonderbare und fast unaussprechliche
> Wirkung. Sie ist als Farbe eine Energie, allein sie steht auf der negativen
> Seite und ist in ihrer höchsten Reinheit gleichsam ein reizendes Nichts. Es
> ist etwas Widersprechendes von Reiz und Ruhe im Anblick.

The English translation by Charles Lock Eastlake, *Theory of Colours*, is as follows:

> This colour has a peculiar and almost indescribable effect on the eye. As a hue it is powerful, but it is on the negative side, and in its highest purity is, as it were, a stimulating negation. Its appearance, then, is a kind of contradiction between excitement and repose.

This does not quite capture Goethe's insight, who speaks of this color in terms of an energy, not as merely being powerful. Also, his "Nichts" is not the same as "negation"; and the last sentence could be better translated as "its appearance presents the paradox of stimulation and repose."

69. *Klong-'grel*, p. 52. *rNam-mkhyen shing-rta*, pp. 528f.

70. Tib. *rdo-rje btsun-mo'i bhaga*. For further details regarding its hermeneutical interpretation see also p. 163, n. 168. Here it may suffice to point out that the Sanskrit term *bhaga* has been retained in the Tibetan text to emphasize that the expression in which it is used is symbolic and as such points to the individual's higher-order spiritual dimension. The concept of a multilevel reality presenting a coordinated hierarchy is probably one of the most difficult to understand and yet is basic to Buddhist thought. The way in which the Buddhists have understood such a reality, in terms of an external, internal, and arcane level of interpretation, to which often a superarcane level is added, stipulates a correspondence between these levels, which each have their own organization dynamics. We may illustrate this by a passage from 'Jigs-med gling-pa's *mKha'-'gro bde-chen rgyal-mo'i sgrub-gzhung* (*Collected Works*, Vol. vii, part 1, pp. 347ff.), which has been interpreted in terms of a coordinated hierarchy by Ngag-dbang bstan-'dzin rdo-rje (*rGyud-don snang-ba*, pp. 140f):

> In an exceptional receptacle for bliss supreme
> Through the revelling in a social gathering
> The designated viands which can neither be chosen nor thrown away
> Have been transmuted into the elixir of life by the gnosemes ŌṂ, ĀḤ, and HŪṂ.

Bliss supreme (*bde-ba chen-po*), which is synonymous with the individual's felt understanding of the thrust toward limpid clearness and consummate perspicacity (*byang-chub-sems*), transcends the mistaken division of experience into higher and baser aspects, which is meant to mask the fore-structure of the moralist's (be he a theologian or philosopher) bias against the body and pleasure in general and to absolutize a mere prejudice.

Crucial to understanding what is meant by a coordinated hierarchy is the term receptacle (*snod*). It points to the individual's concrete life-world, of which he is an integral part and in which he actively participates by interpreting it in the framework of the contextuality of his multifaceted experience. Figuratively, we may say that the contextualized experiencer holds his entire life-world in his hand like a precious and cherished, highly valued object that is simultaneously a thing and a thought. Its thing-character is associated with solidness that serves to protect its fragile thought-character, a delicate texture of apperception and appreciation. Its symbolic quality is expressed by the Sanskrit term *kapāla*, literally meaning a skullcap (see also p. 137, n. 153), but which in this context is interpreted as follows:

> *ka* means *sukha*, "bliss," and *pāla* means *pālana*, "to protect."

This is the external (*phyi*) level of interpretation, which pertains primarily to the physical that is to be assessed objectively. There is also the internal (*nang*) or psychosocial level on which the experiencer explores the near infinite spectrum of pleasure the world has to offer. Here the objective domain, the valued life-world, are the private parts (*skye-gnas*) of the socialized experiencer's girlfriend (*phyag-rgya-(ma)*, Skt. *karmamudrā*).

Lastly, there is the arcane (*gsang*) level that is Being's mystery. Although it defies objectification and any other form of reductionism, the experiencer attempts to express this deeply felt mystery in terms that are taken from his embodied contextuality but are not limited to this contextuality in either meaning or scope. Here the symbol is *bhaga*, the creative source and force of the universe, imaged as the female consort, the indestructibility-diamond mistress (*rdo-rje btsun-mo*), who is permanently united with her male consort, cryptically implied by the term "indestructibility-diamond" (*rdo-rje*), as whom the experiencer images himself by virtue of being a part of the whole and also being the whole.

The same coordinated hierarchy is implied by the expression "social gathering" (*tshogs-kyi 'khor-lo*, Skt. *gaṇacakra*). On the external level it means a mixed party with plenty of food and drink, where eventually couples form and then, on the inner, psychosocial level, get more and more intimate with each other and engage in sex, a concrete expression of the dynamic interplay between appropriate activity and appreciative discernment by which the welter of divisive notions (*tshogs*) is crushed (as if run over by a wheel, *'khor-lo*). This may or may not open the way to the arcane level where the social gathering of the originary awareness modes is enjoyed by the system as a whole, which, as the authentic self, is neither an entity standing within itself nor a hermetically sealed subject but rather encompasses and gives meaning to the "lower" levels of the physical (external) and psychosocial (internal).

The designated viands (*dam-tshig rdzas*) are the "stuff" of which we are made, both physically and psychically. What this complex stuff is in its intricate arrangement over the hierarchically organized levels may be gleaned from the diagram on p. 139, n. 154. We certainly cannot choose this stuff, nor can we throw it away. We can only "make the most of it" and fully enjoy the possibilities it has to offer. Figuratively, this is to transmute these viands into the elixir of life by a first utterance—the gnosemes ŌṂ, ĀḤ, and HŪṂ, which assert nothing but revitalize our whole being by cutting across the hierarchically organized levels. Thus, according to Klong-chen rab-'byams-pa (*Sems-nyid ngal-gso*, p. 747):

ŌM lays the foundation for what, externally, is to become the body as lived in by us (*lus*); internally, our desires and attachments (*'dod-chags*); and arcanely, the experience of ourselves as presenting a gestalt quality (*sku*).

ĀḤ lays the foundation for what, externally, is to become our spoken language (*ngag*); internally, our aversions and irritations (*zhe-sdang*); and arcanely, the experience of our language as utterance (*gsung*).

HŪM lays the foundation for what, externally, is to become our subjective mind (*yid*); internally, our dullness and spiritual darkness (*gti-mug*); and arcanely, the experience of our psychic nature as spiritual resonance (*thugs*).

Using the familiar example of a social gathering, Ngag-dbang bstan-'dzin rdo-rje has indicated the rich possibilities that a multilevel interpretation can offer. This is quite different from the linear approach to man's complex nature by the reductionist, who is both unable and unwilling to understand a multilevel hierarchical organization of a living system and who attempts to reduce everything to one level of interpretation, the allegedly objective one. For such a person, the story might run as follows: He goes to a mixed party to carouse, and then picks up any willing female and has sex with her. Having had his fill of food and drink and sex, he still feels uneasy because somehow something was missing, and so he buys himself a girlie magazine. Thus he remains "objective" and cannot be accused of harboring "subjective" fancies.

71. See Dwags-po Paṇ-chen bKra-shis rnam-rgyal's commentary on the *Hevajratantra*, p. 49.

72. *rNam-mkhyen shing-rta*, p. 277.

73. See Dwags-po Paṇ-chen bKra-shis rnam-rgyal's commentary on the *Hevajratantra*, p. 50, and Dam-pa bsod-nams rgyal-mtshan's commentary on the *Hevajratantra*, p. 60.

74. Reproduced in Kenneth Clark, *The Nude*, p. 91.

75. M. Merleau-Ponty, *Phenomenology of Perception*, p. 160, says: " 'Living' (*leben*) is a primary process from which, as a starting point, it becomes possible to 'live' (*erleben*) this or that world."

76. *Theg-mchog* II, p. 106.

77. See their commentaries on the *Hevajratantra*, pp. 397 and 317, respectively.

78. *Bla-dgongs*, Vol. 10, pp. 706f. A similar account was given by Klong-chen rab-'byams-pa (*mKha'-yang* II, pp. 223f.).

79. English translation by Richard M. Zaner, *The Problem of Embodiment*, p.259.

80. See *Theg-mchog* I, p. 339; *Tshig-don*, p.200; also *Zab-yang* II, pp. 108, 225; *mKha'-yang* II, p. 144.

81. According to *mKha'-yang* III, pp. 117f.

82. According to *Tshig-don*, pp.339f.; *Chos-dbyings*, pp. 261f.

83. The image of the "neural chassis" was proposed by American neu-

rophysiologist Paul D. MacLean in his article "A Triune Concept of the Brain and Behavior."

84. It is worth noting that in rDzogs-chen thought the fundamental forces each constitute a complexity by exhibiting the functional modalities of the other fundamental forces. When one speaks, for instance, of the fundamental force cohesion/water, one is merely referring to a dominant function or modality in this complexity. See, for instance, *Mu-tig phreng-ba* (in *Ati*, Vol. 2), p. 449. The *Rig-pa rang-shar* (in *Ati*, Vol. 1), pp. 466f. explicitly states:

> The five higher order fundamental forces are holistically present in one's live body. The five functional modalities of the motility/wind fundamental force make the system's originary awareness glow projectively. The five functional modalities of the heat/fire fundamental force provide the creative dynamics of originary awareness. The five functional modalities of the solidity/earth fundamental force provide the stuff of which originary awareness is made. The five functional modalities of the cohesion/water fundamental force provide the cognitive domain of originary awareness. The five functional modalities of the space fundamental force provide the abode of originary awareness.

For further details, see also *Theg-mchog* II, p. 110, and *Tshig-don*, pp. 214f.

This conception has interesting implications. We may refer to this complexity of the fundamental forces as an abstract group G, which is a set of elements, the fundamental forces in the above case, which for simplicity's sake may be denoted by $a, b, c, \ldots$ This set is endowed with the law of composition, which involves a double way of combining any two or more elements of the set such that if a and b are elements of the set, their composition can be written ab and ba. However, the following conditions must be satisfied:

1. This is the group's property of *closure*. It means that in a group there is a binary operation for which the elements of the set can be related in pairs, giving results that are also members of the group. For example, for any two elements of the set a, b both ab and ba are also elements of the set.

2. The composition is *associative*. An example is the formula $a(bc) = (ab)c$.

3. There is an *identity* element e for the set such that for every element a of the set $ea = ae = a$.

4. For each element of the group there is another element—its *inverse* such that $aa^{-1} = a^{-1} a = e$.

Both identity and inverse are unique. In the context of the higher order fundamental forces as a set of elements forming the abstract group Being, its identity is also its uniqueness, and the same holds for the lower-order fundamental forces forming the abstract group sentient being. Man's uniqueness lies in his being the inverse of Being.

85. *Theg-mchog* II, p. 47.

86. *Ibid.* II, p. 54.

87. *Ati*, Vol. 1, pp. 679f.

88. The five poisons are the emotions of desire-attachment, aversion-irritation, dullness-spiritual darkness, arrogance-insolence, and envy-jealousy.

89. *Theg-mchog* II, p. 53.

90. *Ati*, Vol. 1, p. 667.

91. We have frequently spoken in the language of "symmetry" and "symmetry transformations" to indicate that Being as a dynamic system is symmetric with respect to its actions, which are symmetry transformations of Being. Any transformation may be conceived of as a symmetry break, and the absence of such symmetry breaking is called the exact symmetry limit. This is what in rDzogs-chen thinking is referred to by the term *super-diaphaneity* (*ka-dag*), while the "first" symmetry break is termed the *spontaneous presencing* (*lhun-grub*) or the *holomovement*. To the extent that it presents a broken symmetry, it is initially an approximate symmetry and as such is "strictly applicable only to spatially and temporally infinite systems" (Rosen, 1975, p. 78). This is precisely what in rDzogs-chen thought is intimated by Being's spontaneous presencing, which is imaged by the experiencer as an emergent (temporal) world-horizon (spatial) of meaning and felt to be the bliss of nirvana. Because of approximate symmetry we can discover approximate displacement symmetry. What this implies may be illustrated by a living being such as man who has approximate displacement symmetry because his finitude has broken the original symmetry of Being.

For the wide application of the concept of symmetry, see the excellent presentation by Joe Rosen, *Symmetry Discovered: Concepts and Applications in Nature and Science.*

92. *Man-ngag*, p. 20.

93. *Ibid.* p. 16.

94. *Ibid.* p. 61.

95. See *Theg-mchog* I, p. 93. On "utterance from the higher order reality level," see Dwags-po Paṇ-chen bKra-shis rnam-rgyal's commentary on the *Hevajratantra*, p. 116, where he defines it as a "non-dual originary awareness in its phonemic gnoseme A symbolizing Being's unoriginatedness which remains inexpressible by ordinary speech." See also Dam-pa bSod-nams rgyal-mtshan's commentary on the *Hevajratantra*, p. 164.

96. Dwags-po Paṇ-chen bKra-shis rnam-rgyal in his commentary on the *Hevajratantra*, p. 117.

97. Tib. *mngon-byang*. The inclusion of terms usually restricted to biology (morphogenesis as the emergence of a new form and ontogenesis as the development of an individual) in the paraphrase of the Tibetan code term is prompted by the consideration that the processes detailed are, in the present context, "seen" from within as regulating the evolution of the whole system's cooperative structures: no mentation, no bodily existence and vice versa. The account of these imaginatively and experientially lived through morpho- and ontogenetic processes given by 'Jigs-med gling-pa (*rNam-mkhyen shing-rta*, pp. 283f.) and by Yon-tan rgya-mtsho (*Nyi-ma'i 'od-zer*, pp. 171f.) tallies with the presentation given here. However, a different account is given by 'Jigs-med gling-pa in his *Klong-chen snying-thig*, part 1 (*Collected Works*, Vol. 7, pp. 1065ff.), where each such morpho- and ontogenetic process functions triadically as transmutation or

the restoration of the system's symbol character, completion as the holistic presence of its potential, and climaxing as the emergence of a new dynamic regime.

98. Dam-pa bSod-nams rgyal-mtshan in his commentary on the *Hevajra-tantra*, p. 299.

99. *mKha'-yang* II, p. 506.

100. *Ibid.* Vol. 1, p. 451.

101. *Ibid.* p. 154.

102. *Ibid.*

103. The following account is based on his *Chos-dbyings*, p. 341.

104. *Ati*, Vol. 1, pp. 154f.

105. See also p. 151, n. 216.

106. *Theg-mchog* II, p. 12.

107. *Ati*, vol. 1, p. 155.

108. It is interesting to note that this idea closely resembles the medieval cosmological speculation expressed in the famous sentence "God (or the world) is an infinite sphere whose center is everywhere and whose circumference is nowhere" "Deus (vel mundus) est sphaera infinita, cuius centrum est ubique et circumferentia nusquam". A special study of this idea was made by D. Mahnke, *Unendliche Sphäre und Allmittelpunkt* to which Marie-Louise von Franz refers in her *Number and Time*, p. 178. This idea continues in Spinoza's philosophy and, without the theological claptrap, is the official position of the modern cosmologist: "There is no cosmic edge and no cosmic center" (Paul Davies, *Superforce*, p. 13). However, under the impact of modern quantum physics, the universe is seen to include design, which makes it a self-organizing universe. This is as close as the West has come to the basic rDzogs-chen idea of an intelligent universe, which is such that its cognitive excitability pervades the whole of Being.

109. Tib. *grol-gzhi*. The above rendering attempts to bring out the dynamic character of *grol*. Although linguistically it is the past tense of the intransitive verb *'grol-ba*, it has no static implications.

110. *Ati*, vol. 1, pp. 155f.

111. Commentary on the *Hevajratantra*, p. 299.

112. *Dag-snang*, p. 266.

113. *Ibid.* p. 268; 'Ba'-ra-ba, *Collected Writings*, Vol. 7, p. 232; g.Yung-ston rdo-rje dpal bzang-po, *gSal-byed me-long*, fol. 22b; *Klong-'grel*, p. 47.

114. For a detailed discussion of these catalysts and their interrelationships see my *Kindly Bent to Ease Us*, Vol. 1, pp. 106ff.

115. *dGongs-pa zang-thal*, vol. 4, p. 16.

116. In the Buddhist context this term, like its Sanskrit equivalent *guru*, never denotes a concrete person but refers to the experiencer's feeling of the identity of the forces acting in the universe and in himself. It is a term for an organizing and meaning-bestowing principle in an individual's (psychic) development. Reductionists cannot understand this because they fail to note the difference between the idea of a guiding principle operating in an evolving universe and the notion of a concrete entity such as a spiritual friend (*dge-ba'i bshes-gnyen*, *kalyāṇamitra*) in a static cosmos that depends on an authoritarian

principle. Even if they can admit something other than the merely objectifiable and quantifiable within their rigidly structured and predictable world picture, they will still typically turn to a cult figure to satisfy their alleged objectivism.

117. The idea of two realities (*bden-gnyis*) is already found in early Hīnayāna Buddhist texts.See, for instance, the *Kathāvatthu*, composed about the time of Aśoka (reigned c. 265–238 BC; also given as c. 273–232 BC), and the *Milindapañhā*, composed in perhaps the first or second century AD and purporting to be the dialogue between the Hellenistic ruler of Bactria, Menander (fl. 160? BC–135? BC), and the senior monk Nāgasena. But it has received its fullest attention in Mahāyāna Buddhism on the basis of Nāgārjuna's *Mūlamadhyamakakārikā*, xxiv, 8. These two realities are the conventional reality (*kun-rdzob*), the one with which we are familiar in everyday life, and the higher order reality (*don-dam*) that we may experience in exceptional circumstances. However, in the process-oriented (*rgyud, tantra*) approach to man's problematic nature, with its emphasis on lived-through experience, as distinguished from the structure-oriented (*mdo, sūtra*) approach, with its concern for epistemological models, the distinction between the two realities is more complex. The process-oriented approach emphasizes a distinction without separation between what lights up (*snang-ba*) and what is open-dimensional (*stong-pa*). The first roughly corresponds to what is called the phenomenal and constitutes the domain of objectifying, thematizing, and representational thought (*sems*). Its organizing principle is logic, which as Erich Jantsch (1975, p. 84) has pointed out, expresses its results in *quantitative* or *structural* terms. The second, the higher-order reality, is accessible only to that mode of thinking that neither objectifies nor subjectifies, in which the subject-object structure has been suspended or has given way to a holistic originary awareness (*ye-shes*). This higher-order awareness is systemic in the sense of pertaining to the whole, rather than abstractive and merely focusing on a selected part. Its corresponding higher-order reality is organized on the basis of both feeling, whose results, according to Jantsch (p. 84), "are obtained in *qualitative* terms," and of tuning-in to the overall dynamic of Being, whose results, according to the same author (p. 84), "are expressed in terms of *sharing* in a universal *order of process* (namely, *evolution*)." Thus by virtue of its open-dimensional character, it presents an irreducibly qualitative aspect of reality. Nevertheless, attempts to reduce the dynamics of the process, with its unlimited wealth of open possibilities, to something static have constantly been made both in Buddhism itself and by its Western interpreters. Consequently, what is purely qualitative has been converted into some static emptiness or void, usually written with capital letters to indicate something that has been set once and forever and to thus prevent further questioning. In their inseparability the phenomenal and the open-dimensional, what is amenable to quantification as well as what is not, illustrate the principle of complementarity, which states that any comprehensive description of reality must have recourse to complementary concepts that exclude each other and yet depend on each other for their very definition. The complementary concepts of what lights up (*snang-ba*) and what is open-dimensional (*stong-pa*) refer to different presentations of one and the same reality. In his *gSang-bdag zhal-lung* (pp. 220f) Lo-chen Dharmaśrī stated quite

explicitly that inseparability is not a dialetic synthesis of opposites. Jantsch (1980, p. 274) characterized such a synthesis as "that clumsy Western attempt at making a rigid structure of notions move and overcome its dualism."

Though our conventional reality is included within the totality's lighting-up, this lighting-up as a phenomenal presentment is not itself identical with the conventional or commonly accepted reality. In the strict Buddhist sense of the term, the conventional reality is a going astray ('khrul-pa) into the opacity of representational thought. The totality's lighting-up retains something of its transparent, symbolic (dag) character, presenting itself as a gestalt quality (sku) commensurate with the originary awareness (ye-shes).

The indivisibility or complementarity of the phenomenal and the open-dimensional lends itself easily to an impassive, rationalistic description of reality. However, another twofold reality touches on man's feeling of being embedded in the abiding dynamics of an all-encompassing universe, which in its abidingness loses nothing of its rich presentments. This is technically referred to as the two realities of the abiding and the phenomenal (gnas-snang bden-gnyis). This idea bears a striking resemblance to Alfred North Whitehead's conception of permanence and flux, which he has elaborated in his monumental work Process and Reality (p. 338 in the corrected edition) as follows:

> In the inescapable flux, there is something that abides; in the overwhelming permanence, there is an element that escapes into flux. Permanence can be snatched only out of flux; and the passing moment can find its adequate intensity only by its submission to permanence. Those who would disjoin the two elements can find no interpretation of patent facts.

118. Although rDo-rje-'chang (Skt. Vajradhara) is mostly known from iconic representations, a deeper meaning is involved in that he can be said to be the visual presentment of the dynamic principle of complementarity. The Thig-le kun-gsal (rNying-rgyud, vol. 5, pp. 132–133) states:

> Within the dynamic reach and range that is the dissipative lucency of the complementarity of Being's openness as its objective cognitive domain and Being's cognitive excitation as its open uncompoundedness, two gestalt qualities reside in an inner lucency such that they cannot be separated from nor added to each other. This indivisible and undivided wholeness is rDo-rje-'chang.

The two gestalt qualities are that of Being in its meaning-rich potential and that of Being in its symmetry transformation into a world-horizon of meaning. On the role of symmetry transformations in rDzogs-chen thought, see my Matrix of Mystery, s.v.

119. Tib. lha'i phyag-rgya. As pointed out in Part One, p. 11, the term lha indicates a formulated energy whose felt impact lends itself to being imaged in forms that in mythological (or religious) language are termed god, or goddess, or deity. See also my Matrix of Mystery, s.v. This felt impact leaves a "marking" (phyag-rgya) that, strictly speaking, pertains to the level of mentation (sems) by

virtue of being so interpreted. Nonetheless, it reflects the triune hierarchical organization of Being as true subject (*bdag-nyid*), which, in view of the fact that Being is not some thing, not *a* being, cannot be equated with the postulate of an egological *thing*-subject (*bdag*). This hierarchical organization is described in terms of a gestalt quality as a dynamic presence (*sku*), a process of information-communication as the announcement of its presence (*gsung*), and its organization dynamics as a resonance with the whole (*thugs*). See Rong-zom Chos-kyi bzang-po's *gSang-'grel* (fol. 25b). As Klong-chen rab-'byams-pa pointed out (*Chos-dbyings*, p. 218), resonance is a holistic, systemic operation.

120. Tib. *chos-nyid*. This term has many meanings according to the context in which it is used. When used in a nonepistemological context, it is a term for Being's meaning-rich potential, which presents a "higher-order" reality. As such it is "meaning itself" (*chos-nyid*) and thus able to impart meaning to the "lower-order" reality, which "has meaning" (*chos-can*). In terms of perception this means that we can "see" either in a truly meaningful way (*chos-nyid lta-ba*) or in a seemingly meaningful way (*chos-can lta-ba*). On this important distinction, see, for instance, *Bla-yang* I (pp. 419f.); *Chos-dbyings* (p. 295). Being's intrinsic meaningfulness "lights up" as a gestalt quality, as is stated in the *Thig-le kun-gsal* (rNying-rgyud, Vol. 5, p. 130):

> Being's meaning-rich potential lights up as a meaning-rich gestalt,
> Just as the sun rises in the sky.
> Being's meaning-rich potential is pervasive of the meaning-rich gestalt,
> Just like milk and butter.

121. Tib. *bde-gshegs snying-po*. This term points to the process character of the totality as it provides an individual's growth potential. Bearing in mind that in rDzogs-chen thought what is usually rendered as "Buddha" develops like a dissipative (*sangs*) structure (*rgyas*) and as the "Buddha"-experience is never some static end-state, the individual as an aspect of the totality is, as it were, "programmed" to develop in the same way. Klong-chen rab-'byams-pa (*Theg-mchog* II, p. 63) gave the following summary account of it:

> This optimization thrust, to the extent that it is the ground and reason (*gzhi*) of Being as a process, is in its actuality (*rang-bzhin*) or spontaneous presencing (*lhun-grub*) a movement in the direction of the Buddha-experience which is Being's abidingness and ultimate originary awareness of itself as true subject. This thrust encompasses each and every sentient being; it never increases nor decreases; it is neither large nor small; and it is neither good nor bad.

In modern terms Being's optimization thrust is the principle of evolution. In it what is termed *originary awareness* (*ye-shes*) as a function of the totality's (that is, Being's) cognitive excitation/excitability (*rig-pa*) proves to be a powerful, auto-catalytic factor in the evolution not only of man and mankind but also of the universe.

122. The term *gshis* occurs either singly or in the following combinations,

dngos-po gshis-kyi gnas-lugs (*dGongs-pa zang-thal*, Vol. 4, p. 191; *Bi-ma*, Vol. 2, p. 364) and *dngos-po gshis-kyi sems-nyid* (*Bi-ma*, Vol. 2, p. 401). It points out that Being is inherently cognitive, a self-existent—in terms of systems philosophy— endogenous originary awareness (*rang-byung-(gyi) ye-shes*), which cannot be re- duced to any mental construct or even *a* mind (*Chos-dbyings*, p. 121). Though synonymous with *dbyings*, *gshis* differs from it only in the sense that it refers to the "presence" or "actuality" (*rang-bzhin*) of Being and *dbyings* to the "facticity" (*ngo-bo*) of Being, both of which in their inseparability again illustrate the principle of complementarity. See *gNas-lugs* (p. 96). The addition of the term *dngos-po* indicates that Being is a concrete presence. In other words, man is the whole of Being and yet only a part of it.

123. The highest attainment possible for an individual is that of becoming a person in whom the various levels in his hierarchical organization—the auto- poietic levels given the "code" names of "gestalt" (*sku*), information-com- munication (*gsung*), and responsive resonance (*thugs*)—have been fully coordi- nated. See *Bla-yang* I (p.220); on these "code" terms see also note 119. The ordinary attainments are abilities that may appear abnormal or even miraculous. They are commonly referred to by their Sanskrit term *siddhi* and have been "marketed" as all sorts of gimmicks in certain sections of Western society. On these see also *Bla-yang* I (p. 219) and *Hevajratantra* II, iv, 95), where they are mentioned in connection with the appeasement of noxious spirits.

124. Tib. *gsang-sngags*. The term *sngags* is used in two different but closely related ways. Following the Indian hermeneutical interpretation of the Sanskrit word *mantra* as protection of the subject's mind, the Tibetans further explicated it as a term for the complementarity of appropriate activity (*thabs*) and apprecia- tive discernment (*shes-rab*) or as a term for the two realities mentioned above. Such was the interpretation given by Dam-pa bsod-nams rgyal-mtshan in his commentary (p. 165) on the *Hevajratantra*. Dwags-po Paṇ-chen bKra-shis rnam- rgyal, in his commentary (p. 116) on the *Hevajratantra*, said:

> *sngags* is a term for the complementarity of appropriate activity and appre- ciative discernment which protects the individual against mental distress and the disruptive tendencies of ego-centered thought.

Being basically the expression of the totality's originary awareness, whose intentionality (of act phase and object phase) may be said to be the totality's autopoiesis, it "informs" itself about how it goes with itself. Figuratively, the totality "addresses" itself, and this addressing or informing itself comes as "utter- ance," which at a later phase in the process congeals into a "spoken" word that has little in common with the original dynamics of utterance. Because in utter- ance it is the totality (or, in philosophical terms, Being) that speaks and because the totality is an abiding mystery (*gsang-ba*), one also speaks of *gsang-sngags* (*guhyamantra*), an epithet for the existential-experiential approach to man's problematic nature. The rich meaning of *sngags* has been summed up by Klong- chen rab-'byams-pa (*Theg-mchog* I, p. 93):

From the viewpoint of its facticity, *sngags* is the most mysterious device for directly understanding the reality of Being's sheer lucency which is the sphere of Being's endogenous originary awareness; the method for encountering this sphere where the developing phase and the fulfilling phase are a spontaneous presence.

From the viewpoint of its hermeneutical explication *sngags* is the most renowned formula that protects against the pollutant emotions and makes one quickly attain limpid clearness and consummate perspicacity.

From the viewpoint of its being an indispensable requisite *sngags* is that which quickly sets free a most astute person amongst those of superior intelligence.

From the viewpoint of its climaxing *sngags* is realization of the sublime status of lordly rDo-rje-'chang within a single life-time or during the phase transition (*bar-do*) or by virtue of one's existential readiness (*rgyud*).

He then stated that *sngags* should be equated with existential readiness (*rgyud*) because an individual encounters the sheer lucency of Being primarily through his Existenz.

125. The direct transmission texts (*bka'-ma*), also termed *pronouncements* (Dargyay, 1977, pp. 12ff.), are works claimed to have their origin in the higher-order reality from which they were made available through intermediaries or spiritual go-betweens. The huge collection of their teachings received its final redaction by rDzogs-chen rgyal-sras gZhan-phan mtha'-yas (born 1740). None of the central texts of this transmission have as yet been translated or studied in the West. The rediscovered treatises (*gter-ma*) are for the most part apocryphal works. Some of them are certainly old texts, but many are popularizing works composed by the persons who discovered them. The term *gter-ma* does not necessarily mean something that has been concealed in caves or physical places; it may also mean the hidden recesses of the mind from which the ideas contained in these rediscovered treatises have been brought to light.

126. The potential for the Buddha-experience presents a dual aspect in that, on the one hand, it lies dormant in each and every living being and must be roused, while, on the other hand, it is already tending toward becoming an actuality. This potential is technically referred to by the term *sbyang-(bya'i) gzhi*. It is neither quantity nor form but, as the text states, an optimization thrust that is both the unfolding of its possibilities and the incentive, the ground and reason, for the evolution of man in a holistic perspective. When Klong-chen rab-'byams-pa (*Grub-mtha'*, p. 316) says:

The stratum that has to be returned to its original purity and which simultaneously is the impetus for the purification process (*sbyang-gzhi*) is Being's dynamic field in its character of being a sheer lucency,

one is immediately reminded by the use of the term Being's dynamic field of Alfred North Whitehead's extensive continuum and of Spinoza's idea of Nature

(*deus sive natura*). The latter has been poetically expressed in a fragment entitled
"Nature" (*Die Natur*) by Georg Christof Tobler, who in 1771 met the German
poet and statesman Johann Wolfgang von Goethe in Weimar. This fragment
was received by Goethe in 1828 and incorporated in one of his essays on science
and natural philosophy. In this fragment which has been included in Horst
Gunther's anthology *Goethe: Anschauendes Denken* (pp. 181–185), we read:

> Nature! We are surrounded and embraced by her—powerless to separate
> from her, and powerless to penetrate deeper into her.

> (Natur! Wir sind von ihr umgeben und umschlungen— unvermögend aus
> ihr herauszutreten, und unvermögend tiefer in sie hinein zu kommen)

Ensconced in a living being and hence curtailed in its scope, this potential is
referred to as man's psychophysical potential (*khams*) or affinity with Being
(*rigs*). On these terms see note 228. That which obscures its light is termed an
incidental grime that must be removed (*sbyang-bya*). Figuratively, Being's potential and optimization thrust "sees" to it that the grime it has playfully deposited on itself will be removed. Again the words of Georg Christof Tobler come
to mind:

> [Nature] shrouds man in dullness and perpetually urges him on toward
> light.

> (Sie hüllt den Menschen in Dumpfheit ein und spornt ihn ewig zum
> Lichte)

What this grime is specifically, has been stated by Klong-chen rab-'byams-pa
as follows:

> That which has to be purified (transmuted, removed, cleaned up, *sbyang-
> bya*) is an incidental grime—the experiencer's headlong actions and emo-
> tional vagaries that make up samsara.

The purifying operations (*sbyong-byed*) are the operators constituting the
Buddhist way as the exercise of one's originary awareness in view of the fact that
by attending to the developing and fulfilling phases the latent qualities are made
to come to the fore as if they were something new. This idea also bears a striking
resemblance to the words of Georg Christof Tobler:

> [Nature] perpetually creates new forms; what is there has never been as
> yet; what has been does not come again—everything is new, and yet it is
> the old.

> (Sie schafft ewig neue Gestalten; was da ist, war noch nie, was war,
> kommt nicht wieder—alles ist neu, und doch immer das Alte.)

Because Being's dynamic field, cleansed of every trace of grime by this purifying operation, turns into limpid clearness and consummate perspicacity, its spontaneous presencing in a gestalt quality commensurate with its originary awareness takes place; this state of affairs, in which self-fulfillment and other-enrichment have reached their utmost scope, results from the purification of the grime deposited on the potential in its embodied condition. This resultant state is termed *sbyangs-pa'i 'bras-bu.*

127. The qualities that pertain exclusively to the Buddha-experience, among which powers as the exercise of Being's originary awareness play an important role, were enumerated by Vasubandhu in his *Abhidharmakośa* VII, 28–33 and explicated in his autocommentary, the *Bhāṣya.* This presentation, which limits the qualities to eighteen, has become standard.

128. The rendering of the Tibetan term *rgyud* by *Existenz,* a term widely used in phenomenology and used first in the philosophical probings of Karl Jaspers and Martin Heidegger, is prompted because it indicates a *how* and, as Calvin O. Schrag (1969, p. 267) pointed out, "recaptures the primordial unity in which sentience, volition, and thought are interpenetrating and reciprocal movements," and (p. 268) "unlike the traditional category of existence [it] is neither a simple designation for a *quid est* nor a designation of finite existents in general."

129. Both terms, *khams* and *rigs,* are similar in referring to "programs" as well as to what might be called their repository. The term *khams* is more general in that it refers to the psychic makeup of an individual, which, to be precise, is simultaneously both psychic and physical. The term *rigs* is more specific in pointing to the actual "growth program" in the direction of the Buddha-experience. Both terms are synonymous with the system's (Being's) optimization thrust (*bde-gshegs snying-po,* for which the epistemology-oriented (rationally reductionist) texts use the term *de-bzhin gshegs-pa'i snying-po*). See *Bla-yang* I (p. 308); *Grub-mtha'* (pp. 229, 238).

130. Tib. *sdom-pa.* At first glance these "restrictions and obligations" seem to refer to a behavioral code aiming at and reinforcing a standardized social structure. This notion, widely held in Western societies, merely reflects the myopic character of a deterministic and prescriptive ethics that fits so well into a static conception of the world (and society) and that excludes any program of imaginative variation. But in the Buddhist context these very restrictions and obligations imply a hierarchical organization of the individual and vary according to the individual's development. Such a conception of ethics and morality as evolving and acknowledging responsibility has a distinct impact on a multilevel social milieu. In the triadic organization so much favored by the Buddhists, the lowest level is represented by seven social statuses that a person may occupy. This level is called *so-sor thar-pa* (Sanskrit *prātimokṣa*), which means that a person from within his or her status in society can find releasement from samsara's frustrations. The intermediate level is that of a Bodhisattva (*byang-chub sems-dpa'*), a person who, because of the widening horizon of his social awareness, has risen above a mere prescriptive ethics and, as the texts state, is concerned with the welfare of others. The highest level is that of a person who is tuned-in to the dynamics of Being (*rig-'dzin*) and creatively participates in the

shaping of the human world. There exists an extensive, sometimes controversial literature on these three levels (*sdom-gsum*) in the Tibetan tradition. Here a few works of major importance may be cited: Sa-skya Paṇḍita Kun-dga' rgyal-mtshan's (1182–1251) *sDom-gsum-gyi rab-tu dbye-ba'i bstan-bcos* (Gangtok, 1967); sPos-khang-pa Rin-chen rgyal-mtshan's (fifteenth century) *sDom-pa gsum-gyi rab-tu dbye-ba'i gzhung-lugs legs-par bshad-pa*, a detailed commentary on Sa-skya Paṇḍita's work (Delhi, 1977–79); mNga'-ris Paṇ-chen Padma-dbang-rgyal's (1487–1542) *Rang-bzhin rdzogs-pa-chen-po'i lam-gyi cha-lag sdom-gsum rnam-par nges-pa zhes-bya-ba'i bstan-bcos* (n.p., 1970), and sMin-gling Lo-chen Dharmaśrī's (1654–1717) *sDom-pa gsum rnam-par nges-pa'i 'grel-pa legs-bshad ngo-mtshar dpag-bsam-gyi snye-ma*, a commentary on mNga'-ris Paṇ-chen's work (n.p., 1970).

131. Tib. *byang-chub sems-dpa'*. The Sanskrit term *Bodhisattva* conveys little of what seems to have been understood and intimated by the Buddhists when they used this term. The Tibetan term has been the focus of an intensive and extensive hermeneutical probing, particularly in the older tradition (*rnying-ma*). Each component was scrutinized and given a specific interpretation such that *byang* pointed to a state of limpid clearness and *chub* to its consummate perspicacity. This interpretation touches on the very meaning of *bodhi*, whose Western rendering by "enlightenment," still haunting popular and academic writings on Buddhism, merely reflects the stale rationalism of a past age. Similarly, the term *sems* was understood as a deeply felt understanding of this clarity and as an incentive to move further into it, while *dpa'* indicated the strength needed to overcome any obstacles. A detailed assessment of the implications of this term on the basis of its Tibetan hermeneutical interpretation is given in my "Bodhisattva—The Ethical Phase in Evolution" (pp. 111–124).

132. Tib. *dkyil-'khor*. A detailed analysis of this term, popularized in its Sanskrit equivalent *maṇḍala*, has been given in my *Matrix of Mystery*, *s.v.*

133. This rendering of the Tibetan term *yi-dam* attempts to bring out the very dynamics of what is so imaged. Its intrinsic meaning may be stated to be what Anna-Teresa Tymieniecka described (1983, p. 129) as "the *entelechial individualization of the living individual being as the agent* of the *natural life* as well as of the *specifically human life-world* in its entire spread."

The term *yi-dam* is often used interchangeably with *lha*, on which see note 119 above.

134. See note 130. In this context they dispose him to be a follower of either the Śrāvakayāna, or Pratyekabuddhayāna, or Bodhisattvayāna.

135. Tib. *dam-tshig.* Unlike the term *sdom-pa* (see note 130), with its social connotations and implications, the term *dam-tshig* points to the center from which the organizing notions of lived-through experience issue and, beyond this center, which is the contextualized experiencer, to Being itself as a process of unfoldment. The rendering of *dam-tshig* as "rules of the game" has a special significance in the context of this unfoldment because it emphasizes the underlying intentionality of Being's cognitive character and, maybe, reflects an inherent limitation. See *Theg-mchog* I (pp. 271f.); also my "The Dynamics of Being:

rDzogs-chen Process Thinking." With respect to the problem of these rules of the game in the context of a holistic assessment, it may be relevant to quote Jantsch's (1980, p. 310) observations:

> In a process-oriented view, the evolution of specific structures is not predetermined. But then are functions—processes which may realize themselves in a multitude of structures—predetermined? In other words, does the evolution of mind follow a predetermined pattern? Or does such an assumption again lead to the wrong conclusion already prefigured in process thinking, just as the predetermination of structures has been pre-figured by mechanistic, structure-oriented thinking? Is the formula of Eastern mysticism that the universe is made to become self-reflexive, only the expression of an inherent limitation of Eastern process philosophy?

With respect to the experiencer, *dam-tshig* refers to the "fine structure" of the experiential process as it manifests in terms of qualitative presences—the individual's gestalt quality (*sku*), his communicative capacity as genuine speech (*gsung*), and his responsive and holistic resonance (*thugs*) with the whole of Being. Each level in this fine structure has again a hierarchical organization, described in terms of the *external*, the *internal*, and the *arcane*. See *Theg-mchog* I (pp. 261, 264, 265). Through a tuning-in to the rich potential of the qualitative, the individual's finitude loses its rigidity. Thus the *sGra-thal 'gyur-ba* (in *Ati*, Vol. 1, p. 89) states:

> Although it is impossible to detail
> Each and every *dam-tshig* pertaining to the experiencer,
> They can be summed up in the triad of gestalt, communication, and resonance.
> A yogi links them to his body, speech, and mind.

For further details see also note 242 below.

Lastly, the Tibetan hermeneutical interpretation of this term may be given here as summarized by Klong-chen rab-'byams-pa (*Tshig-don*, p. 304): *dam-pa* is an aid that holds firm one's Existenz, and *tshig-pa* is this stability that burns away all evil.

136. This word, like its feminine form *ḍākinī*, is a vernacular term that has been translated into Tibetan as *mkha'-'gro* and *mkha'-gro-ma*, respectively. The explanation given is that each figure presents a mode of an originary awareness (*ye-shes*) in specific gnosemic form. In mythological language these figures may be said to come as "inspirations" that the experiencer feels and visualizes as a presence. See *mKha'-yang* II (pp. 209f.); *dGongs-pa zang-thal* (Vol. 1, p. 353). In connection with them reference is often made to "heroes" (*dpa'-bo*, *dpa'*). They are imaged presences of strengths.

137. According to the *Ye-shes snying-po* (pp. 89f), they are the *bla-ma* as the mainspring of one's liveliness, the *yi-dam* as the mainspring of one's attainments

in life, and the presence of all the *mkha'-'gro* and *mkha'-'gro-ma* as the mainspring of one's actions to the extent that they reflect the higher-order level of the Buddha-experience.

138. Tib. *brgyud-pa'i bla-ma*. The concept of lineage plays a prominent role in Tibetan Buddhism. Pratapaditya Pal (1984, p. 69) has admirably summed up its significance:

> The concept of lineage may have derived from the Indian idea of *guruparamparā*, whereby spiritual authority was handed down through gurus and the disciples from one generation to the next. A second possible source may have been the idea of patriarchs in Ch'an Buddhism of China. Whatever the origin, the concept was nurtured and reared so assiduously by the Tibetans that the final product must be regarded as Tibetan.

139. This refers to how the varied works dealing with the experiential approach to man's situation were classified in their emphasis on either the external (physical) or on the internal (psychic). The fourfold division comprises Kriyātantra, Caryātantra, Yogatantra, and Anuttarayogatantra. The sixfold division is arrived at by substituting the triple division of Mahāyoga, Anuyoga, and Atiyoga for the Anuttarayoga.

140. The quotes are to indicate that language in this context is not what the reductionist who is caught in the objectivist's fallacies imagines it to be. Rather language is understood in its ciphering function, which may later become deciphered into the familiar patterns of spoken and written language. Georg Christof Tobler's words about nature may give an idea of what is intended here:

> [Nature] has neither language nor discourse, but she creates tongues and hearts, by which she feels and speaks.

> (Sie hat keine Sprache noch Rede, aber sie schafft Zungen und Herzen, durch die sie fühlt und spricht.)

141. They are Mañjuśrī, Avalokiteśvara, Vajrāpani, Maitreya, Gaganagarbha, Kṣitigarbha, Nivaraṇaviṣkambhin, and Samantabhadra. Their stories have been related by Mi-pham 'Jam-dbyangs rnam-rgyal rgya-mtsho, *Collected Works* (Vol. 13, pp. 257–676).

142. In all probability the sixteen Arhants of the Hīnayāna.

143. The *tshogs-lam* and the *sbyor-lam* are phases in the path as a whole, such that the former involves studying and thinking about what one studies, and the latter effectuates the phase of "seeing" reality with fresh eyes (*mthong-lam*).

144. See above note 140.

145. To properly understand this attitude of reverence and respect, we must remind ourselves that the person who was given the appellation "Buddha" (the awakened one), on the basis of his description of the experience he had undergone and articulated in the words "darkness has gone and light has shone forth" (*tamo vigato āloka uppanno, Anguttaranikāya* I, p. 164), was never conceived of in

terms of a popular god or even in terms of the theoretical God-construct of each and every kind of theology, based as they are upon the misidentification of a model with the thing itself and consequently becoming the source of much confused thinking. Voltaire (1694–1778) ridiculed this phenomenon, saying that theology makes us talk about what we do not know and confused about what we know.

The image of the Buddha, painted or sculpted, and the vast amount of Buddhist writings are therefore incentives to gain wider perspectives, to penetrate deeper into Being's wonderful mystery, and to never rest content with answers that are no answers whatsoever, because the basic questions have not been asked. Unfortunately, we forget that images are stilts we need to raise ourselves to a higher vantage point, from which we can orient ourselves and see possible directions in which to go. Rather than trying to understand them for what they are, we tend to elevate them into eternal truths, which are no truths at all but merely the source of dogmatism and fanaticism, sectarianism and idolatry. The travesty of converting a lived-through experience into an entity termed *The Buddha* (with capital letters to make sure that there is such a "thing"-Buddha and to reemphasize the part of the theological argument that claims there is and could only be one such thing that corresponds to the description "God" [The Buddha]—a claim also upheld by Hīnayāna Buddhism) illustrates this forgetfulness.

146. This refers to the two major traditions in Mahāyāna Buddhist philosophy, where philosophy was understood not merely as an intellectual pursuit but also as the mainstay of a distinct way of life. The one tradition goes back to Śāntideva (probably seventh century A.D.), said to be in the lineage beginning with Mañjuśrī and continuing through Nāgārjuna, the other tradition goes back to Dharmakīrti (fl. 7th century AD) who is said to belong to the lineage beginning with Maitreya and continuing through Asanga. For further details see my *Jewel Ornament of Liberation* (1959, 1970, pp. 115f).

147. This reference to obnoxious spirits must be understood from the Buddhist perspective, which understands them to be projections of one's own mind whereby, like its other projections, they become part of our experienced world. As such they are anthropomorphic images of what today we would describe as man's unresolved inner conflicts, compulsions, phobias, and other neurotic symptoms. Through their imaged presence they provide the possibility for "getting on speaking terms" with them—pleading with them if necessary, or, if more drastic measures are called for, resolving them by defusing a potentially dangerous situation. This is possible only by recognizing the "reality" of these spirits, not by suppressing or, as the psychologists would say, repressing them by means of total control through rational thought, which builds on metaphysical assumptions that merely impoverish and narrow man down. The approach indicated in this passage has much in common with the Jungian notion of psychotherapy as being a dialogue, an interaction between two partners in life's drama. It certainly does not advocate an egological control hierarchy.

148. The reabsorption of the projections in which the imaginative process of transformation expresses itself, into the source from which they have come,

reflects the sound psychological insight that if these projections were allowed to assume an independent existence, they would undermine the unity and integrity of the experiencer's Existenz and turn it into a neurotic self.

149. bsTan-pa'i nyi-ma (Zin-bris, fol. 14bf.) states that the loopholes are of three kinds (external, internal, and arcane) and relates them to the experiencer's body, speech, and mind. The aim of this imaginative procedure is to protect the integrity of the personality from disintegrating.

150. This paragraph describes and very concisely sums up the intermeshing between two orders of reality. The "lower-order" reality is represented by the triad of one's physical body (lus), one's language/speech (ngag), and one's subjective mind (yid). Each item in this triad allows itself to be objectified. As object "the body is represented by objectifying thought, instead of being apprehended in its presential immediacy" and is "excerpted from its living involvements and quoted out of context" (Schrag 1969, p. 130). Language on this level is "objectified, abstracted, and disembodied speech" (p. 164), speech being mostly talk or chatter. Subjective mind is thematizing-representational thinking, which starts from the assumption that the subject-object dichotomy is something granted. The "higher-order" reality is presented in terms of a gestalt quality (sku), which in its presentational immediacy does not allow itself to be dissected, and a communicative in-formative process (gsung), which mediates between the system's gestalt quality and the system's spirituality (thugs), which is in resonance with the whole of Being. The two orders of reality thus manifest in two "systems," the one being the "sentient being" (sems-can) system, the other the "Buddha" (sangs-rgyas) system, with respect to which the mainsprings of authentic existence are approximations. Nonetheless, the two systems are connected and intermesh by way of homologous principles that derive from the same source, that is, Being.

151. sman. The major problem of this whole section is one of notation. Though all the terms are related to literal language, they are used in a nonliteral, metaphorical sense that, unfortunately, can be easily reduced to a literal meaning. Even the term sman, here rendered as "tonic," is in its Tibetan application much broader than the English word. Thus the bDud-rtsi rin-po-che ye-shes snang-ba'i 'khor-lo'i rgyud (rNying-rgyud, Vol. 26, p. 16), interestingly retaining the Sanskrit word for alchemy, rasāyana, gives a fourfold classification:

> Alchemical pharmacy (rasāyana) is "external" medicine;
> The five genuine substances (dam rdzas) are "internal" medicine;
> The five motilities (rlung) in their pure state are "arcane" medicine;
> The (realization of Being's) gestalt quality (sku) and originary awareness
> (ye-shes) is "ultimate" medicine;
> Unfathomable by ordinary thinking it is beyond ordinary words.

The five "genuine substances" are the five kinds of the Being's originary awareness or "higher-order" functions whose "lower-order" falsifications are the preeminently emotional pollutants, often referred to as "poisons"—a metaphorical expression that we too use when we say that someone's bad temper "poisoned the whole atmosphere." The transmutation (or sublimation) of these "poisons" into modes of "originary awareness," not their repression, is indicated in the same text (p. 120):

> The five poisons are (or become), if not repressed, the five originary
>   awareness modes;
> One has to deal with them as the five genuine substances.

In a certain sense health, a person's well-being, is a manifestation of Being in its wholeness and also a celebration of this wholeness. The chemistry of a human being is basically the same as that of every other animal, but the individual's emotional attunement toward "life" is not at all chemical—(though it may involve something of chemistry) but depends very much on the complexity of the nervous system, which is basically electrical in its operation. There are thus in a living organism the chemical components, the "fundamental forces" imaged as various kinds of "flesh." Then there is the capacity of the organism to store and release energy in many ways, to eliminate waste products, and to build up generative products. The electrical operations come as "intelligence," which is at once both cognitive and emotional. They are referred to as the individual's various affinities with Being (*rigs*), each one presenting a male-female complementarity or higher-order operation (*ye-shes*), which on the lower-order level breaks down into fragmentary and fragmentizing affective (emotionally pollutant) processes (*nyon-mongs*).

152. The Tibetan text uses the Sanskrit term *rakta*, which literally means "blood," but in the Tibetan context here is used in a purely figurative sense. As the explication in the text intimates, we depend so much on rational and thematizing-representational thinking that we naively assume it to be the "stuff" of which life is made.

153. This is the literal rendering of the Sanskrit word *kapāla*, which the Tibetan author has retained to emphasize its symbolic character. The latter has been explicated in one of the direct transmission texts (see note 125 above), the *bKa'-ma* (Vol. 12, p. 547), as follows:

> *ka* is non-localizability and
> *pā* is (Being's) field that is without origination;
> *la* means being beyond the domain of the intellect.
> In this *kapāla*—the invariance of Being's triune gestalt character—
> The real stuff of the indivisibility of Being's gestalt quality and originary
>   awareness,
> Made ready as the nectar of birthlessness and deathlessness, is poured.

In highly figurative and evocative language this passage illustrates what we would call the complementarity of matter and mind.

154. There is no uniformity in the "arrangement" of the various ingredients or their correspondences with the various levels in the hierarchical organization of the individual. The symbolic implication of these ingredients, according to

both the old (*rnying-ma*) and new (*gsar-ma*) traditions, has been stated by bsTan-pa'i nyi-ma (*Zin-bris*, fol. 17b f.). According to the old tradition, the five kinds of "flesh" are "observable qualities" of the underlying dynamics and as such not rigidly circumscribed entities. Other "kinds," such as that of a lion, elephant, horse, peacock, eagle, and a superior man, are used to illustrate this point. According to the new tradition (beginning with Rin-chen bzang-po's [958–1055] activity as translator), which uses the images listed in this text, the five kinds of "flesh" are likened to "hooks attracting realizations," and their underlying dynamics are likened to "lamps illuminating the realizations." 'Ba-ra-ba rgyal-mtshan dpal-bzang (probably 1310–1391), in his *Collected Writings* (Vol. 7, pp. 233f.) presented the following grouping, starting from the east and ending in the center, as diagramed on the opposite page.

155. Tib. *mngon-rtogs*. This term indicates an immediately felt understanding of a visual presentment, not a conclusion arrived at by way of deductive logic. Dvags-po Paṇ-chen kKra-shis rnam-rgyal was quite explicit on this point in his lengthy discussions of this term in his commentary on the *Hevajratantra* (pp. 148f., 472f.). For further details see also Part One, p. 18.

156. Tib. *de-bzhin-nyid-kyi ting-nge-'dzin*. On the hermeneutical interpretation of the term *de-bzhin-nyid*, which I had formerly rendered by "as-is" in an attempt to remain as close as possible to its linguistic components but which now I prefer to paraphrase by "Being-in-its-beingness" in order to emphasize its holistic connotation, see my *Matrix of Mystery* (pp. 77f.). As to the term *ting-nge-'dzin*, consistently rendered by "in-depth appraisal," 'Jigs-med gling-pa (1729–1798), summing up the observations made long before his time by Klong-chen rab-'byams-pa (1308–1363/64), stated that this in-depth appraisal cannot be placed on the same footing as concentration or, in more evocative terms, meditation (*bsam-gtan*, Skt. *dhyāna*), which, according to the Pāli and by implication Hīnayāna tradition, indicates a static state called either *cittass' ekaggatā* (Skt. *cittasyaikāgratā*), "the state of a mind focused on a single topic," or *samādhi*, "concentration." In his *rNam-mkhyen shing-rta* (p. 293) he said:

> The in-depth appraisal of Being-in-its-beingness serves to underpin the vision of Being's holistic presence within us (*gzhi dngos-po gshis-kyi bzhugs-tshul*) constituting that which makes us tick. Although, with respect to its facticity, it is an appreciative discernment (*shes-rab*), in its pursuance marked by the experiencer's dedication (*mos-pa*) to it, it seems to be like some concentration process (*bsam-gtan*) and hence is referred to as in-depth appraisal (*ting-nge-'dzin*).

What 'Jigs-med gling-pa tried to express is that we are the whole and yet only part of it. We need the whole (Being, Being-in-its-beingness) to give concrete reality and meaning to the parts (the many beings, the experiencer included). Not only does such a holistic view completely discredit the static notion of the whole being merely the sum of its parts, it also does away with any dualism.

According to *Zin-bris* (fol. 26a), this in-depth appraisal is a tuning-in to what is termed *stong-pa chen-po*, a "super-nothingness" that is the "darkness" that

Directions of the compass	East	South	West	North	Center
Kinds of flesh	bull	dog	horse	elephant	man
Emotions/pollutants	dullness	avarice	desire	envy	irritation
Affinity regents	Vairocana	Ratnasambhava	Amitābha	Amoghasiddhi	Akṣobhya
Originary awareness modes	quasi-mirroring	identity	specificity	task-accomplished	field
Waste and generative products	feces	estrus	semen	tissue	urine

precedes the passage into the utter openness of Being's sheer lucency. Other names used in Mahāyāna Sūtras for this in-depth appraisal are *rdo-rje lta-bu'i ting-nge-'dzin* (Skt. *vajropamasamādhi*), "an in-depth appraisal as firm as a diamond," and *stong-pa-nyid-kyi ting-nge-'dzin* (Skt. *śūnyatāsamādhi*), "an in-depth appraisal suffused with Being's openness."See, for instance, Mahāyānasūtrālaṅkāra XIII, 1; XIV, 45; XVIII, 77, 80.

157. The Tibetan terms for these experiences of an inner light, growing in magnitude and intensity, are *snang-ba*, *mched-pa*, *thob-pa*, and *nyer-thob*.Like their Sanskrit equivalents (mentioned in *Pañcakrama* III) *āloka*, *ālokābhāsa*, *up-alabdhi*, and *upalabdha*, they are "concepts by intuition," whose meaning derives from the immediately apprehended, rather than "concepts by postulation," whose meaning derives, as the name indicates, from the postulates of the particular and narrowly defined theory in which they occur (Northrop 1947, 1959). Of these four concepts, the first two are relatively easy to understand. They vividly describe the dawning of the inner light (*snang-ba*, *āloka*) and its spreading (*mched-pa*, *ālokābhāsa*). According to Klong-chen rab-'byams-pa (*Shing-rta chen-po*, pp. 944f.), with the dawning and spreading of the inner light, the external reference of perception becomes ever more vague, and perception melts into pure sensation such that in the first instance the distinctions (*rtog-pa*) we make on the basis of a dispassionate (*zhe-sdang*) and critical assessment (*shes-rab*) dissolve, and in the second instance the distinctions we make on the basis of a libidinal (*'dod-chags*) and actional involvement (*thabs*) dissolve. More difficult to understand are the two remaining concepts. With the inner light approaching what seems to be its steady-state (*thob-pa*, *upalabdhi*), the distinction we make on the basis of impassivity (*gti-mug*) dissolve, and with the omnipresence (*nyer-thob*, *upalabdha*) of the inner light in sheer lucency, the last trace of what could hold us in the bondage and darkness of samsara has thoroughly dissipated.

Attempts to reduce these concepts by intuition to concepts by postulation have been made. One such form of reductionism was of a numerical nature and resulted in lumping *thob-pa* and *nyer-thob* together. As a precedent, chapter III of the *Pañcakrama*, attributed to a certain Śakyamitra of unknown date, could be adduced. A more conspicuous example of this reductionist trend is found in the *Kālacakratantra*, a syncretistic work of rather late origin that quite incongruously equates *snang-ba* with the *sattva*, *mched-pa* with the *rajas*, and *thob-pa/nyer-thob-pa* with the *tamas* of the Sāṃkhya system of Brahmanical speculative philosophy.This widespread reductionism is also found in the commentary by Tha-shas-pa Daridra Kun-dga'- mi-'gyur rdo-rje on the *Bar-do gsol-'debs* by Kun-dga' dpal-'byor (1428–1476), fol. 10b, and from 'Jigs-med gling-pa's *rNam-mkhyen shing-rta* (p. 50) where various other equations are made. Significantly, these "modernistic" terms (among them also the term *stong-pa chen-po*), are not found in the older Tibetan literature.

158. Tib. *rnam-thar gsum*. They again emphasize Being as a process in that Being's utter openness (*stong-pa-nyid*) as pure potential is the ground and reason (*gzhi*) for its unfolding, that its irreducibility to any such defining characteristics as substance and quality (*mtshan-ma-med-pa*) is the way (*lam*) of its unfolding, and that its holistic character of having no preferences for either samsara or

nirvana (*smon-pa-med-pa*) is the climaxing (*'bras-bu*) of its process. See Klong-chen rab-'byams-pa's *Klong-'grel* (p. 52); 'Jigs-med gling-pa's *rNam-mkhyen shing-rta* (pp. 528f., 665); Yon-tan rgya-mtsho's *Nyi-ma'i 'od-zer* (pp. 362, 456f.). Each of them is also related to the three in-depth appraisals. See notes 156, 159, 162.

159. Tib. *kun-tu snang-ba'i ting-nge-'dzin*. For further details see my *Matrix of Mystery* (pp. 76, 78). In *Zin-bris* (fol. 26b) this in-depth appraisal is stated to have as yet no objective reference and its feeling-tone of compassion has a magiclike quality. It is also known as *dpa'-bar 'gro-ba'i ting-nge-'dzin*, "an in-depth appraisal moving in the manner of a hero." In Buddhism a "hero" has always been understood as a person who overcomes the deadening powers at work in himself. It is further known as *smon-pa med-pa'i ting-nge-'dzin*, "an in-depth appraisal that has no preferences for either samsara or nirvana." Both these in-depths appraisals are also listed in the Sutra literature, the former (as *śūraṃgamasamādhi*) in *Vijñaptimātratāsiddhi* (p. 632) and the latter (as *apraṇihitasamādhi*) in *Mahāyānasūtrālaṅkāra* (XVIII, 77, 80).

160. Tib. *yid-kyi lus*. According to Kah-thog 'Gyur-med tshe-dbang mchog-grub's *gSang-sngags nang-gi lam-rim-po rgya-cher 'grel-pa sangs-rgyas gnyis-pa'i dgongs-rgyan* (p. 819), this psychic factor about to embody constitutes itself when the sheer lucency of Being is not recognized as what it is, and the *nyer-thob* phase (see note 157), because of a subtle connection with the *thob-pa* phase, glides off into the phase transition (*bar-do*) of the system's devolution, by which its movement along the *mched-pa* and *snang-ba* phases proceeds in the direction of decreasing luminosity and increasing "materialization." Each phase carries with it specific tendencies that disrupt the original unity and may be said to be thought prototypes and as such constitute the "mind" (*sems*) aspect of the being-to-be. As a "body" it also has perceptions, feelings, notions, and motivations that, in particular and in more technical language, constitute the "motility" (*rlung*) of the complexity that is about to become embodied. The idea of the *yid-kyi lus* being a combination of mentation (mind, *sems*) and motility (*rlung*) is strikingly similar to what C. D. Broad (1925, pp. 535f.) called the "Compound Theory." His words are:

> Might not what we know as a "mind" be a compound of two factors, neither of which separately has the characteristic properties of a mind, just as salt is a compound of two substances, neither of which by itself has the characteristic properties of salt? Let us call one of these constituents the "psychic factor" and the other the "bodily factor." The psychic factor would be like some chemical element which has never been isolated; and the characteristics of a mind would depend jointly on those of the psychic factor and those of the material organism with which it is united. This would allow of all the correlation between mind and body which could ever be discovered . . . . Now this does seem to accord fairly well with what we know about minds when we reflect upon them. On the one hand, it seems a mistake to ascribe perception, reasoning, anger, love, etc., to a mere body. On the other hand, . . . it is almost equally difficult to ascribe

them to what is left when the bodily factor is ignored. Thus the mind, as commonly conceived, does look as if it were a compound of two factors neither of which separately is a mind. And it does look as if specifically mental characteristics belonged only to this compound substance.

161. Tib. *dri-za*. For further details see Part One, p. 40.

162. Tib. *rgyu'i ting-nge-'dzin*, also termed *yi-ge rgyu'i ting-nge-'dzin*. For further details concerning this in-depth appraisal, see my *Matrix of Mystery* (pp. 76,79). In *Zin-bris* (fol. 26b f.) this in-depth appraisal is also known as *sgyu-ma lta-bu'i ting-nge-'dzin*, "an in-depth appraisal which has the quality of being like magic and wonderment." Actually, from the viewpoint of an intensely lived-through experience that touches upon one's deepest feelings, wonderment may well be stated to be the world's cause (*rgyu*), its enunciation (*yi-ge*), and the overarching originary awareness (*ye-shes sems-dpa'*). Another name for it is *mtshan-ma med-pa'i ting-nge-'dzin*, "an in-depth appraisal in which as yet no thematic specifications obtain." Both these in-depth appraisals are also mentioned in Mahāyānasūtras, the former, Skt. *māyopamasamādhi*, in *Laṅkāvatārasūtra* (p. 81) and the latter, Skt. *ānimittasamādhi*, in *Mahāyānasūtrālaṅkāra* (XVIII, 77).

163. The Buddhist tradition recognized four kinds of birth: from a womb, from an egg, from the combination of heat and moisture, and spontaneous origination.

164. These two gnosemes sum up the dynamics of Being, not as an abstract idea but as a concrete reality in man's lived-through experience of his embeddedness in a world. HŪM expresses a holistic resonance with life's meaningfulness that is not predetermined but is an utter openness (*stong-pa-nyid*). HRĪH expresses the exercising of this very meaningfulness in man's contextual situationality through compassion (*snying-rje*). From the viewpoint of the gestaltism in lived-through experience, HŪM points to and expresses Being's meaning-rich gestalt quality (*chos-sku*), while HRĪH points to and expresses Being's optimizing activity through its guiding images and cultural norms (*sprul-sku*). In this sense we may say with M. Heidegger that Being speaks and that the task of the experiencing individual is to decipher this language.

As Advayavajra (*Pañcatathāgatamudrāvivaraṇa*, in *Advayavajrasaṃgraha*, p. 24) pointed out, there is both identity and difference in Being's openness and compassion:

> The difference between openness and compassion is like the one
>   between a lamp and its light;
> The identity between openness and compassion is like the one between
>   a lamp and its light.

165. Tib. *'byung-ba*. For a detailed account see Part One, pp. 36f.

166. Tib. *sems ma-dag-pa*. This impurity and opacity of mentation evolve in the course of Being's unfoldment and in the wake of a drop in its cognitive

excitation and intensity. Klong-chen rab-'byams-pa (*Theg-mchog* II, p. 47) clearly stated:

> Although there is no opacity in Being's meaning-rich field, this opacity makes itself felt ceaselessly in any density, the moment Being's holomovement sets in. That is, from the frolicking of its stepped-down excitation (*ma-rig-pa*) there evolves mentation (*sems*), from mentation as an ornament there evolves one's subjective mind (*yid*), and from one's subjective mind there evolve the emotional pollutants.

By contrast, lucid mentation (*sems dag-pa*) is the aspect that is not yet falsified by the disruptive and divisive tendencies of representational thinking, with its reification of the observed. Through the appreciation of the observed as symbolic presentments, it not only retains a linkage with but is also eminently suited to link itself backward to its origin, experience as such (*sems-nyid*). Because of the overall low level of excitation (*ma-rig-pa*) in mentation (*sems*), both opaque and lucid mentation pertain to the level assessed as samsara. *Thegmchog* II (p. 46). See also Part One, pp.44f.

167. According to *Abhidharmakośa* III, 49 the axial mountain consists of gold, silver, lapis lazuli, and crystal.

168. Tib. *rdo-rje btsun-mo'i bhaga*. There are two versions of the first component in this term, *rdo-rje btsun-mo* and *rdo-rje'i btsun-mo*. Dam-pa bSod-nams rgyal-mtshan, in his commentary on the *Hevajratantra* (pp. 59f., 64, 70) used the expression *rdo-rje btsun-mo* and explicated it as follows (p. 59):

> Since She is the very quintessence of Being's meaning-rich field, an unfailing openness, She is Being's indestructibility (*rdo-rje*); since She is the source of unsurpassable joy, She is the indestructibility Lady (*rdo-rje snyems-ma*); and since She is the very nature of the transcending function of appreciative discernment, She is the regal Mistress (*btsun-mo*).

In his commentary on the *Hevajratantra*, Dwags-po Paṇ-chen bKra-shis rnam-rgyal, on the other hand, used the term *rdo-rje'i btsun-mo* and explicated it as follows (p. 49):

> *rdo-rje* means energy and its indestructible character (*rdo-rje*) is rDo-rje-'chang chen-po, who, in this context, is the exalted Hevajra. Mistress (*btsun-mo*) is the consort of this very *rdo-rje* (namely, Hevajra).

The retention of the Sanskrit term *bhaga*, here rendered by "cleft," in an otherwise purely Tibetan context, is very significant. One of the many meanings of this word is "portion" or "fortune," said to consist of power, beauty, splendor, fame, knowledge, and zeal. This notion of "portion" derives from the hermeneutical association of *bhaga* with *bhañjana* "splitting," "cleaving asunder," and with the emphasis on the act of cleaving asunder, another meaning of *bhaga* is "destruction," in particular, the vanquishing of the deadening forces of one's unbridled emotions. See Dwags-po Paṇ-chen bKra-shis rnam-rgyal's commentary on the *Hevajratantra* I, Vol. 15 (p. 174). The image of what effects this cleaving asunder is a wedge, which in some people arouses an association with a woman's pubes, while in others it evokes the idea of a critical probing and appreciation (*shes-rab, prajñā*).

169. The goddesses of worship (*mchod-pa'i lha-mo, sems-ma*) are symbolic presences and, in the intentional structure -Merleau-Ponty in *The Phenomenology of Perception* (1962, p. 156) even speaks of the erotic structure—of perception, constitute the "female" object phase, the psychic functionaries (*sems-dpa'*) presenting the "male" act phase. In this relationship and interaction between the male and female, the male act phase may be understood as a searching for what to perceive (to see, to hear, to smell, to taste) and the female object phase as an already present solicitation for such searching. For further details see my *Matrix of Mystery* (pp. 111f. and p. 268 n. 106).

170. Tib. *rta-rkang*.

171. Tib. *chu-skyes*.

172. Tib. *sgrom*.

173. Tib. *zar-tshags*.

174. Tib. *sna-'phyang*.

175. Tib. *chun-'phyang*.

176. Tib. *shar-bu*.

177. Tib. *rgya-phibs*.

178. This proper name refers to the story of a certain Thar-pa nag-po and his servant Dan-phag, told at length in *dGongs-'dus* (pp. 130f.). Thar-pa nag-po was a dull-witted and incompetent person and took everything he was told literally. By contrast, Dan-phag was highly intelligent and thought about what he had been told. Being so different in outlook and behavior, master and servant constantly quarreled. In order to resolve their differences they went to their teacher, the monk Thub-dka' gzhon-nu. When Thar-pa nag-po was told that his mind was on the wrong track, he became furious, gave his teacher a tongue-lashing, and chased him and Dan-phag away. From this moment onward, he became ever more steeped in his literal interpretation, on the basis of which his behavior became increasingly deviant. After his death, he was reborn ever and again in evil forms of life. In the course of his rebirths he acquired the epithet Rudra and has ever since terrorized the living beings. See also my *Matrix of Mystery* (pp. 145f.). In passing it may be mentioned that Rudra is also a cognomen of Śiva. Singling him out as representing the spiritually deadening power of literalism may well reflect the fact that in its last phase in India, Buddhism fought a losing battle against Saivism.

179. Tib. *chos-kyi dbyings*. Because of the complexity of its connotations, this term is one of the most difficult ones to render adequately in any Western language. To translate it by Being's meaning-rich field is to indicate that what is summed up by this concept of intuition is multidimensional and dynamic. Specifically it connotes the dimension or field (*dbyings*) where meanings (*chos*) are born. The term is also synonymous with experience as such (*sems-nyid*). In this

connection Calvin O. Schrag's (1969) words are most relevant for understanding the Buddhist term. He said (pp. 17f.):

> To speak of an experiential field or a field of experience is to suggest an alternative to speaking of experience as a juxtaposition of discrete elements. Experience in its primordial presentment, we suggest, is not a granular arrangement of psychic data or an atomistic accumulation of sensations and images. There has been a widespread tendency in traditional theories of experience to view experience as broken up into discrete units, like grains of sand. These granular units are assumed to be scrambled or wholly disconnected, passively presented to an experiencer who then has the burden of arranging them into some kind of conceptual unity.

Klong-chen rab-'byams-pa (Chos-dbyings, p.294) quite explicitly stated that this field is Being's unitary identity with itself (mnyam-nyid gcig).

Lastly, to speak of chos-(kyi) dbyings as a dynamic field is to indicate that it is a process. This process character was elaborated by Klong-chen rab-'byams-pa (Chos-dbyings, p. 43) in terms of a starting point, a path, and a goal. As a starting point, it is Being's ground and the reason (gzhi) for its unfolding, and as such it is a natural diaphaneity, a predisposition toward optimization, and a sheer lucency. Being's unfolding or the way (lam) is the activation of the latent potentialities and possibilities in the direction of Being's self-individualization through a deeply felt understanding of itself. The climaxing or goal ('bras-bu) of the process is Being's experience of itself in terms of its gestaltism.

Being's dynamic character as being both a field and its excitation has been beautifully illustrated in the dGongs-pa zang-thal (Vol. 5, p. 118):

> Being's lighting up as an exteriority is Being's meaning-rich field; Being's meaning-rich gestalt is the field's excitation as an interiority. Both come about at the same time just as the open sky and the bright sun and moon in it.

180. Tib. tshad-med bzhi. They are loving kindness, compassionate sympathy, participatory joy, and dynamic balancing out. For a detailed discussion of these and their interrelationship, see my Kindly Bent to Ease Us (Vol. 1, pp. 106–122).

181. Tib. theg-pa brgyad. Their classification is closely related to an individual's intellectual acumen. Thus on a low level there are the three traditional pursuits of the Śrāvaka(yāna), Pratyekabuddha(yāna) and Bodhisattva(yāna); on an intermediary level there are the Kriyāyoga(yāna), Caryāyoga- or Ubhaya-(yāna), and the Yoga(yāna) proper; and on a higher level there are the Mahā(yogayāna) and the Anu(yogayāna). The highest level is the holistic Atiyoga or rDzogs-chen teaching, which is sometimes also listed as a pursuit (yāna), although there is no longer involved any teleology that marks the preceding pursuits.

182. Tib. bsdu-ba'i dngos-po bzhi. They are liberality, kind words, conscien-

tious behavior, and the awareness of all human beings being alike in being human beings.

183. Tib. *grub-mtha'*. Like its Sanskrit equivalent *siddhānta*, this term indicates the final formulation (*mtha'*, Skt. *anta*) of what one has set out to prove (*grub*, Skt. *siddha*). As such it presents a rational model of the world that, nonetheless, has been created on the basis of some specific metaphysical assumption. Though model building is itself a creative act, its outcome is a mere artifact of only limited validity. But in view of man's dependence on the models he creates, he conveniently forgets that he is the creator of his models and fictions and attempts to elevate them into eternal truths that must be defended by all means, even by resorting to violence if necessary. Instead of promoting knowledge, these alleged truths merely engender dogmatism and sectarianism. The history of Buddhist philosophy is no exception. Traditionally four major models or systems have been listed. Those based on specific metaphysical assumptions were the "realist" Vaibhāṣika and Sautrāntika systems and the "idealist" Yogācāra or Cittamātra system. The Madhyamaka system, in both its Svātantrika and Prāsangika versions, on the other hand, was based on a predominantly logical approach, which is most marked in the latter. Each of these systems has its own particular limitations and biases.

184. Tib. *chos-kyi 'khor-lo*, Skt. *dharmacakra*. According to *Abhidharmakośa* VI, 54cd, this term is synonymous with the expression "path of seeing" (*dharmacakras tu dṛṅmārgaḥ*) and, as the author, Vasubandhu, went on to explicate, their similarity lies in the speed with which a wheel rolls and the path of seeing proceeds and in the similarity of the spokes of a wheel with the members of the path of seeing (*āśugatvādy arādibhiḥ*). In his *Bhāṣya* he explicated the first part of this line to the effect that the speed of the wheel's or the path's movement implies leaving behind the past, conquering new domains and consolidating the conquest, and a successive moving up and down as the path continues. With respect to the similarity of the wheel with the path of seeing, he approvingly cited a certain Bhadanta Ghosaka, who stated that the first four members of the Noble Eightfold Path (see below note 191) are similar to the spokes, the next three members to the hub, and the last member to the rim of the wheel.

185. Tib. *dran-pa nye-bar bzhag-pa bzhi*. These are modes of an individual's critical and appreciative discernment in its endeavor to learn more about the "nature" of the physical world, specifically one's body (*lus*), the world of one's feelings (*tshor-ba*), the world of one's mental operations (*sems*), and the world of concepts, ideas, and meanings (*chos*). The aim is to open up a new perspective on life, not to reinforce old fixations.

186. Tib. *yang-dag-pa'i spong-ba bzhi*. They serve (1) to prevent all that is unwholesome from coming to the fore; (2) to leave behind all that is unwholesome; (3) to let all that is wholesome come to the fore; and (4) to strengthen all that is wholesome. Each facet involves willingness, eagerness, perseverance, keeping one's mind to the task involved, and having one's mind thoroughly engaged.

187. Tib. *rdzu-'phrul-gyi rkang-pa bzhi*. They are specific in-depth appraisals marked by willingness, perseverance, intentiveness, and reasoning.

188. Tib. *dbang-po lnga*. They are confidence, sustained effort, attentive inspection, in-depth appraisals, and appreciative discernment and mark a possible breakthrough to a vision of reality.

189. Tib. *stobs lnga*. They are the same as the ones listed in the previous note. As strengths they effectuate the breakthrough.

190.Tib. *byang-chub-kyi yan-lag bdun*. They are attentive inspection, critical investigation of the ideas that constitute our reality, sustained effort, joy, serenity through the refinement and clarification of the vision, an in-depth appraisal of it, and a dynamic balancing out. They are facets of the phase of vision in what is the Buddhist "path."

191. Tib. *'phags-lam yan-lag brgyad*. These are (1) the proper way of seeing, (2) the proper way of forming an idea of the vision, (3) the proper way of expressing the vision and its idea in words, (4) the proper way of acting in the light of the vision, (5) the proper way of conducting one's life, (6) the proper way of exerting oneself, (7) the proper way of attending to the vision and what it implies, and (8) the proper way of concentrating. On the internal logic of this eightfold path, see above note 184. Strictly speaking, only the first member, the way of proper seeing (that is, seeing with "fresh eyes") constitutes the path of seeing that follows the buildup and breakthrough phase on the path as a whole; the subsequent members already belong to the path of creative imagination culminating in a fully concentrated state. Because the eightfold path is the formulation of an experience that has come about after a long period of intensive preparation, it is obviously more than just a topic for sermonizing.

192. Tib. *rnam-par thar-pa brgyad*. These have been detailed in *Abhidharmakośa* VIII, 32 and its accompanying *Bhāṣya*. Basically they are forms of concentration in the service of overcoming one's finitude, but they apparently became an end in themselves at an early phase of Buddhist thought. All of them have a thematic reference and move within a static world view. For a detailed account see Louis de la Vallée Poussin, *L'Abhidharmakośa de Vasubandhu* (huitième chapitre, pp. 203f.).

193. Tib. *mi-'jigs-pa bzhi*. They are special "insights" or, more precisely according to Vasubandhu's interpretation, the results of such insights, which carry with them the feeling that one need not be afraid. They are (1) an understanding of man's situationality and by implication of what is possible and what is not, (2) an understanding of the (emotional) pollutants having become ineffectual through the understanding of man's situationality, (3) an understanding of the inevitability of one's actions having their result, and (4) an understanding of the possibility of following a path leading out of man's predicament. See *Abhidharmakośa* VII, 32ab.

194. Tib. *stong-nyid bco-brgyad*. The fragmentation of the factor in experience that is not differentiated into transitory components, referred to by the technical term *stong-(pa-)nyid* (Skt. *śūnyatā*), along with its reduction to the level of the theoretically postulated, in the manner of David Hume and the modern positivists in the West, is specific to the Madhyamaka system in Buddhism. It is little more than a continuation of the method of analyzing the data of experience, first advocated by a minority in Hīnayāna Buddhism, the

Sthaviravadins, who prided themselves in their "analytical approach" (*vibha-jyavādin*). This granulation resulted in postulating from eighteen to twenty kinds of *stong-nyid*. Eighteen, together with their Sanskrit equivalents, have been listed in Sarat Chandra Das, A *Tibetan-English Dictionary* (p. 552); twenty, listed only in their Tibetan form, are found in the terminological dictionary by the Second lCang-skya sprul-sku Ye-shes bstan-pa'i sgron-me, *alias* Rol-pa'i rdo-rje (1717–1786), the *Dag-yig mkhas-pa'i 'byung-gnas* (pp.69f.). This list is derived from the *Abhisamayālaṅkārāloka* by Haribhadra, who based himself on the *Aṣ-ṭasāhasrikaprajñāpāramitāsūtra* and the *Madhyāntavibhāga*.

195. Tib. *phar-phyin bcu*. These are the traditional six transcending functions of liberality, ethics, acceptance of the human situation, strenuousness, concentration, and appreciative discernment, to which are added expertise, dedication to the task at hand, strength in pursuing one's goal, and insights.

196. Tib. *yon-tan*. No single word in any Western language can convey the rich array of meanings that the Tibetan term carries with it. It indicates not only qualities and capabilities but also all the potentialities that are at first latent in an individual and later come to the fore in the course of his development. Colloquially, *yon-tan* comprises all that allows us to refer to a person as talented. In rDzogs-chen thought it is viewed as the expression of Being's creativity, while in traditional Buddhist philosophy it remains a static notion. See the detailed presentation by Klong-chen rab-'byams-pa in *Grub-mtha'* (pp. 230f.) and *Zab-yang* II (p. 221).

197. Tib. *so-so yang-dag-pa'i rig-pa*. Four such analytical comprehensions are mentioned, which deal (1) with isolatable features in experience, be they of a realistic or (2) ideational nature, (3) with linguistic expressions, and (4) with the facility to express oneself clearly and concisely. Because they are related to concentrative efforts, they remain thoroughly thematic and within the realm of the representational. See *Abhidharmakośa* VII, 37cd–40b.

198. Tib. *rang-rig-pa'i ye-shes-kyi klong*. This term indicates the hierarchical organization of the total system in its complexity and dynamics. A lengthy elucidation was given by Klong-chen rab-'byams-pa in *Theg-mchog* I (pp. 11f.). The term occurs frequently in rNying-ma works.

199. Tib. *thugs-rje chen-po*. The above rendering of this term is prompted by the consideration that this kind of compassion is a holistic activity. It pertains to the whole, that is, Being as it presents itself as the Buddha-system, which has evolved like a dissipative structure (*sangs-rgyas*). The Buddha system, presenting a higher-order reality, develops like any living being system (*sems-can*) presenting a lower-order reality, by way of homologous dynamics stemming from a common source, which is Being's pure potential.

200. Tib. *snying-rje chen-po*. This qualification is used exclusively with reference to the spiritual force commonly spoken of as the Buddha. Within the human context the Buddha-experience is of a higher-order reality in that it is an approximation to the whole, which is the exact higher-order limit.

201. Tib. *sku gsung thugs mi-zad-pa rgyan-gyi 'khor-lo*. This term sums up the dynamics of a hierarchical organization that forms the basic structure of a live person. As indicated by the first three terms, there is operative a gestalt dynam-

ics, a communication dynamics, and a spiritual resonance dynamics, which in their coordination present a multilevel autopoiesis whose richness is a source of inexhaustible beauty. This multilevel autopoiesis is also expressive of each of the symmetry transformations that Being is undergoing. A detailed explication of the whole program involved was offered by Klong-chen rab-'byams-pa (*Theg-mchog* I, pp. 11f.).On symmetry transformations see my *Matrix of Mystery, s.v.*

202. Tib. *ye-shes-kyi rtsal-snang.* This is a cryptic reference to the phase that marks the onset of Being's holomovement prompted, not caused, as it were, by Being's originary awareness. The term *rtsal-snang* was frequently used by 'Jigs-med gling-pa. See his *rNam-mkhyen shing-rta* (pp. 561, 570, 572, 581).

203. Tib. *stong-pa-nyid-kyi ye-shes.* In this term the genitive particle *kyi* (Engl. *of*) does not imply a relationship between two separate entities, but their identity.

204. Tib. *rten-'brel bcu-gnyis.* This is commonly known by its Sanskrit term *Pratītyasamutpāda* and quite mistakenly associated with nineteenth-century ideas of causation. The principle of universal connectedness operates on each level of the triune hierarchical organization of man and universe, the external, internal, and arcane in different ways. See, for instance, *mKha'-yang* II (pp. 175f.).

205. Tib. *rang-bzhin 'od-gsal-ba'i chos-nyid.* This technical term "encodes" the complementarity of Being in its facticity (*ngo-bo*) as pure potential (*chos-nyid*) and its actuality (*rang-bzhin*) experienced as sheer lucency (*'od-gsal*).

206. Tib. *skyon-gyis ma-gos-pa'i chos-nyid.* As pure potential Being is the totality of undifferentiated qualities. In the process of undergoing symmetry transformations, symmetry breaks occur that are experienced as an incidental, not essential, diminution of the original wholeness. The source of this idea is *Uttaratantra* I, 51.

207. Tib. *rnam-shes tshogs-brgyad.* These are the five sense-specific perceptual operations of seeing, hearing, smelling, tasting, and touching; the meaning-specific perceptual operation that interprets the sensory data as meaning this or that; the affectively toned subjective response to the perceived meanings; and the genus- and species-specific potential in its moving in the direction of perceptual differentiations.

208. Tib. *dpe brgyad.* These, claimed to have been given their final form and content by Nāgārjuna, are a dream, a magiclike presentment, an illusion, a mirage, the reflection of the moon in water, an echo sound, a cloudland, and a phantom. They were poetically elaborated by Klong-chen rab-'byams-pa in his *sGyu-ma ngal-gso.* See my *Kindly Bent to Ease Us* (Vol. 3).

209. Tib. *mi-rtog-pa'i ye-shes.* This term contains a hidden critique of the concentrative state associated with the realm of formlessness (*gzugs-med*, Skt. *ārūpya*), in which no divisive concepts obtain but which lacks in originary awareness.

210. The four "deadening powers" (*bdud*) are manifestations of the system's stepped-down excitation, with its dichotomic trend into assuming an independent existence of the "subjective" and the "objective." Each of them—the deadening power of one's organism in terms of its psychophysical aggregates (*phung-po*), the deadening power of the image of a Lord of Death (*'chi-bdag*), the

deadening power of the (emotional) pollutants (*nyon-mongs*), and the deadening power of overevaluated ideas (*lha'i bu*)—presents an obstacle in one's gaining one's existential freedom. See *Chos-dbyings* (p. 291). There is of course no limit to what may turn out to be an obstacle or a "deadening power." A lengthy discussion was offered by dPal-sprul O-rgyan 'Jigs-med chos-kyi dbang-po in his *Collected Works* (Vol. 2, pp. 639–673).

211. Tib. *ye-shes-kyi me*. The double connotation of *me* as fire and heat implies that this originary awareness as heat grows in intensity and radiates outward, while as fire it blazes forth and consumes the various emotional pollutants that have been conceived of as displaced modes of originary awareness. See, for instance, *Rig-pa rang-shar* (p. 466).

212. Skt. *Akaniṣṭha*. This is not a place in the ordinary sense. The term attempts to sum up the deeply felt understanding of the spatiality of a lived through experience. For further details see my *Matrix of Mystery* (p. 254 n. 21).

213. The Tibetan terms *rtsa*, *rlung*, *thig-le*, and *'khor-lo*, used singly or jointly in this context, are without exception process words, not denotatively used nouns for concrete entities. All four are intimately inter-related such that *rtsa* describes the pathways or development lines, termed *chreods* by Conrad H. Waddington, in a "structuration" process and as such also serve as "conductors" for the energy "current" termed *rlung*; *thig-le* indicates the "information input" acting as the principle of organization of the total process; and *'khor-lo* marks the intersections of the development lines, which in their dynamic operation may be compared to a nucleation process that eventually leads to such structural patterns as those termed the live body (*lus*), its gestalt dynamics (*sku*), and the gestaltism of a guiding image or cultural norm presentment (*sprul-sku*), to give only one example within the complex organization of the whole. See *Theg-mchog* I (pp. 357, 370); *Tshig-don* (pp. 208f.).

214. The gnoseme A may be said to express and, in a wider sense, stand for organismic mentation, which, as Erich Jantsch (1980, pp. 163f.) has shown, does not reflect but is pure self-expression of the organism as a whole in terms of irresistible drives, impulses, and compulsive behavior. All of them, in view of the location of this gnoseme, are connected with but not restricted to sex. Similarly, the gnoseme HAM may be said to express and stand for reflexive mentation, which concerns the imaginative recasting of the outer world in terms of the models and images that make up man's inner world. This involves both creative and compulsive (schizophrenic) features. The latter are most conspicuous in a stale intellectualism connected with the brain—in modern terms the overrated left half of the brain. Only a balancing out, if not an intermingling of these two extremes (the merely organismic and the merely reflexive) in what becomes the gnosemic utterance *ahaṃ*, ("I"), ensures the integrity of the individual. Here self-reflexive mind, the individual's self-interpretation in existence, comes into play. According to Jantsch, "It designs actively a model of the environment in which the original system itself is represented. Thus, the original system, which we may also call self, becomes involved in the creative interpretation and evolution of the image." This self-imaging that preserves the individual's integrity has of course nothing to do with egological presuppositions.

215. The experientially lived-through morpho- and ontogenetic processes (*mngon-byang*) pinpoint stages in the imaginative reenactment of a living being's embodiment, with special emphasis on the psychic-spiritual aspects. Taken as a whole, they illustrate three dimensions of an evolutionary process that are characterized by coherence and continuity. These dimensions are referred to as the ground/reason (*gzhi*), the as yet unformed and latent wealth of open possibilities; the path (*lam*) as being both an opening up of this hidden wealth and drawing on it while moving into new realities; and the climaxing or goal (*'bras-bu*) as the deeply felt presence of a new dynamic regime in which the "enfolded" (to borrow a term from British physicist David Bohm) has become the "unfolded." These experientially lived-through morpho- and ontogenetic processes, seen as forming a set of five members, involve the following stages: (1) the psychic factor in search of an embodiment; (2) its entering the womb of its mother; (3) its embryonic development in terms of its five psychophysical aggregates, each having its own morpho- and ontogenetic dynamics; (4) the maturation phase preceding birth; and (5) the felt presence of the new regime as a guiding image. Seen as a set of four members, these same processes involve the following stages: (1) the instability phase between the dying of old structures and the subsequent restructuring of old material (*'chi-srid*), involving the nonrecognition of Being in its meaning-rich gestalt (*chos-sku*), as well as the phase transition (*bar-do*), presenting the gestalt quality of a world-horizon of meaning (*longs-sku*) by being a symmetry transformation of the former; (2) the psychic factor as a potential guiding image (*sprul-sku*); (3) the concrete presence of the unity of Being's gestalt, communication, and resonance dynamics (*sku gsung thugs rdo-rje*) as Being's overarching gestaltism (*ngo-bo-nyid-kyi sku*); and (4) the optimizing activity (*phrin-las*) of this complex. The three activation procedures (*cho-ga*) are concerned with Being's gestalt quality, communication, and spiritual resonance dynamics. For a more detailed discussion, see Yon-tan rgya-mtsho's *Nyi-zla'i sgron-me* (pp. 154f.).

According to *Zin-bris* (fol. 24a), the medium version is the topic of the so-called Mother-Tantras, emphasizing the felt appreciation of the processes involved (*shes-rab*), and the condensed version is the topic of the so-called Father-Tantras, emphasizing the activity aspect in these processes (*thabs*). The elaborate version is related to the five phases of the Buddhist path as a whole such that the consciousness principle in search of a body (embodiment) is the buildup (or preparatory) phase; the entry into a womb, the breakthrough (linkage) phase; the being-in-the-womb, the vision phase; the period of gestation, the creative imagination phase; and the birth as a full-fledged living being, the no-more-learning phase. This latter classification was already offered by 'Jigs-med gling-pa in his *rNam-mkhyen shing-rta* (p. 282).

216. Tib. *phyag-mtshan*. Although the rendering of this term by "signature" is a revival of an archaism in the English language, it still comes closest to the connotation of the Tibetan term. It must not be forgotten that in this context imaginative processes are involved, not iconographic reductions.

217. rDo-rje 'chang (Vajradhara) and rDo-rje 'dzin-pa (Vajradhṛk) are identical in that the one is the inverse of the other. Their unified coherence may be likened to the mathematical concept of an abstract group G operating as having

an identity element and its inverse, as previously detailed; see p. 122, n. 14. The implication is that with respect to the calm and fierce formulated energies, there is not a transition from calmness to fierceness or vice versa, rather the one is the inverse of the other.

218. This Sanskrit term for the central chreod in the system's structuration process is infrequently used in rNying-ma texts, which prefer the circumlocution *rtsa dbu-ma*, "the central *rtsa*," or the indigenous term *kun-'dar-ma*. The latter was explicated by Klong-chen rab-'byams-pa as follows:

> *kun-'dar-ma* is so named because in it everything gathers. Since on it as their support system the holistic in-formation input (*thig-le*) as well as the optimization of the other structuration lines (*rtsa*) and the optimal energy movement (*rlung*, along these conductors) come into existence, it is called *kun* (holistic). Since, furthermore, it is of an encompassing and all-pervasive nature it is called '*dar-ma*.

See *Theg-mchog* I (p. 361); *Tshig-don* (p. 253). Being flanked by two other "chreods," the *ro-ma* and the *rkyang-ma* (see below note 230), a bilateral symmetry of the system (the living human being) is established. At the same time, the bilateral arrangement of the *ro-ma* and *rkyang-ma* is reversed with respect to whether the system is male or female, so that one system may be conceived of as a mirror image of the other, whereby asymmetry comes into play. On this intriguing problem of the reversal of "right" and "left" but not of "up" and "down" in a mirror image, see Gregory Bateson, *Mind and Nature* (pp. 81f.). The structuration of the system, intimated by these development lines, is both hierarchical and three-dimensional (as is every living organism). As such it pertains to the lower-order reality level. In pure rDzogs-chen thought this structure is overshadowed by a "fourth" development line, the *ka-ti shel-gyi sbu-gu-can* (*mKha'-yang* II, p. 141; III, pp. 94, 119, 127; *sGra thal-'gyur-ba*, pp. 126f.), which pertains to the higher-order reality level. The implication is that man simultaneously lives on two reality levels and cannot be reduced to only one level.

219. *lhan-cig-skyes-pa*. Remember that in rDzogs-chen process thinking the evolution of the Buddha-experience or, as we may say, the Buddha system (*sangs-rgyas*) in view of the wide applicability of the term *system*, like that of a sentient being system (*sems-can*), depends on the intensity of the excitation (*rig-pa*) or loss of intensity in excitation (*ma-rig-pa*), respectively, in Being's holomovement (*gzhi-snang*), which, as the term implies, is wholly present in either system. While the Buddha system is characterized by an optimal level of excitation operative as the system's originary awareness, this operation is systemic, that is, not confined to a particular part of the system; hence the texts speak of a "systemic originary awareness" (*lhan-cig-skyes-pa'i ye-shes*). By contrast, the sentient being system is marked by a loss in excitation; hence the texts speak of a "systemic low-level excitation" (*lhan-cig-skyes-pa'i ma-rig-pa*).

220. *chos-sku thig-le nyag-gcig*. The English rendering of this Tibetan term is merely an attempt at breaking its highly complex code. As noted repeatedly, the

term *chos-sku* points to the gestaltism of lived-through experience in that it sums up Being's meaning-rich potential in a gestalt quality. As such this gestalt quality is both the expression and the expressed of Being's originary awareness (*ye-shes*) as a function of Being's optimally cognitive excitation (*rig-pa*). In rDzogs-chen process-oriented thinking, with its holistic perspective, Being (or, if one prefers, the Universe) is "intelligent" in its own right such that no division between something subjective, the knowing, and something objective, the known, exists. Because of this systemic intelligence, Being is a self-organizing process, not a static entity, and as such has within it all the information needed for its self-organization, similar to the DNA molecule, which contains the information necessary for the production of proteins and through them the formation and continuous regeneration of the cell. This "information package" is termed *thig-le nyag-gcig*, which may be rendered literally as "a point-instant virtual singularity." See my *Matrix of Mystery* (pp. 47, 49). According to Klong-chen rab-'byams-pa, it is Being's "auto-luminescence as the projective glow of its invariance" (*Zab-yang* II, p. 217, which is based on *Thig-le kun-gsal*, in rNying-rgyud, Vol. 5, p. 132). In *Chos-dbyings* (p. 112) this term is used as a synonym of "self-existent (endogenous) originary awareness" (*rang-byung-gi ye-shes*), and on p. 216 it occurs together with *rig-pa gcig-pu*, "the uniquely optimally cognitive excitation of Being," and with *chos-sku*, "the gestalt experience of Being's meaningfulness" (*rig-pa gcig-pu chos-sku thig-le nyag-gcig*). Other combinations are *chos-nyid thig-le nyag-gcig* (*Chos-dbyings*, p. 198) and *sangs-rgyas nyag-gcig* (*Chos-dbyings*, pp. 220, 221, 229).

221. On these see p. 116, n. 48, and above note 190.

222. These are the *chos-sku* (the gestalt experience of Being's meaningfulness), the *longs-sku* (the gestalt experience of Being in its presence as a world-horizon of meaning), and the *sprul-sku* (the gestalt experience of Being in guiding images or cultural norms).

223. Tib. *snying-rje chen-po*. See above note 200 for the explication of this term.

224. They are the remaining four originary awareness modes when the central originary awareness mode, Being's originary awareness of itself as constituting its cognitive field or domain, which is the core of the *yi-dam* himself, is omitted. The remaining modes are the quasi-mirroring, identity, specificity, and task-accomplished originary awareness modes.

225. See above note 180.

226. See above note 187. Whenever brackets are used, the enclosed passages have been excerpted from Tshe-dbang mchog-grub's larger work containing many details not found in this smaller work.

227. *nyams*. For further details see my *Matrix of Mystery* (p. 271, notes 16, 17, 19, and 20). The coordination of five sentiments with the four phases of birth, illness, death, and old age, as presented here, tallies with the one given by Yon-tan rgya-mtsho in his *Nyi-ma'i 'od-zer* (p. 187). The apparent contradiction between five sentiments and only four phases in an individual's life was resolved by Padma phrin-las snying-po, a student of 'Jam-dbyangs grags-pa, who himself had been a student of both 'Jam-dbyangs mkhyen-rtse'i dbang-po (1820–1892)

and his contemporary mChog-gyur gling-pa, in his notes on the *Ye-shes snying-po*, the *brJed-byang* (written in about 1920, p. 205), by stating that five senti-ments are due to taking nonflabbiness and harmonious blending, which charac-terize the transmutation of death, as two separate sentiments.

228. See above note 190.

229. The three poisons are passion-lust (*'dod-chags*), irritation-aversion (*zhe-sdang*), and infatuation-dullness (*gti-mug*).

230. Of these two terms, *ro-ma* was explicated by Klong-chen rab-'byams-pa as follows:

> The appellation *ro-ma* is used to indicate that its function is to take up that which constitutes the "flavor" (*ro*) of the system's totality and hence is like salt (that gives flavor to food). Since it brings about an extraordinary relishing of the experiential process, in view of the fact that its support base is the optimal function of the in-formation input (*thig-le*), this is what is meant by using the term *ro*. Moreover, since this development line develops out of desire-attachment it is furthermore termed *ma* ("moth-erly"), and the reason is that it enables those who have desire-attachment prevailing in their psychological disposition toward finding their integral wholeness, the Buddha-experience, by using their desire-attachment. Fur-thermore, the term *ro* refers to the fact that there is little of ego-centered purposing involved and its experience rests on the dynamics of the in-formation input. Since this is difficult to express in words, the term *ma* (a negative particle) is applied. Therefore, since along this chreod the sys-tem's in-formation and organization input in what is its commonly accept-ed reality, moves, it fills this whole dynamics with a superb flavor of bliss.

See *Tshig-don* (p. 251); *Theg-mchog* I (pp. 360f.). The physiological implications of this structuration process, mentioned in these texts in detail, are outside the scope of this treatise.

The fifty gnosemes in this chreod express themselves in the shapes and sounds of the sixteen vowels and the thirty-four consonants of the Tibetanized Sanskrit alphabet.

The term *rkyang-ma* was explicated as follows:

> This development line is termed so because it is solitary and, furthermore, has neither bends nor branchings. As the cause-momentum in what con-stitutes the higher-order in-formation input and the lower-order com-monly accepted reality in-formation input, it is active in the maturation of both the higher-order and lower-order fundamental forces and in their separation. Since it is solitary (*rkyang*) it is invariant, and since it is the underlying ground of all that is it is "motherly" (*ma, mo*). On the basis of the support it provides within the system, the Buddha-experience is easily won.

See *Theg-mchog* I (pp. 360f.); *Tshig-don* (p. 252). Lastly, as these sources indicate, the *ro-ma* reflects "appropriate activity" (*thabs*) and the *rkyang-ma* "originary awareness" (*ye-shes*) as pertaining to the whole system and by implication to "appreciative discernment" (*shes-rab*).

The hyphenated term *in-formation* has been taken over from Erich Jantsch (1980, pp.201, 218) to indicate that no information transfer is involved. Being in-forms itself about how it is going with it.

The fifty operators in this chreod are the fifty (or, if one splits one into two, fifty-one) mentation-related operators (mental events, *sems-'byung*, Skt. *caitasika*) as listed in *Abhidharmakośa* II, 23–34 and *Triṃśikola* 10–14.

231. Four of the five affinities are arranged around the fifth or central affinity. Each affinity as an operational domain has its regent and queen. Seen from the vantage point of the central dancing couple, there are only four dancing couples around this center.

232. *snying-rje chen-po*. See above note 200. The different rendering in this context is intended to avoid confusion that might arise from using the term *higher-order* in the context of the *lower-order* commonly accepted reality.

233. This rather condensed presentation will be easier to understand if we remember that rDzogs-chen process-oriented thinking involves the principle of complementarity, which may appear in many guises. There is the lower-order commonly accepted reality (*kun-rdzob*) or Being's lighting-up and presencing aspect (*snang-cha*), which is actional (*thabs*) as compassion (*snying-rje*). Its image is the masculine. Complementary to it is the higher-order reality (*don-dam*) or Being's open and opening aspect (*stong-cha*), which is appreciatively discerning (*shes-rab*) as utter openness (*stong-nyid*). Its image is the feminine. It is unfortunate that no word in any Western language can satisfactorily convey the dynamic character of Being's openness, which certainly is not some static emptiness or void.

234. These, according to the Sāṃkhya system, are the constitutive factors (*guṇa*) of the *prakṛti* that underlies the evolution of the psychophysical universe, *sattva* being the "intelligence"-stuff, *rajas* the "activity"-stuff, and *tamas* the "inertia"-stuff. The Sāṃkhya system is highly speculative and full of logical contradictions. Nonetheless, its influence on non-Buddhist Indian thought has been tremendous. Its appeal lies in its later dualism, which places the *ātman/puruṣa* (similar to the Western notion of the transcendental ego) outside the world such that it is neither an a priori condition for knowledge (as it is still in Kant's transcendental philosophy) nor has anything about it that could be called knowledge, because all this is part of the evolution and transformation of the *prakṛti*.

235. Obscurations are of two kinds: (1) the intellectual constructs set up by representational-thematizing thought (*shes-sgrib*) and (2) the affective-emotional responses and drives (*nyon-sgrib*).

236. The twelvefold division of the Buddhist scriptures according to their form and contents is as follows: (1) prose sermons (Sūtra); (2) sermons in a mixture of prose and verse (Geyyā); (3) explanations, commentaries, and

prophesies (Vyākaraṇa); (4) stanzas (Gāthā); (5) pithy sayings (Udāna); (6) introductory statements (Nidāna); (7) edifying tales (Avadāna); (8) short speeches beginning with the words: "Thus spoke the Exalted One" (Ityukta, wrongly Itivṛttaka); (9) birth stories (Jātaka); (10) lengthy discourses (Vaipulya); (11) stories of miracles (Adbhutadharma); (12) and instructions (Upadeśa).

237. These openness modes have been listed in *Bla-dgongs* (Vol. 5, p. 64). In paraphrasing these modes we may be allowed to use the word *nothing* instead of *open* to point out that Being's openness has nothing about it that might make us speak of it as a thing. Thus, (1) because it itself is nothing, it has nothing objective about it and cannot be claimed to be a construct (as are all other objects and things); (2) because it has been nothing from all beginning, it has not come into existence incidentally; (3) because it is nothing in its actuality or presence, it has not been created by anyone; (4) because it is holistically nothing, it has nothing ephemeral about it; and (5) because it is nothing in its identity-with-itself, the manifold has but one flavor in it as Being's pure potential.

238. *thig-le chen-po drug.* The earliest reference to them was made by gNubs-chen Sangs-rgyas ye-shes (born 772) in his *rNal-'byor mig-gi bsam-gtan* (also known as *bSam-gtan mig-sgron*, pp. 374f.). There he said that these six information quanta, without being a plurality or even a singularity, are operative in Being's symmetry transformation from pure potential to spontaneous presence. The same idea is found in the *Byang-chub-sems-kyi man-ngag rin-chen phreng-ba* (bearing the subtitle *Bang-mdzod 'phrul-gyi lde-mig*, in rNying-rgyud, Vol. 2, pp. 149–207, pp. 184f.), and in the *Nges-don 'dus-pa* (in rNying-rgyud, Vol. 8, pp. 124–477, pp. 328–334), both of which seem to have been translated in the eighth century. They were mentioned again by Rong-zom Chos-kyi bzang-po (eleventh century) in his *bKa'-'bum* (pp. 217f.). Lastly, they were dealt with in the experiential context of the coevolution of man and his environing world by Klong-chen rab-'byams-pa in his *Bla-yang* I (p. 461). After his time, with the exception of a passing reference to them in the present text, no further discussions concerning them are found.

239. This little sentence is of utmost importance. There can be no doubt that what counts foremost in the creative vision and the symbolic re-creation of the world are processes, while what we would call structures are kept as fluid as possible. In other words, the images are process structures.

240. This statement means that either the male or the female may be chosen.

241. Within the imaginary structure of the live body, there are two centers: the one, situated in the heart region, is termed *tsitta* and associated with the calm and quiet forces operating within us; the other, situated in the head region, is termed *dung-khang* and associated with the fierce forces. For further details see my *Matrix of Mystery*, *s.v.*, *tsitta* and *dung-khang*.

242. After discussing the transmutation of the individual's body into a gestalt experience and the transmutation of speech into utterance, the text now touches on a very important feature of lived-through experience, the individual's sociality. As an experiencer the individual exists amidst the activities and

attitudes of "others." Sociality, as Calvin O. Schrag (1969, p. 186) pointed out, "does not function here as a classificatory concept, nor is it the region of the social as a nexus of objectifiable properties and relations. It has to do, initially at least, with the prereflective involvement and functioning intentionality from which all forms of reflection take their rise." As an existential structure—the *Bla-dgongs* (Vol.5, p.60) speaks of "a spontaneous, nondualistic superconfiguration"—this sociality is referred to, on the one hand, by the term *configurational setting* (*dkyil-'khor*), and, on the other hand, by two related concepts. The one may be paraphrased as "oneself being the expression of a primary concern with being committed" (*dam-tshig sems-dpa'*), and the other as "the other being the expression of a primary concern with originary awareness" (*ye-shes sems-dpa'*). The anthropomorphic implication of the term *sems-dpa'* is particularly well suited to keeping the feedback loop between oneself and the other alive. In terms of experience the Buddhists long ago anticipated Max Scheler and Gabriel Marcel's notion of a "we"-experience.

The term *dam-tshig sems-dpa'* is explicated as follows in *Bla-dgongs* (Vol. 5, p. 59):

> Since one's true body (*lus*), speech (*ngag*), and subjective mentation (*yid*) have existed in an originary manner as the gestalt quality (*sku*), communication (*gsung*), and spirituality (*thugs*) of a formulated energy, not to go beyond this experiential fact is what is meant by commitment (*dam-tshig*); and since in the radiance of such a formulated energy there is no going astray into mistaken notions about it, this is what is meant by primary concern (*sems-dpa'*).

243. See also preceding note. The term *ye-shes sems-dpa'* has been explicated in the work quoted as follows:

> Since it has been there from all beginning and has existed in an originary manner it is spoken of as originary awareness (*ye-shes*); and since there does not exist the grime of dualism, this is what is meant by primary concern (*sems-dpa'*).

244. They are group of popular gods higher up in the hierarchy. See *Abhidharmakośa* III, 69.

245. A lengthy hermeneutical explication of this term, which forms the basis of the interpretation given here—*bdud* (the deadening powers) and *rtsi* (a solvent)—is found in the *sNang-srid kha-sbyor bdud-rtsi bcud-thig 'khor-ba thog-mtha' gcod-pa'i rgyud phi-ma* (in rNying-rgyud, Vol. 6, pp. 3f.). There we read:

> *bdud* is the crowd of divisive concepts in mentation;
> *rtsi* is the undivided meaning-rich gestalt experience of Being.
> *bdud* is mentation with its triad of attention, cognition, and flitting
>   from one content to another;
> *rtsi* is the nonexistence of these three.

bdud is the darkness of unknowing;
rtsi is a super originary awareness.
bdud is the gate through which one enters samsara with its darkness;
rtsi is the gate through which Being's optimally cognitive excitation
shines forth.
bdud is the triple manner of going astray;
rtsi is the triple manner of reversing this trend.
bdud is the going astray into the three world spheres;
rtsi is the total eradication of this going astray.
bdud is the triad of the poison of the pollutants;
rtsi is Being's gestaltism, communicativeness, and spiritual resonance.
bdud is the five poisons of the pollutants;
rtsi is the five gestalt experiences and their five originary awareness
modes.
bdud is the eighty-thousand pollutants;
rtsi is the eighty-thousand gates to life's meaning.
bdud is the mentation involved in samsara ranging over three world
spheres;
rtsi is the spirituality of the victorious ones throughout the three aspects
of time.
bdud is the living beings in samsara;
rtsi is the Buddhas in nirvana.

The triple manner of going astray and of reversing this trend relate to the
triune character of Being as facticity (*ngo-bo*), actuality (*rang-bzhin*), and resonance (*thugs-rje*).
    246. According to the *Thams-cad bdud-rtsi lnga'i rang-bzhin rin-po-che 'phreng-
ba'i rgyud* (in rNying-rgyud, Vol. 26, pp. 99–145), pp. 102f., the eight basics
are, externally, a tree's trunk, bark, branches, leaves, marrow, fruits, petals, and
flowers; internally, the eight spiritual pursuits, the Śrāvakayāna, the Pratyekabuddhayāna, the Bodhisattvayāna, the Kriyāyoga, the Caryāyoga (or
Ubhayayoga), the Yoga, the Mahāyoga, and the Anuyoga together with the
scriptural material related to them; and, on the arcane level, the eight perceptual patterns.
    247. The same statement without further explication is found in the work
listed in the preceding note. The five kinds of elixir are the same "substances" as
the ones listed in note 154.
    248. See above note 152.
    249. *zung-'jug.* The usage of this term is similar to that of *dbyer-med*. While
the latter, almost exclusively used in works of the old (*rnying-ma*) tradition,
emphasizes the indivisibility of the two members making up the complementarity; the former, mostly used in the new (*gsar-ma*) traditions, the bKa'-brgyud-
pa and others, indicates that the two members are "in phase."
    250. rDzogs-chen thinkers have paid special attention to the problem of
freedom, which for them was not a category that might be contrasted with other
categories or its opposite, bondage, but was conceived of as a systemic (and

hence holistic) quality. The term *ye-grol*—*ye* refers to its originary and atemporal aspect—is closely related to *yongs-grol*, emphasizing the holistic nature of this quality. Thus Klong-chen rab-'byams-pa, who has made the most exhaustive study of the problem of freedom (see, for instance, *Theg-mchog* II, pp. 289f.; *Chos-dbyings*, pp. 165f.; *Zab-yang* I, p. 302; *Bla-yang* II, pp. 121f.), said in his *Bla-yang* I (p. 423):

> There is not a single entity in the whole of that which lights up and is interpreted (*snang-srid*) as samsara or nirvana ('*khor-'das*), that is not free. Since that which is termed a "going astray" has first of all never been experienced as some entity or other, there is now also nothing that abides as such an entity termed "going astray," and finally there can also be no possibility for such an entity termed "going astray" to turn up. For this reason one speaks of the six kinds of living beings as being a super originary freedom (*ye-grol chen-po*).

251. The originary awareness sensitive to the things of the world as they are in themselves (*ji-lta-ba mkhyen-pa'i ye-shes*) is the crystallization of Being's originary awareness of itself as a meaning-rich field (*chos-kyi dbyings-kyi ye-shes*) and Being's originary awareness of its identity-with-itself (*mnyam-pa-nyid-kyi ye-shes*). The originary awareness sensitive to the things of the world as they are interconnected (*ji-snyed-pa mkhyen-pa'i ye-shes*) is the crystallization of the quasi-mirroring awareness (*me-long lta-bu'i ye-shes*), the specificity-initiating awareness (*so-sor rtog-pa'i ye-shes*), and the task-accomplished awareness (*bya-ba grub-pa'i ye-shes*). See *Yid-bzhin* (p. 698).

252. Admittedly, the term *nga-rgyal* "pride," presents certain difficulties because of its egological connotations, in which case it is considered in Buddhist texts as a pollutant (*nyon-mongs*). In this context it has no egological connotations whatsoever; in fact the proud feeling of being an aspect of an all-encompassing evolutionary process is incommensurable with an ego-centered reductionism. This has clearly been recognized in *rDo-rje snying-po* (pp. 333f.), where a distinction is made between a "lower order ego" (*nga*) and a "higher order self" (*bdag*), which both become meaningless in what is termed *lha'i nga-rgyal*.

253. Recent research has shown that high frequencies have a "recharging" effect, while sounds in low frequencies tire the listener. These conclusions are based on the examination of the sound in Gregorian chant with the aid of an oscilloscope by French physician Alfred Tomatis. See *Brain/Mind Bulletin*, 10, no. 6, 4 March, 1985.

254. This important section on reemerging from a state of composure follows a lengthy discussion of topics not exactly relevant to the creative vision itself.

255. The three affinities with Being (*rigs*) are the experiencer's inclination toward spiritual growth (*de-bzhin gshegs-pa'i rigs*), his rootedness in Being's indestructibility as his inalienable value (*rdo-rje'i rigs*), and his uncontaminatedness by samsaric existence (*padma'i rigs*).

256. *Dohākośa* (verse 16).

257. *Theg-mchog* II (p. 124).

258. Without going into details, which would require a lengthy monograph outside the scope of this book, a few explicatory words concerning this highly metaphorical passage may be said. "The wide-open sky" (*nam-mkha'*) also has the meaning of "infinite space," which, in rDzogs-chen thought, is as much out there as it is within ourselves. In whichever way we encounter it, it is never an empty container but a swirling, intimately felt superforce. The "two lamps" are (1) this very superforce in its aspect of Being's field-continuum (*dbyings*) from which all meanings originate, similar to the modern quantum vacuum, which is alive with throbbing energy, and (2) the excitation (*rig*) of this field, one's optimally cognitive capacity. Neither the field nor its excitation are independent of each other, and the overall effect of the inherent dynamics is a virtual polarization; hence "two lamps." In the ceaseless activity of the field and its excitation, light is emitted; hence the metaphor of a "lamp."

259. Martin Heidegger, *The Will to Power as Art*, "Nietzsche" (Vol. 1, p. 209).

REFERENCES

Works in Western Languages

Bateson, Gregory (1979), *Mind and Nature. A Necessary Unity*. New York: E.P. Dutton.

Bohm, David (1980), *Wholeness and the Implicate Order*. London, Boston and Henley, Routledge & Kegan Paul.

Brain/Mind Bulletin 10, no. 6 (1985), "High frequencies cited in 'recharging' effects reported with Gregorian chant."

Broad, C.D. (1925, 6th ed. 1951), *The Mind and its Place in Nature*. London, Routledge & Kegan Paul.

Clark, Kenneth (1956), *The Nude*. Harmondsworth, Middlesex: Penguin Books.

Dargyay, Eva M. (1977), *The Rise of Esoteric Buddhism in Tibet*. Delhi: Motilal Banarsidass.

Davies, Paul (1984), *Superforce: The Search for a Grand Unified Theory of Nature*. New York: Simon and Schuster, Inc.

Fallico, Arturo B. (1962), *Art & Existentialism*. Englewood Cliffs, N.J.: Prentice Hall.

Franz, Marie-Louise von (1974) *Number and Time: Reflections Leading toward a Unification of Depth Psychology and Physics*. Translated by Andrea Dykes. Evanston: Northwestern University Press.

Goethe, Johann Wolfgang von, *Faust*. Edited and translated by Stuart Atkins (1984). Cambridge, Massachusetts: Suhrkamp/Insel Publishers Boston, Inc.

Goethe, Johann Wolfgang von, *Texte zur Farbenlehre. Theory of Colours*. English translation (1840) by Charles lock Eastlake. Cambridge, Massachusetts, and London, England: The M.I.T. Press (sixth printing 1982).

Goethe, Johann Wolfgang von, *Anschauendes Denken. Goethes Schriften zur Naturwissenschaft in einer Auswahl herausgegeben von Horst Gunther* (1981). Frankfurt am Main, Insel Verlag.

Guenther, Herbert V. (1975–76), *Kindly Bent to Ease Us*. 3 vols. Emeryville, CA: Dharma Publishing.

Guenther, Herbert V. (1978), "Bodhisattva—the Ethical Phase in Evolution." In: Leslie S. Kawamura, ed. (1978), *The Bodhisattva Doctrine in Buddhism*. Waterloo, Ont.: Wilfrid Laurier University Press.

Guenther, Herbert V. (1981) "The Old and the New Vision." In: Erich Jantsch, ed. *The Evolutionary Vision: Toward a Unifying Paradigm of Physical, Biological, and Sociocultural Evolution*. Boulder, Colorado: AAAS Selected Symposium 61.

Guenther, Herbert V. (1983), "The Dynamics of Being: rdzogs-chen Process Thinking." In: Eva K. Dargyay, ed. (1983), *Canadian Tibetan Studies 1*. Calgary, Alberta: Society for Tibetan Studies.

Guenther, Herbert V. (1984), *Matrix of Mystery. Scientific and Humanistic Aspects of rDzogs-chen Thought*. Boulder & London, Shambhala.

Günther, Horst (1981), *Goethe: Anschauendes Denken. Goethes Schriften zur Naturwissenschaft in einer Auswahl herausgegeben*. Frankfurt am Main: Insel Verlag.

Heidegger, Martin (1962), *Being and Time*. Translated by John Macquarrie & Edward Robinson. New York: Harper & Row.

Heidegger, Martin (1979), *The Will to Power as Art, 'Nietzsche,'* Vol. 1, New York: Harper & Row.

Husserl, Edmund (1923, 1924), *Erste Philosophy, Zweiter Teil*. In: *Husserliana Band VIII* (1959). den Haag: Martinus Nijhoff. [The English rendering is taken from Richard M. Zaner (1964), *The Problem of Embodiment*. The Hague: Martinus Nijhoff].

Jantsch, Erich (1980), *The Self-organizing Universe*. Oxford, New York, Toronto, Sydney, Paris, Frankfurt: Pergamon Press.

Jantsch, Erich and Conrad Waddington, ed. (1976), *Evolution and Consciousness: Human Systems in Transition*. London, Amsterdam, Don Mills, Ontario, Sydney, Tokyo: Addison-Wesley Publishing Company.

Langer, Suzanne K. (1967, 1972), *Mind, an Essay on Human Feeling*, 2 Vols. Baltimore and London: Johns Hopkins University Press.

Lauf, Detlef-I. (1975), *Geheimlehren tibetischer Totenbucher*. Freiburg im Breisgau: Aurum Verlag. English translation (1977) *Secret Doctrines of the Tibetan Books of the Dead* by Graham Parkes. Boulder and London: Shambhala.

Levin, David Michael (1985), *The Body's Recollection of Being: Phenomenological Psychology and the Deconstruction of Nihilism*. London: Routledge & Kegan Paul.

Lipps, Hans (1938), *Untersuchungen zu einer hermeneutischen Logik*. Frankfurt: Klostermann.

MacLean, Paul D. (1973), "A Triune Concept of the Brain and Behavior." In: T. Boag and D. Campbell, eds., *The Hincks Memorial Lectures*, Toronto: University of Toronto Press.

Merleau-Ponty, Maurice (1962), *Phenomenology of Perception*. Translation by Colin Smith. London: Routledge & Kegan Paul.

Nietzsche, Friedrich, *Also Sprach Zarathustra*, (*Thus Spoke Zarathustra*). In Walter Kaufmann, ed. (1954), *The Portable Nietzsche*. New York: Penguin.

Norman, K.R. (1984), "On Translating from Pāli." In: *One Vehicle: Journal of the National University of Singapore Buddhist Society*. Singapore, pp. 77–87.

Northrop, F.S.C. (1959), *The Logic of the Sciences and Humanities*. New York: Meridian Books.

Rosen, Joe (1975), *Symmetry Discovered: Concepts and Applications in Nature and Science*. Cambridge: Cambridge University Press.

Schrag, Calvin O. (1969), *Experience and Being*. Evanston, Ill.: Northwestern University Press.

Schrag, Calvin O. (1980), *Radical Reflection and the Origin of the Human Sciences*. Indiana: Purdue University Press.

Thomsen, Dietrick E. (1983), "The New Inflationary Nothing Universe." In: *Science News* (1983) 123, 12 February 1983.

Tymieniecka, Anna-Teresa (1983), "Natural Spontaneity in the Translacing Continuity of Beingness." In: *Analecta Husserliana* vol. XIV. Dordrecht, Holland: D. Reidel.

Whitehead, Alfred North (1978), *Process and Reality*. (Corrected Version, ed. David Ray Griffin and Donald W. Sherburne). New York: Free Press.

Zaner, Richard M. (1964), *The Problem of Embodiment. Some Contributions to a Phenomenology of the Body*. The Hague: Martinus Nijhoff.

Tibetan Works (by known authors)

Klong-chen rab-'byams-pa
Klong-'grel
= *Phyogs-bcu'i mun-pa thams-cad rnam-par sel-ba*,
Paro, 1975

mKha'-yang
= *mKha'-'gro yang-tig*
In: *sNying-thig ya-bzhi*, vol. 4–6,
New Delhi, 1971

Grub-mtha'
= *Theg-pa mtha'-dag-gi don gsal-bar byed-pa grub-pa'i mtha' rin-po-che'i mdzod*,
Sde-dge ed., Delhi, 1983

sGyu-ma ngal-gso
= rDzogs-pa chen-po sgyu-ma ngal-gso 'grel-pa dang bcas-pa,
Gangtok, n.d.

Chos-dbyings
= Chos-dbyings rin-po-che'i mdzod-kyi 'grel-pa lung-gi gter- mdzod,
Sde-dge ed., Delhi, 1983

Theg-mchog
= Theg-pa'i mchog rin-po-che'i mdzod, 2 vols.
Sde-dge ed., Delhi, 1983

gNas-lugs
= sDe-gsum snying-po'i don-'grel gnas-lugs rin-po-che'i mdzod,
Sde-dge ed., Delhi, 1983

Bi-ma
= Bi-ma snying-thig
In: sNying-thig ya-bzhi, vols. 7–9

Bla-yang
= Bla-ma yang-tig
In: sNying-thig ya-bzhi, vol. 1

Man-ngag
= Man-ngag rin-po-che'i mdzod,
Sde-dge ed., Delhi, 1983

Tshig-don
= gSang-ba bla-na-med-pa'i 'od-gsal rdo-rje snying-po'i gnas-gsum gsal-bar byed-
pa'i tshig-don rin-po-che'i mdzod,
Sde-dge ed., Delhi, 1983

Zab-yang
= Zab-mo yang-tig
In: sNying-thig ya-bzhi, vol. 10–11

Yid-bzhin
= Theg-pa chen-po'i man-ngag-gi bstan-bcos yid-bzhin rin-po- che'i mdzod,
Sde-dge ed., Delhi, 1983

Sems-nyid ngal-gso
= rDzogs-pa chen-po sems-nyid ngal-gso 'grel-pa dang bcas-pa,
Gangtok, n.d.

bKra-shis rnam-rgyal (Dwags-po Paṇ-chen)
dPal kye'i rdo-rje zhes-bya-ba' rgyud-kyi rgyal-po'i 'grel- pa legs-bshad nyi-ma'i 'od-
zer (commentary on the Hevajratantra),
n.p., n.d.

Khrag-thung rol-pa'i rdo-rje
Dag-snang ye-shes dra-ba-las gnas-lugs rang-byung-gi rgyud rdo-rje snying-po,
Dehradun, 1970

mKhan-po Yon-dga' v. Yon-tan rgya-mtsho

sGam-po-pa
gSung-'bum (hand-written copy of the complete works),
n.p., n.d.

'Gyur-med tshe-dbang mchog-grub
bsKyed-pa'i rim-pa cho-ga dang sbyar-ba'i gsal-byed zung- 'jug snye-ma,
n.p., n.d.

gSang-sngags nang-gi lam-rim rgya-cher 'grel-pa sangs-rgyas- gnyis-pa'i dgongs-
rgyan
In: Smanrtsis Shesrig Spendzod, vol. 35,
Leh, 1972

Ngag-dbang bstan-'dzin rdo-rje
mKha'-'gro bde-chen rgyal-mo'i sgrub-gzhung-gi 'grel-pa
In: Ngagyur Nyingmay Sungrab, volume 28, New Delhi, 1972

Chos-kyi dbang-phyug (6th Zhwa-dmar Karma-pa)
lHan-cig-skyes-sbyor-gyi zab-khrid nges-don rgya-mtsho'i snying-po phrin-las
'od-'phro, Paro, 1979

'Jigs-med gling-pa
Yon-tan = Yon-tan rin-po-che'i dga'-ba'i char
In: The Collected Works of Kun-mkhyen 'Jigs-med gling-pa,
(Ngagyur Nyingmay Sungrab, vol. 30),
Gangtok, 1971

rNam-mkhyen shing-rta (commentary on the above)
In: The Collected Works of Kun-mkhyen'Jigs-med gling-pa,
(Ngagyur Nyingmay Sungrab, vol. 30), Gangtok, 1971

bsTan-pa'i nyi-ma
bsKyed-rim-gyi zin-bris cho-ga spyi-'gros ltar bkod-pa man-ngag kun-btus,
n.p., n.d.

Tha-shas-pa Daridra Kun-dga' mi-'gyur rdo-rje
Bar-do'i chos-bshad mi-rtag sgyu-ma'i bang-chen dang-po, n.p., n.d.

Dam-pa bSod-nams rgyal-mtshan (Sa-skya bla-ma)
rGyud-kyi rgyal-po dpal Kye-rdo-rje'i rgya-cher 'grel-pa nyi-ma'i 'od-zer (commentary on the Hevajratantra), New Delhi, 1980

gNubs-chen Sangs-rgyas ye-shes
rNal-'byor mig-gi bsam-gtan, Leh, 1974

dPal-sprul O-rgyan 'Jigs-med chos-kyi dbang-po
gSung-'bum (Collected Works) 6 vols., Gangtok, 1971

'Ba-ra-ba rgyal-mtshan dpal-bzang
gSung-'bum (Collected Works) 14 vols., Dehradun, 1970

Mi-pham 'Jam-dbyangs rnam-rgyal rgya-mtsho
Mun-sel = gSang-'grel phyogs-bcu'i mun-sel-gyi spyi-don 'od-gsal snying-po,
Gangtok, n.d.

rDzogs-chen rgyal-sras gZhan-phan mtha'-yas
bKa'-ma 14 vols., Gangtok, 1969

Yon-tan rgya-mtsho (mkhan-po Yon-dga')
  Nyi-ma'i 'od-zer = Yon-tan rin-po-che'i mdzod-kyi 'grel-pa zab-don snang-byed
  nyi-ma'i 'od-zer, Gangtok, 1969

g·Yung-ston rdo-rje dpal bzang-po
  gSal-byed me-long = dPal gsang-ba snying-po'i rgyud-don gsal-byed me-long, n.p.,
  n.d.

Rong-zom Chos-kyi bzang-po
  bKa'-'bum, n.p., n.d.
  gSang-'grel = rGyud-rgyal gsang-ba snying-po'i 'grel-pa dkon-cos 'grel, n.p., n.d.

Lo-chen Dharmaśrī
  gSung-'bum (Collected Works) 19 vols., Dehradun, 1977

gSang-bdag zhal-lung In: Smanrtsis Shesrig Spendzod, Vol. 36, Leh, 1972

Sangs-rgyas gling-pa
  Bla-dgongs = Bla-ma dgongs-'dus 13 vols., Gangtok, 1972

Tibetan works (by unknown authors)

dGongs-pa zang-thal = rDzogs-pa chen-po dgongs-pa zang-thal In: Smanrtsis Shesrig
  Spendzod, vol. 60–64, Leh, 1973

sGra-thal 'gyur-ba = Rin-po-che 'byung-bar byed-pa sgra-thal 'gyur chen-po'i rgyud
  In: Ati, vol. 1, pp. 1–205

Thig-le kun-gsal = Thig-le kun-gsal chen-po'i rgyud In: rNying-rgyud, vol. 5, pp.
  124–289

bDud-rtsi rin-po-che ye-shes snang-ba'i 'khor-lo'i rgyud In: rNying-rgyud, vol. 26,
  pp. 2–58

sNang-srid kha-sbyor bdud-rtsi bcud-thig 'khor-ba thog-mtha' gcod-pa'i rgyud phyi-ma
  In: rNying-rgyud, vol. 6, pp. 1–52

Byang-chub-sems-kyi man-ngag rin-chen phreng-ba (subtitle: Bang-mdzod 'phrul-gyi
  lde-mig) In: rNying-rgyud, vol. 2, pp. 149–208

Tibetan Collections

Ati = rNying-ma'i rgyud bcu-bdun 3 vols., New Delhi, 1973–77

rNying-rgyud = rNying-ma'i rgyud-'bum 36 vols. Thimbu, 1973

sNying-thig ya-bzhi 11 vols. Klong-chen rab-'byams-pa, New Delhi, 1970

Sanskrit and Prākrit works

Abhidharmakośa, Critically edited by Swami Dwarikadas Shastri Bauddha
  Bharati, Varanasi, 1970

Jñānasiddhi In: *Two Vajrayana Works, Gaekwad's Oriental Series*, No. XLIV, B. Bhattacharyya, ed., Baroda, n.d.

Dohākośa, M. Shahidullah, ed., *Les Cants Mystiques de Kāṇha et de Saraha. Les Dohā-Kośa (en apabhraṃśa, avec les versions tibetaines) et Les Caryā (en vieux-bengali) avec introduction, vocabulaires et notes.* Adrien-Maisonneuve, Paris, 1928

Pañcakrama, L. de la Vallée Poussin, ed., University de Gand, Louvain, 1896

Mahāyānasūtrālaṅkāra, Sylvain Lévi, Librairie Honoré Champion, Paris, 1907

Hevajratantra, D.L. Snellgrove, ed., *London Oriental Series*, Volume 6, London, New York, Toronto: Oxford University Press, 1959

INDEX

OF TECHNICAL TERMS

Sanskrit & Pali

Akaniṣṭha, 150 n.212
apraṇihitasamādhi, 141 n.159
avadhūti, 86
ahaṃ, 150 n.214
ātman, 57, 115 n.22, 155 n.234
ānimittasamādhi, 142 n.162
ārūpya, 149 n.209
āloka, 140 n.157
ālokābhāsa, 140 n.157
utpattikrama, vii
utpannakrama, vii
upalabdha/upalabdhi, 140 n.157

kapāla, 120 n.70, 137 n.153
kakkola, 38
karmamudrā, 120 n.70
kalyāṇamitra, 124 n.116

gaṇacakra, 120 n.70
gandhabba, 40
guṇa, 155 n.234
guru, 124 n.116
guruparamparā, 134 n.138
guhyamantra, 128 n.124

cittasyaikāgratā/cittass' ekaggatā,
    138 n.156
caitasika, 155 n.230

ḍāka, 67, 133 n.136
ḍākinī, 67, 133 n.136

tantra, viii, 30, 125 n.117
tapas, 113 n.6
tamas, 91, 140 n.157, 155 n.234

dharmacakra, 146 n.184
dhyāna, 138 n.156

puruṣa, 155 n.234
prakṛti, 155 n.234
prajñā, 144 n.168
prātimokṣa, 131 n.130
pratītyasamutpāda, 149 n.204

bodhi, 132 n.131
bola, 38

bhaga, 119 n.70, 143 n.168

maṇḍala, 132 n.132
mantra, 128 n.129
māyopamasamādhi, 142 n.162

yāna, viii

rakta, 137 n.152
rajas, 91, 140 n.157, 155 n.234
rasāyana, 136 n.151

Vajradhara, 151 n.214
Vajradhṛk, 151 n.214
vajropamasamādhi, 140 n.156
vibhajyavādin, 148 n.194

Śākyamuni, 113 n.6
śūnyatā, 5, 147 n.194
śūnyatāsamādhi, 140 n.156
śūraṃgamasamādhi, 141 n.159

sattva, 91, 140 n.157, 155 n.234
samādhi, 138 n.156
siddhānta, 146 n.183
siddhi, 128 n.123
sukha, 120 n.70
sūtra, 125 n.117

Tibetan

ka-ti shel-gyi bu-gu-can, 152 n.218
ka-dag, 44, 47, 123 n.91
kun-tu snang-ba, 26
kun-tu snang-ba'i ting-nge-'dzin,
    141 n.159
kun-'dar-ma, 152 n.218
kun-rdzob, 125 n.117, 155 n.233
kun-gzhi, 42
kun-gzhi'i rnam-par shes-pa, 42
dka'-thub, 113 n.6
dkyil-'khor, 14, 115 n.25, 132 n.132,
    157 n.242
bka'-ma, 129 n.125
rkyang-ma, 152 n.218, 154 n.230
rkyen, 41, 42, 50
sku, xiii, 27, 28, 51, 53, 113 n.9,
    115 n.29, 121 n.70, 127 n.119,
    128 n.123, 133 n.135, 136 n.150,
    136 n.151, 150 n.213, 157 n.242
sku gsung thugs rdo-rje, 151 n.215
sku gsung thugs mi-zad-pa rgyan-gyi
    'khor-lo, 148 n.201
skye-gnas, 120 n.70
skye-srid, 26
skyon-gyis ma-bcos-pa'i chos-nyid,
    149 n.206
bskyed, bskyed-pa, xii, xiv, 14
bskyed-rim (bskyed-pa'i rim-pa), vii, 10,
    11, 14

khams, 56, 130 n.126, 131 n.129
khrag, 40
mkha'-'gro, 133 n.136
mkha'-'gro-ma, 133 n.136
'khor-'das, 159 n.250
'khor-lo, 120 n.70, 150 n.213
'khrul-pa, 126 n.117

grub-mtha', 146 n.183
grub-pa, 53
grol, 'grol-ba, grol-gzhi, 124 n.109
dge-ba'i bshes-gnyen, 124 n.116
dgongs-pa mi-'gyur-ba'i gzer, 28
rgya-phibs, 144 n.177
rgyas, 127 n.121
rgyu, 26, 41, 42, 50, 142 n.162
rgyu'i ting-nge-'dzin, 142 n.162
rgyud, viii, 125 n.117, 129 n.124,
    131 n.128
sgo-lnga'i rnam-par shes-pa, 42

sgom-pa, 27, 46
sgom-pa dag-pa, 46
sgyu-ma lta-bu'i ting-nge-'dzin, 142 n.162
sgrib-pa-can, 21
sgrom, 144 n.172
brgyud-pa'i bla-ma, 134 n.138

nga-rgyal, 159 n.252
ngag, 27, 50, 121 n.70, 136 n.150,
    157 n.242
ngo-bo, 128 n.122, 149 n.205
ngo-bo-nyid-kyi sku, 151 n.215
dngos, 43, 128 n.122, 138 n.156,
    145 n.182
dngos-po gshis-kyi gnas-lugs, 128 n.122
dngos-po gshis-kyi sems, 128 n.122
mngon-rtogs, 138 n.155
mngon-byang, 123 n.97, 151 n.215
sngags, 25, 128 n.124

bcud, 11, 42

chags, 41
chu, 36
chu-skyes, 144 n.171
chung-ba, 35
chun-'phyang, 144 n.175
chub, 131 n.131
chen-po, 116 n.42
cho-ga, 151 n.215
chos, 28, 53, 144 n.179, 146 n.185
chos-kyi 'khor-lo, 146 n.184
chos-kyi dbyings, 144 n.179
chos-kyi dbyings-kyi ye-shes, 159 n.250
chos-sku, 26, 142 n.164, 151 n.215,
    153 n.232
chos-sku thig-le nyag-gcig, 152 n.220
chos-can, 127 n.120
chos-can lta-ba, 127 n.120
chos-nyid, 127 n.120
chos-nyid lta-ba, 127 n.120
chos-nyid thig-le nyag-gcig, 153 n.220
mched-pa, 140 n.157, 141 n.160
mchod-pa'i lha-mo, 144 n.169
'chi-bdag, 149 n.210
'chi-srid, 151 n.215

ji-snyed-pa mkhyen-pa'i ye-shes,
    159 n.251
ji-lta-ba mkhyen-pa'i ye-shes, 159 n.251

nyams, 153 n.227
nyams-rtogs, 113 n.9
nyid, 50
nyer-thob, 140 n.157, 141 n.160
nyon-sgrib, 155 n.235
nyon-mongs, 137 n.151, 150 n.210,
    159 n.252
nyon-yid, 42
mnyam-nyid, 50
mnyam-nyid gcig, 145 n.179
mnyam-pa-nyid-kyi ye-shes, 159 n.251
rnying-ma, 112 n.4, 132 n.131,
    138 n.154, 158 n.249
snyigs-ma, 42
snying-rje, 142 n.164, 155 n.233
snying-rje chen-po, 148 n.200,
    153 n.223, 155 n.232
snying-po sngags-kyi gzer, 29

ting-nge-'dzin, 138 n.156
ting-'dzin lha'i gzer, 29
gti-mug, 121 n.70, 140 n.157, 154 n.229
gter-ma, 129 n.125
rta-rkang, 144 n.170
rten, 35
rten-'brel bcu-gnyis, 149 n.204
rtog-pa, 51, 140 n.157
lta-ba, 27
stong-cha, 155 n.233
stong-nyid bco-brgyad, 147 n.194
stong-pa, 18, 125 n.117
stong-pa chen-po, 138 n.156, 140 n.157
stong-(pa)-nyid, 5, 118 n.68, 140 n.158,
    142 n.164, 147 n.194, 155 n.230
stong-pa-nyid-kyi ting-nge-'dzin,
    140 n.156
stong-pa-nyid-kyi ye-shes, 149 n.203
stong gsal rig-pa, 115 n.24
stobs lnga, 147 n.189
brten-pa, 35

thabs, xii, 16, 111 n.1, 117 n.65,
    128 n.124, 140 n.157, 151 n.235,
    155 n.230
thabs-kyi rgyud, x
thig-le, 150 n.213, 152 n.218, 154 n.230
thig-le chen-po drug, 156 n.238
thig-le nyag-gcig, 153 n.220
thugs, xiv, 27, 51, 121 n.70, 127 n.119,
    128 n.123, 133 n.135, 136 n.150,
    157 n.243
thugs-rje chen-po, 148 n.199

thub-pa, 113 n.6
thub-pa rgyud, x
theg-pa, viii
theg-pa brgyad, 145 n.181
thob-pa, 140 n.157, 141 n.160
mthar-thug, 28
mthong-lam, 134 n.143

dag, 24, 31, 126 n.117
dangs-ma, 42
dam-tshig, 132 n.135, 157 n.242
dam-tshig rdzas, 120 n.70
dam-tshig sems-dpa', 157 n.242
dam rdzas, 136 n.151
dung-khang, 156 n.241
de-bzhin-nyid, 26, 138 n.156
de-bzhin-nyid-kyi ting-nge-'dzin,
    138 n.156
de-bzhin gshegs-pa'i snying-po, 131 n.129
de-bzhin gshegs-pa'i rigs, 159 n.255
don-dam, 125 n.117, 155 n.230
don-dam-pa'i sngags, 47
dran-pa nye-bar bzhag-pa bzhi, 146 n.185
dri-za, 40, 142 n.162
bdag, 51, 115 n.22, 127 n.119, 159 n.252
bdag-nyid, 127 n.119
bdag-nyid chen-po, 51
bdud, 149 n.210, 157 n.245
bdud-rtsi, 157 n.245
bde-ba chen-po, 119 n.70
bde-(bar) gshegs-(pa'i) snying-po,
    114 n.16, 115 n.22, 127 n.121,
    131 n.129
bden-gnyis, 125 n.117
mdo, 125 n.117
'du-'bral med-pa, 113 n.9
'dod, 41
'dod-khams, 27
'dod-chags, 41, 121 n.70, 140 n.157,
    154 n.229
rdul, 40
rdo-rje, 120 n.70, 143 n.168
rdo-rje snyems-ma, 143 n.168
rdo-rje lta-bu'i ting-nge-'dzin, 140 n.156
rdo-rje btsun-mo, 120 n.70, 143 n.168
rdo-rje btsun-mo'i bhaga, 119 n.70,
    143 n.168
rdo-rje'i btsun-mo, 143 n.168
rdo-rje'i rigs, 159 n.255
sdom-pa, 131 n.130
sdom-gsum, 132 n.130
bsdu-ba'i dngos-po bzhi, 145 n.182

nang, 35, 120 n.70
nam-mkha', 43, 160 n.258
gnas-snang bden-gnyis, 126 n.117
rnam-thar gsum, 140 n.158
rnam-par thar-pa brgyad, 147 n.192
rnam-shes tshogs-brgyad, 149 n.207
sna-'phyang, 144 n.174
snang-cha, 155 n.233
snang-ba, 114 n.17, 125 n.117, 140 n.157,
    141 n.160
snang-srid, 43, 159 n.250
snod, 11, 42, 119 n.70

padma'i rigs, 159 n.255
dpa', 132 n.131
dpa'-bar 'gro-ba'i ting-nge-'dzin,
    141 n.159
dpa'-bo, 133 n.136
dpe brgyad, 149 n.208
spyod-pa, 27
sprul-sku, 26, 142 n.164, 150 n.213,
    151 n.215, 153 n.222

pha-rgyud, 30
phar-phyin bcu, 148 n.195
phung-po, 149 n.210
phyag-rgya-(ma), 120 n.70, 126 n.119
phyag-mtshan, 52, 151 n.216
phyi, 35, 120 n.70
phrin-las, 151 n.215
'phags-lam yang-lag brgyad, 147 n.191
'phro-'du phrin-las-kyi gzer, 30

bag-chags 'khrul-pa, 43
bar-do, bar-(ma-)do, 117 n.53,
    129 n.124, 141 n.160, 151 n.215
bar-srid, 26
bya-ba, 53
bya-ba grub-pa'i ye-shes, 159 n.251
byang, 132 n.131
byang-chub-kyi yan-lag bdun, 147 n.190
byang-chub-sems, byang-chub-kyi sems,
    115 n.22, 119 n.70
byang-chub sems-dpa', 131 n.130,
    132 n.131
bla-ma, 62, 67, 68, 133 n.137
dbang-po lnga, 147 n.184
dbyings, 53, 54, 128 n.122, 144 n.179,
    160 n.258
dbyer-med, 111 n.1, 158 n.249
'byung-ba, 34, 43, 142 n.165
'bras-bu, 27, 141 n.158, 145 n.179,
    151 n.215

sbyang-bya, 130 n.126
sbyang-(bya'i) gzhi, 129 n.126
sbyangs-pa'i 'bras-bu, 131 n.126
sbyong-byed, 130 n.126
sbyor-lam, 134 n.143

ma-rgyud, 30
ma-dag, 31
ma-rig-pa, 44, 45, 55, 143 n.166,
    152 n.219
mar, 24
mi-'jigs-pa bzhi, 147 n.193
mi-rtog-pa'i ye-shes, 149 n.209
mun-pa-can, 21
me, 36
me-long lta-bu'i ye-shes, 159 n.251
mos-pa, 138 n.156
sman, 136 n.151
smin-byed, 24
smon-pa med-pa, 141 n.158
smon-pa med-pa'i ting-nge-'dzin,
    141 n.159

tsitta, 156 n.241
btsun-mo, 143 n.168
rtsa, 150 n.213, 152 n.218
rtsa dbu-ma, 152 n.218
rtsal-snang, 149 n.202
rtsi, 157 n.245

tshad-med bzhi, 145 n.180
tshogs, 120 n.70
tshogs-kyi 'khor-lo, 120 n.70
tshogs-lam, 134 n.143
tshor-ba, 146 n.185
mtshan-ma med-pa, 140 n.158, 142 n.162
mtshan-ma med-pa'i ting-nge-'dzin,
    142 n.162

rdzu-'phrul-gyi rkang-pa bzhi, 146 n.187
rdzogs/rdzogs-pa/rdzogs-chen/rdzogs-pa
    chen-po, xii, xiv, 24
rdzogs-rim, 16

zhing, 56
zhing-khams, 56
zhe-sdang, 121 n.70, 140 n.157,
    154 n.229
gzhi, 27, 127 n.121, 140 n.158,
    145 n.179, 151 n.215
gzhi dngos-po gshis-kyi bzhugs-tshul,
    138 n.156
gzhi-snang, 152 n.219

zar-tshags, 144 n.173
zung-'jug, 111 n.1, 158 n.249
gzugs, 43
gzugs-kyi khams, 27
gzugs-med, 149 n.209
gzugs-med-kyi khams, 27

'od-gsal, 149 n.205

yang-dag-pa'i spong-ba bzhi, 146 n.186
yab, 30
yab-yum, 31
yar, 24
yi-ge, 142 n.162
yi-ge rgyu'i ting-nge-'dzin, 142 n.162
yi-dam, 66, 67, 68, 86, 87, 88, 93,
    153 n.224
yid, 27, 42, 44, 50, 121 n.70, 132 n.133,
    133 n.137, 136 n.150, 143 n.166,
    157 n.242
yid-kyi lus, 141 n.160
yid-dpyod, 46
yum, 30
yul, 27
ye, 17, 52, 53, 54, 159 n.250
ye-grol/ye-grol chen-po, 159 n.250
ye-shes, 43, 45, 52, 53, 54, 113 n.9,
    115 n.2, 125 n.117, 127 n.121,
    133 n.136, 136 n.151, 153 n.220
ye-shes-kyi me, 150 n.211
ye-shes-kyi rtsal-snang, 149 n.202
ye-shes chen-po, 17
ye-shes sems-dpa', 117 n.56, 157 n.242,
    157 n.243
yongs-grol, 159 n.250
yon-tan, 148 n.196

rang-byung-gi ye-shes, 128 n.122,
    153 n.220
rang-bzhin, 127 n.121, 128 n.122,
    149 n.205
rang-bzhin 'od-gsal-ba'i chos-nyid,
    149 n.205
rang-rig-pa'i ye-shes-kyi klong, 148 n.198
rig-(pa), 18, 34, 43, 45, 47, 55,
    127 n.121, 152 n.219, 153 n.220,
    160 n.258
rig-pa gcig-pu, 153 n.220
rig-pa gcig-pu chos-sku thig-le nyag-gcig,
    153 n.220

rig-'dzin, 131 n.130
rigs, 131 n.129, 137 n.152, 159 n.255
ro-ma, 152 n.218, 154 n.230
rlung, 36, 136 n.151, 141 n.160

lam, 27, 28, 140 n.158, 145 n.179,
    150 n.213, 151 n.215, 152 n.218
lus, 27, 28, 34, 39, 50, 53, 56, 121 n.70,
    136 n.150, 146 n.185, 150 n.213,
    157 n.242
lus-can, 20, 21
longs-sku, 26, 151 n.215, 153 n.222

shar-bu, 144 n.176
shes, 52, 53, 54
shes-sgrib, 155 n.235
shes-rab, xii, 16, 111 n.1, 117 n.65,
    128 n.124, 138 n.156, 140 n.157,
    144 n.169, 151 n.215, 155 n.230,
    155 n.233

sa, 36
sangs, 127 n.121
sangs-rgyas, 35, 115 n.22, 136 n.150,
    148 n.199, 152 n.219
sangs-rgyas nyag-gcig, 153 n.220
sems, 27, 34, 39, 43, 44, 45, 125 n.117,
    116 n.119, 132 n.131, 141 n.160,
    143 n.166, 146 n.285, 152 n.219
sems-nyid, 143 n.166, 144 n.179
sems dag-pa, 143 n.166
sems ma-dag-pa, 142 n.166
sems-can, 20, 21, 35, 136 n.150,
    148 n.199, 152 n.259
sems-dpa', 144 n.169, 157 n.242
sems-'byung, 155 n.230
sems-ma, 144 n.169
so-so yang-dag-pa'i rig-pa, 148 n.197
so-sor, 51
so-sor rtog-pa'i ye-shes, 159 n.257
so-sor thar-pa, 131 n.130
srog-sdom gzer, 28
gsang, 120 n.70
gsang-sngags, 128 n.124
gsang-ba, 128 n.124
gsar-ma, 112 n.4, 138 n.154, 158 n.249
gsal-ba, 18
gsung, xiii, 27, 51, 121 n.70, 127 n.119,
    128 n.123, 133 n.135, 136 n.150
bsam-gtan, 138 n.156

lha, xiii, 11, 12, 126 n.119
lha'i nga-rgyal, 159 n.252
lha'i phyag-rgya, 126 n.119
lha'i bu, 150 n.210
lhan-cig skyes-pa, 18, 152 n.219
lhan-cig skyes-pa'i bde-ba, 18

lhan-cig skyes-pa'i ma-rig-pa, 18,
    152 n.219
lhan-cig skyes-pa'i ye-shes, 16, 17, 18,
    152 n.219
lhun-grub, 44, 47, 123 n.91, 127 n.121

INDEX
OF SUBJECTS

Abidingness, 6, 8, 9, 19, 39, 63
achievements, ordinary, 63
activity, appropriate, 16, 19, 26, 30, 38,
  63, 90, 91, 92, 105, 106, 111 n.1,
  117 n.65
  optimizing, 100, 151 n.215
actuality, 128 n.122
aesthetic forms, world of, 23, 27
Akṣobhya, 90
Amitābha, 90
Amoghasiddhi, 90
Anuttarayogatantra, 134 n.139
Anuyoga (Anu), xi, 112 n.4, 134 n.139,
  145 n.181, 158 n.246
Atiyoga (Ati), xi, xiv, 134 n.139,
  145 n.181
attachment, 41
attainments, 128 n.123
attitude, 69
auto-excitation, 82
autopoiesis, xiii, 6, 15, 49, 113 n.11
Avalokiteśvara, 134 n.140
awareness, originary, 6, 9, 43, 45, 46,
  47, 48, 49, 51, 52, 54, 55, 76, 82,
  83, 88, 94, 95, 115 n.21, 125 n.117,
  133 n.136, 136 n.151, 139 n.154,
  152 n.219, 153 n.220, 155 n.230,
  159 n.251
  modes, 39, 87, 89, 90, 92, 153 n.224
  holistic, 53
  quasi-mirroring, 48, 49, 54, 92
  specificity-initiating, 51, 92
  super originary, 17
  systemic, 16, 17, 18, 86
  task-posed and accomplished, 52, 92

Beauty, 88
beginning, 17, 53
Being, 82, 92, 94, 95, 96, 98, 99,
  140 n.158
  affinity with, 63, 65, 89, 92, 137,
  137 n.151, 159 n.255
  in its beingness, 25, 26, 27, 74, 75,
  77, 100, 122 n.84, 138 n.156
  intentionality of, 10
  mystery of, 9, 95
being(s), living, 4, 117 n.50, 159 n.250
  sentient, 35, 66, 67, 68, 75, 100
  spiritual, 67
birth, 22, 26, 27, 116 n.48, 142 n.163,
  151 n.215
bliss, 86, 99, 102
  supreme, 81, 89, 91, 92, 119 n.70
blood, 40
Bodhisattva, 132 n.131
Bodhisattvayāna, viii, 112 n.4,
  132 n.134, 145 n.181, 158 n.246
body, xii, xiii, 9, 13, 14, 20, 21, 27, 28,
  34, 40, 41, 50, 56, 117 n.50,
  121 n.70, 122 n.84, 136 n.150,
  141 n.160, 150 n.213, 156 n.242
Brahma, 66
Buddha, 35, 66, 67, 68, 113 n.6,
  127 n.121, 134 n.145
  experience, 63, 68, 69, 75, 83, 84,
  85, 89, 100, 101, 102, 129 n.126,
  130 n.127
  message, 68, 81
  powers, 63
  sons, 67, 69
  system, 148 n.196, 152 n.219

"Buddha"-realms, 56
Buddhalocana, 90

Cake(s), 73, 98
capabilities, 82, 148 n.196
  catalytic, 42
  synthesizing, 42
Caryātantra, 112 n.4, 134 n.139
Caryāyoga(yāna), 145 n.181, 158 n.246
catalysts, 81
chreod, 84, 86, 89, 150 n.213,
    152 n.218, 154 n.230
color, 30, 32, 34, 118 n.68
commitment, 69, 94
communication, 67, 127 n.119,
    128 n.123, 136 n.150, 157 n.242
community, 67
compassion, 23, 28, 68, 75, 76, 87, 90,
    142 n.164, 155 n.233, see also super-
    compassion
complementarity, 16, 28, 34, 105, 106,
    118 n.65, 126 n.118, 155 n.233
completeness, 25
composure, 73
comprehension, analytical, 82
concretization, low-level, 63
conditions, adverse, 70
  favorable, 71
configuration, 8, 9, 14
configurational setting, 65, 67, 157 n.242
connectedness, cosmic, 41
  existential, 41
  universal, 7, 31, 34, 82, 92
contextuality, 43
coupling, 89, 99
creativity, 44
cremation grounds, 79, 80, 81, 83

Death, 22, 26, 74
  Lord of, 89, 149 n.210
defects, six, 89
deiform energy, 11, 12, 13, 14, 24, 25,
    57, 77, 84, 85, 90, 94, 96, 101, 102,
    103
  activation of, 84, 85, 86
  calm, 87
  fierce, 88, 89
deiform nature, xiii, xiv
desire, 27
  world of, 81
developing phase, vii, xii, 9, 10, 14, 15,

    19, 26, 27, 28, 64, 93, 101, 102,
    110, 116 n.30
Dharma, 67
Diamond-mistress cleft, 79
dichotomy, 99
  subject-object, 11, 64
dimension, 54
discernment, appreciative, 16, 17, 19, 30,
    38, 63, 90, 91, 92, 105, 106, 107,
    108, 111 n.1, 117 n.65, 128 n.124,
    155 n.230
disengagement, 66
rDo-rje-'chang, 67, 68
rDo-rje 'dzin-pa, 86

Earth, 37, 38, 39, 41, 42, 122 n.84
effort, sustained, 88
eliminations, four, 81
elixir, 11, 97, 98
embodied being, 53
embodied existence, 56
embodiment, 39, 57
emotions, 44
empowerment, 65
energy, formulated, 87
engagement, 69
environment, 43
enworldedness, 50
estrus, 40
evolution, 31, 125 n.117, 127 n.121
  principle of, 6
  three-phase, 20
excitability, 34
  lack of cognitive, 18
excitation, 18, 43, 45, 47, 152 n.219,
    153 n.220
  stepped-down version of, 44, 45,
    143 n.166, 160 n.258
excitement, sexual, 18
existence, authentic, 67, 95
Existenz, 63, 131 n.128
experience, 10
  as such, 143 n.166, 144 n.179
  transformative, 14

Facticity, 128 n.122
father-tantra, 30, 36, 112 n.4, 151 n.215
field, Being's meaning-rich, 81, 160 n.58,
    144 n.179
fire, 37, 38, 39, 41, 42, 79, 122 n.84,
    150 n.211

flow patterns, kinesthetic, 18
focal point, 84, 86
force, concomitant, 41
  deadening, 83
  fierce, 80
  modifying, 41
forces, fundamental, 11, 34, 35, 36, 40,
    41, 42, 43, 44, 76, 78, 79, 122 n.84
  matter-dominated, 35, 42
  radiation-dominated, 35, 42
fore-structure, 112 n.5, 115 n.20,
    117 n.50
formlessness, 27
freedom, 99, 156 n.250
fulfilling phase, 10, 15, 16, 17, 18, 19,
    26, 101
functions, six transcending, 89, 92,
    148 n.195

Gaganagarbha, 134 n.140
Gestalt, xiii, 3, 9, 10, 14, 24, 26, 28, 51,
    57, 74, 87, 94, 102, 109, 113 n.9,
    126 n.118, 127 n.119, 127 n.120,
    133 n.135, 136 n.150, 148 n.201,
    150 n.213, 151 n.215, 153 n.230,
    157 n.242
gnoseme, 23, 24, 25, 29, 31, 32, 78, 79,
    92, 94, 95, 119 n.70, 142 n.164,
    150 n.214, 154 n.230
goal, 27, 28, 151 n.215
gods/goddesses, 9, 29, 97, 108,
    124 n.108, 126 n.119, 144 n.169
"growth program," 131 n.129
Guhyamantra, 28, 63
guiding image, 26, 52, 151 n.215

Happiness, 13, 18, 19, 26, 66, 68
Hīnayāna, viii, 4, 147, n.194
holomovement, 4, 5, 31, 42, 44,
    114 n.18, 123 n.91, 149 n.202,
    152 n.219

"I," 40, 115 n.22, 150 n.214
identity, 50
images, felt, 94, 156 n.239
imagination, holistic, 46
in-depth appraisal, 22, 23, 25, 26, 29,
    73, 76, 77, 102, 138 n.156,
    141 n.158 and 159, 142 n.162,
    146 n.187
individuality, 52
  authentic, 6
indivisibility, 6, 7, 8

insight, 147 n.193
inspection, 81
intelligence/excitation, 6
intrepidities, four, 82

Jewels, three, 66, 67

Kriyātantra (Kriyā), x, 112 n.4,
    134 n.139
Kriyāyoga (yāna), 145 n.181, 158 n.246
Kṣitigarbha, 134 n.140

lamps, two, 160 n.258
language, 14, 25, 29, 67, 106, 121 n.70,
    136 n.150
level, higher, 68, 69
life-force, 28, 76
life-form, 77
life-stuff, 73, 98, 120 n.70
life-world, 119 n.70
light, inner, 140 n.157
lighting-up, 4, 5, 11, 125 n.117,
    127 n.120
lineage, 134 n.139
loopholes, 70, 71, 136 n.149
lucency, 101, 102, 103, 104, 126 n.118
  sheer, 6, 8, 19, 23, 74

Macro-system, 41
Mahādeva, 80
Mahāyāna, viii, 4, 64, 65, 125 n.117,
    135 n.146
Mahāyoga (Mahā), xi, xii, xiv, 28, 105,
    112 n.4
Mahā(yogayāna), 145 n.181, 158 n.246
Maitreya, 134 n.140
male-female, 99
Māmakī, 90
Mañjuśrī, 134 n.140
Mantrayāna, 103
matter, 34
  matter-"stuff," 42
  matter-system, 43
maturation, 24, 25, 27, 75, 83, 84, 94
meaning, 53, 68, 69
mentation, 9, 11, 12, 14, 29, 34, 39, 43,
    44, 45, 46, 78, 83, 89, 92,
    142 n.166, 150 n.214, 157 n.242
message, 67
milieu, 14
mind, 20, 21, 34, 50, 68, 69, 121 n.70,
    136 n.150, 141 n.160
  projections of, 29

Mistress, 143 n.168
mother-tantra, 30, 36, 112 n.4, 151 n.215
motility, 39, 41, 122 n.84, 136 n.150,
141 n.160
motility-mentation, 77, 86
mystery, 120 n.70

Nature, 130 n.126, 134 n.140
Nirmāṇaratidevas, 96
nirvana, 7, 15, 16, 33, 50, 75, 90, 91,
115 n.23, 123 n.91
Nivaraṇaviṣkambhin, 134 n.140
nothingness, 5, 7, 118 n.68

Object, 27
obligation, 65, 131 n.130
obscuration, 91, 155 n.235
'Og-min realm, 83
ontogenesis, 14, 19
opacity, state of, 5, 44
open-dimensionality, 18, 28
openness, 49, 50, 57, 77, 82, 87, 90, 92,
102, 118 n.65, 142 n.164, 155 n.233,
156 n.237
super originary, 3
optimization, 28, 47
thrust toward, 4, 8, 15, 19, 20, 56, 64,
127 n.121
organism, 40

Pain, 66
palace, 78, 79, 80, 81, 83, 93
Pāṇḍaravāsinī, 90
path, noble eightfold, 146 n.184,
147 n.190 and 191, 151 n.215, see
also way
patterns, structural, 43
eight perceptual, 83, 117 n.50,
158 n.246
perception, 127 n.120, 149 n.207
concept-forming, 42
affectively toned, 42
phase transition, 84, 85, 117 n.53,
129 n.124, 141 n.160, 151 n.215
pleasure, 18, 66, 88
poison, 45, 89, 123 n.88, 136 n.15,
154 n.229
pollutants, emotional, 83, 150 n.210
potential, genus- and species-specific, 41,
42
activation of inner, xii
meaning-rich, 127 n.120
psychophysical, 130 n.126

powers, five psychic controlling, 82
four deadening, 89, 93, 149 n.210,
157 n.245
Pratyekabuddha, 67
Pratyekabuddhayāna, viii, 112 n.4,
132 n.134, 145 n.181, 158 n.246
presence, spontaneous, 8, 44, 47,
127 n.121
pride, 101, 102, 159 n.252
process, morpho- and ontogenetic, 48,
54, 123 n.97, 151 n.215
protection, 82
psychic factor, 75, 76
purity, 25, 129 n.126
pursuits, spiritual, viii, 112 n.4,
156 n.246

Radiance, 18, 39
radiation-"stuff," 40, 42
Ratnasambhava, 90
reality, commonly accepted, 3, 4, 5, 7,
90
higher-order, 3, 4, 5, 7, 42, 47, 48,
90, 119 n.70
indivisibility of, 6, 7, 8
two modes, 6, 7, 63, 111 n.1,
125 n.117, 127 n.120, 136 n.150
refuge, 66, 68
releasements, three, 75, 87
eight, 82
resonance, 27, 51, 127 n.119, 128 n.133,
133 n.135, see also spirituality
revitalization, 71, 72
Rudra, 81, 84, 103, 144 n.178
rules of the game, 66, 132 n.135

Safeguards, 28, 30, 117 n.64
Samantabhadra, 134 n.140
samsara, 5, 7, 15, 16, 20, 33, 50, 75, 90,
91, 98, 99, 115 n.23
Sangha, 67, 68
scent-eater, 75, 85, 86
scriptures, Buddhist, 155 n.236
self, 115 n.22, 150 n.214
selfhood, 51
self-organization, 6, 44
self-transcendence, xii, xiii, 6, 31, 37,
82, 109
sentiments, 89, 153 n.227
sexuality, 36, 37
similes, eight, 83
singularity, 153 n.220

situatedness, 9, 13
Śiva, 66, 144 n.178
skull, 93
skullcap, 72, 120 n.70
sky, 32, 35, 160 n.258
space, 32, 35, 38, 39, 42, 43, 122 n.84,
    160 n.256
speech, xiii, 9, 27, 50, 133 n.135,
    157 n.242
spirits, obnoxious, 70, 71, 135 n.147
spirituality, 51, 136 n.150, 157 n.242, see
    also resonance
Śrāvaka, 67
Śrāvakayāna, viii, 112 n.4, 132 n.134,
    145 n.181, 158 n.246
strength, 82
structuration, xii, 21, 41, 74, 150 n.213,
    152 n.218
subject, 127 n.119
subjectivity, 44, 45
success, four bases of, 82, 87
super-compassion, 82
super-diaphaneity, 44, 123 n.91
super-diaphanous, 47
symmetry, 45
symmetry transformation, 123 n.91
system, 4
systems, philosophical, 81
systemic, 18

Talk, 27
rTa-mchog Heruka, 70
Tantra, six divisions of, 67
Tara, 90
tendencies, 20
    ingrained, 7
throne, 83, 84, 85, 86

thrones, three, 16
tonic, 72, 97, 136 n.150
transfiguration, 70
transmutation, 64, 74, 75, 76, 78, 85,
    94, 95
treatises, rediscovered, 63, 129 n.125
triangle, 32, 33
tuning-in, 74

Ubhayatantra (Uba), x
Ubhaya(yāna), 145 n.181, 158 n.246
understanding, 106, 107, 113 n.9
utterance, 25, 29, 51, 128 n.124
    first, 31, 47
    original, xiii

Vacuum, false, 31, 35
    true, 31
Vairocana, 89
Vajrapāṇi, 134 n.140
Vajrayāna, ix, x, xi, 4
vibration-"stuff," 43
vision, 27, 28, 88, 147 n.191
    cultivation of the, 27, 28
Viṣṇu, 66

Water, 37, 38, 39, 42, 122 n.84
way, 27, 28, 145 n.179, see also path
    noble eightfold, 82
wheel, 81, 92, 146 n.184
wind, 37, 38, 42
world, 9, 34, 36, 41, 90
world horizon of meaning, 76, 123 n.91
worship, 72, 96, 97

Yogatantra (Yoga), x, xi, xiv, 112 n.4,
    134 n.139
Yoga(yāna), 145 n.181, 158 n.246

This book was written on a
Victor 9000 word processor using Wordstar.
Editorial updates and type coding were done on a Pronto 16
in WordPerfect. The data was converted on a Shaffstall 5000XT
and processed for typesetting with Magnatype software. The text was
then set in Goudy Old Style on a Linotron 202. The cover was produced by
Mark Winkler on an Aurora AU/220 computer graphics system,
then output using a Dunn Instruments CompactColor
Camera. The color separation was generated
on a Crossfield 635IE scanner
by Gregory & Falk.